Benjamin Franklin

AUTOBIOGRAPHY

AND OTHER WRITINGS

RIVERSIDE EDITIONS

RIVERSIDE EDITIONS

UNDER THE GENERAL EDITORSHIP OF

Gordon N. Ray

Benjamin Franklin

AUTOBIOGRAPHY

AND OTHER WRITINGS

EDITED WITH AN INTRODUCTION AND NOTES BY

RUSSEL B. NYE

MICHIGAN STATE UNIVERSITY

HOUGHTON MIFFLIN COMPANY

BOSTON • The Riverside Press Cambridge

Benjamin Franklin: 1706–1790

The Autobiography of Benjamin Franklin: A Restoration of a "Fair Copy" by Max Farrand. Copyright, 1949, by the Regents of the University of California. Reprinted by permission of the University of Cailfornia Press.

The Riverside Press

CAMBRIDGE • MASSACHUSETTS

PRINTED IN THE U.S.A.

CONTENTS

CONTENTS

INTRODUCTION
by Russel B. Nye

OF THOSE whom Americans venerate as our Founding Fathers, Benjamin Franklin alone walks among us at our own level. Washington, Jefferson, Madison, Hamilton, Patrick Henry, John Adams, and others of that half-legendary galaxy exist in the minds of most Americans as posed portraits by Stuart or Peale, or as formalized heroes frozen into statuary. But not Franklin. With Franklin — with his old-fashioned bifocals, his tricorn hat, and snuff-colored coat — the man in the street, the schoolboy in school, the tradesman in the market feel a friendly nodding acquaintance. Perhaps no figure in American history is more familiar than that of the runaway apprentice, rolls under his arm, wandering wide-eyed down the streets of a strange city; or that of the bespectacled scientist in kneebreeches gravely testing the clouds with his kite and key; or that of the kindly, graying sage whose "Early to bed and early to rise" is still probably the most widely quoted aphorism in the English-speaking world. Americans feel a kinship with Franklin as they do with few others of their heroes. What John Adams once said of him, that there was "scarcely a citizen who was not familiar with his name and who did not consider him a friend to human kind," is still largely true.

One of the major reasons for this, of course, is Franklin's *Autobiography*, which for generations has made Franklin the personal friend of its readers. As an enlightened product of a rational civilization, Franklin was able to look at himself and his life more or less dispassionately, judging himself as he would another, analyzing himself with a blend of detached curiosity and personal involvement that is uniquely Franklin's. In the pages of the *Autobiography* Franklin asks himself, "Who am I, how did I come to be, and why am I a human being as I am?" and he answers without arrogance, and with a charm and honesty, a sensibility and wit, that have endeared him to millions since. It is little wonder that, in a memoir-writing age that produced hundreds of such autobiographies, Franklin's was a classic.

At least some of the perennial appeal of the *Autobiography*, of course, lies in the fact that it is a good story, well told. After all, Franklin had much to tell. He was born into the reign of

Queen Anne, and he died only twenty years before Lincoln's birth. His life spanned nearly a century of exciting and momentous events, in many of which he played a part. The story of that life and of the personality that was Franklin's has an interest and an attraction of their own. The runaway apprentice's flight to Philadelphia, the earnest young man's disillusion on his first trip to London, the steady rise from poor boy to solid citizen, the tragedy of Braddock, the maneuverings of colonial politics, the inner promptings and struggles of the all-too-human philosopher who hoped to live "under the Restraints of Reason" — this is dramatic material, handled skilfully but unobtrusively by a writer with a knack for narrative.

Franklin had a clear and sensitive mind, with the ability to write vivid, economical, uncluttered prose in the tradition of the neoclassic "plain style" he learned from his masters, Addison, Steele, Swift, and Defoe. Like many other young men of his time, he assiduously modeled his prose on *The Spectator*, heeding Defoe's warnings against "a superfluous crowding in of insignificant words." His style, however, is not simply a copy of his models, for Franklin was concerned with so developing his writing that he might be "a tolerable English writer" in his own way. The norm of English style, he believed, should be that of intelligent, informed conversation, using words "as near as possible to those spoken," most of all, as he wrote the philosopher Hume, emphasizing clarity, for "one cannot be too clear." Then too, Franklin was a professional journalist who considered writing to be his trade, who was proud of it, and who never stopped learning it. A good editor, he explained in the *Pennsylvania Gazette*, should like any other skilled writer have "great Easiness and Command of Writing and Relating Things clearly and intelligibly, and ni few Words," without "affected Words and high-flown Phrases." He also admired the kind of scientific writing advocated by the Royal Society's Thomas Sprat, who urged writers "to reject amplifications, digressions, and swellings" in favor of "clear senses and a native easiness." The best writing, Franklin believed.

> should proceed regularly from things known to things unknown, distinctly and clearly without confusion. The words used should be the most expressive that the language affords, provided they are the most generally understood. Nothing should be

expressed in two words that can be as well expressed in one;
that is, no synonyms should be used, or very rarely, but the
whole should be so placed as to be agreeable to the ear in
reading; summarily it should be smooth, clear, and short, for
the contrary qualities are displeasing. . . . In this sense, that
is best wrote which is best adapted for obtaining the end of
the writer.

The result, as is evident in the pages of the *Autobiography*, is a
prose style with grace, force, flexibility, and order, an instrument
ideally suited to the expression of Franklin's ideas and a reflection
of the personality behind the pen.

I

Despite its charm and interest, the *Autobiography* does not
present a completely satisfactory version of Franklin. It is in-
complete, since it carries Franklin only to the age of fifty-one,
when he stood really but on the threshold of greatness. It tends
to oversimplify him by failing to do justice to his amazing
versatility, his restless energy of mind, his tremendous sweep of
accomplishments. Franklin was a person of diffuse talents; he
involved himself so thoroughly with his world that it is difficult
to draw together in focus all the facets of his mind and character.
For a man who was, as Herman Melville said, "everything but a
poet," one uncompleted document is certainly not enough to
explain him. We see in its pages little of the scientific interests
which absorbed him before 1757, only a few hints of his social
and family life, almost nothing of his political career, and of
course nothing of the years of middle and later life.

The most serious deficiency of the *Autobiography* is the image
of Franklin as "Poor Richard" that it is likely to project. By
oversimplifying a personality of depth and complexity into a
shrewd tradesman of homely apothegms and a full pocketbook,
the narrative has sometimes left its readers with the false likeness
of Franklin which led John Keats to call him (with regrettable
misunderstanding) "a philosophical Quaker full of mean and
thrifty maxims." Franklin did believe, as he said, that portions of
his narrative might serve to exemplify to the young "the effects
of prudent and imprudent conduct in the commencement of a
life of business," but he did not mean to be judged by posterity
solely in terms of his rags-to-riches success story or of *The Way*

to Wealth. Unfortunately, Parson Weems, Noah Webster's schoolbooks, McGuffey's readers, and a thousand inspirational orators and copywriters have fixed Franklin in the popular mind as the first apostle of frugality and the patron saint of savings accounts.

There is some truth, to be sure, in this picture of Benjamin Franklin. By reason of his industry, skill, and acumen he rose from penniless obscurity to fame and wealth. He was a hard-working, shrewd, successful businessman, and he did, in his guise of Poor Richard, embody a good many of those practical virtues with which the way to wealth is paved. "A Penny saved is a Tuppence clear," "God helps those who help themselves," "Keep thy Shop well and thy Shop will keep thee," "A word to the wise is enough," "Lost time is never found again," and dozens of other Franklinian maxims are imbedded deep in the American business tradition as the distilled wisdom of a man who made good. The *Autobiography* is a success story of no small proportions. Franklin knew how to size people up and how to get along with them; he perceived the value of putting one's best face to the world; he saw the advantages of influential friendships. He hated inefficiency and ineptness; he had a keen sense of administration and he was a genius at organization. He worked hard, kept accurate accounts, invested wisely, produced careful work of high quality, honored his contracts, dressed neatly, avoided hurtful temptations, and retired after twenty years of business with a comfortable fortune and a secure future.

Yet this view of Franklin shows but a small fragment of the character of a man who freely admitted to various "errata," who found thrift "a virtue I could never acquire," who confessed to disorderly and careless habits, who depended on his wife to keep the books straight and to curb his openhanded generosity, and who jeopardized his life and fortune by joining a risky revolution at seventy. "An egg today is better than a hen to-morrow" does not sound like Poor Richard, but it is, and so is "There's more old drunkards than old doctors," "Let thy maid-servant be faithful, strong, and homely," and "Keep your eyes wide open before marriage and half-shut afterwards." Moralizers have often abstracted from Franklin's *Autobiography* and his letters a laudable set of rules of conduct for the virtuous and thrifty, just as Franklin himself drew up his ledgers of moral bookkeeping. But his self-acknowledged "foolish intrigues with low women," his passionate bouts of indulgence, his willingness (as he admitted) "to change opinions which I had thought right but found otherwise," confuse the moralists and blur the portrait of the rather stuffy young man who appears in early portions of the *Autobiography*. Franklin could never take "the great Dr. Franklin" quite so seriously as some of his admirers have done; he does not always tell the whole story, and he is often amused at himself when he does. It is interesting to note that contemporary gossip had it that Franklin was not asked to draft the Declaration of Independence for fear he might hide a joke in it — just as at its signing, one of the most solemn moments in modern history, he reputedly dropped his quip about hanging together or separately. The truth is that Franklin was not a simple, uncomplicated man, nor is he to be explained only in terms of the tradesman's dream of success.

Franklin's business career, successful as it was, was but a brief interlude in a long, full life. He was perfectly willing to gather unto himself a competent share of the world's goods, and he knew how to do it with the cleverest of them. The game of business, however, with its "little cares and fatigues," neither excited nor interested him. He wanted money because it gave him independence and security to live as he wished, in pursuit of those things he found important in life. He wanted, he said, "leisure to read, study, make experiments, and converse at large with such ingenious and worthy men as are pleased to honor me with their friendship or acquaintance, on such points as may produce something for the common benefit of mankind." There is no doubt but that had he so desired, Franklin might have been very rich indeed. Had he patented only a few of his commercially-adaptable inventions (such as his stove, bifocal spectacles, or lightning rods) he could have been one of the world's wealthiest men. Instead he decided at forty-two that he had money enough, retired, and lived comfortably for more than a half-century longer on the relatively modest income from his holdings. He was more interested in knowledge than in money. He did not wish to have it said of him, as Poor Richard said of another, "He does not possess wealth, wealth possesses him."

II

Franklin's greatest pleasures in life came from those "philosophical studies and amusements" to which he hoped to devote himself after his retirement from business. He was, as the *Autobiography* fails to convey, one of the dozen or so great scholars of his age, responsible for some of the most important basic scientific research ever performed. Science was often crowded out of his life by his engagements with state and society, so much that he was actually able to find no more than a few uninterrupted years for study in mid-life. Yet science was the one activity from which he never retired and from which he gained his greatest personal rewards. He began his first experiments in 1729, with a series of observations on the relations of color to heat absorption and conductivity (an amazing piece of work for a self-taught youth of twenty-three) and continued his scientific work for the rest of his life, in moments stolen from other business. In 1747 he began the brilliant electrical experiments with which, Sir Humphry Davy said, "by very small means he established very grand truths," and on which his scientific fame subsequently rested. His last publication, in fact, was a paper on certain maritime observations, done at seventy-nine.

Franklin's scientific experiments were recognized by his contemporaries as his greatest contribution to his times. Men stopped to stare at him on the streets of Philadelphia and Paris, not because he was the rich and successful author of "Poor Richard," but because he was the learned Dr. Franklin, who ranked with Newton, Leibnitz, Hume, and Voltaire. He was friends with Linnaeus, Lord Kames, James Watt, Buffon, Priestley, Condorcet, and practically all the other first-rate scientists and philosophers in the world. He was a member of the Royal Society of London, of the French, Swedish, Italian, Spanish, and Dutch Academies, winner of the Copley medal for scientific research, holder of a half-dozen honorary degrees, master of five languages, author of a hundred or more papers in chemistry, electricity, medicine, meteorology, heat, agriculture, and botany. He was a scholar, a man of consuming intellectual curiosity and flashing insights, and earnest and dedicated searcher after knowledge for its own sake. His reply to the question posed by a fellow spectator at the world's first balloon ascension has never been equaled.

"But what good is it?" his friend asked. Franklin replied, "What good is a newborn baby?"

There was so much to know, so much unknown about the universe he inhabited, that Franklin gladly would have devoted all his time and energy to the task of finding out a little of it. "As yet," he once remarked, "the quantity of human knowledge bears no proportion for the quality of human ignorance." Nature had many mysteries, but they held no terror for Franklin. He respected the universe for its power, wondered at its complexity and order, and hoped that its secrets could be found and turned to man's benefit. In science, he felt certain, lay the key to man's future, for by it he could "extend the power of man over matter, avert or diminish the evils he is subject to, or augment the number of his enjoyments." Through science Franklin could meet nature on equal terms in quest of truth, coolly, confidently, reasonably. "Mr. Franklin," his French friend M. Marbois once said, "adores only great nature."

Franklin was also a "practical" scientist, or more accurately, a gadgeteer. Like other scientists of his time, he was eager to put science to work in the smallest and least important areas of daily life as well as in the largest. He could see no reason why men should not take full advantage of any opportunities science offered to make life easier and pleasanter. Then too, Franklin liked to solve problems and he disliked ineffectiveness, in things as well as in persons. A smoky chimney not only challenged his ingenuity but offended his respect for efficiency — therefore he invented a smokeless one, much as he might write a constitution, organize a hospital, improve the city police, or show a young man how to save money. The list of his inventions is a long one, including in addition to the well-known stove and lightning rods such things as a flexible catheter, musical glasses, an improved boat hull, a chair that opened into a ladder, another chair that gently fanned the occupant as he rocked, a way of killing turkeys by electrocution, a device for removing books from high shelves (still used in groceries), and improved paving blocks. He patented none of these, remarking that "as we enjoy great advantages from the inventions of others, we should be glad of an opportunity to serve others by any invention of ours."

The ideal of service, of which his inventions were an illustration, was an integral part of Franklin's social creed. His so-called retirement lasted but six years before he was called into public service by the government of Pennsylvania. Never again for thirty years did he have the leisure for thought, experiment, and "agreeable and constructive conversation" that he desired. He was under no compulsion to leave his beloved study, but there was too much to do in his busy world for him to disengage himself from it. No man should gain such eminence in study, he believed, that it became necessary to "neglect the knowledge and practice of essential duties" of "a good Christian." "The great *Aim* and *End* of all learning," he wrote another time, is "to serve mankind, one's Country, Friends, and Family." As a young man he read carefully the Reverend Cotton Mather's *Essays to Do Good* (1710) which, he told Mather's son, influenced him very strongly. The good Christian, Mather explained, was like a man in a boat, rowing toward Heaven with two oars, "prayer" and "settled business." Thus, said Mather, an honest Christian might "glorify God by doing *Good* for *others*, and getting of *Good* for himself." Like other eighteenth-century Calvinists, Mather recognized a man's "double calling" to do well for himself here as well as hereafter, and so did Franklin. However, like Mather and the Calvinists, he believed that all of the world's goods belonged to God and hence His temporary bestowal of a portion of it on one man for his personal use involved very definite responsibilities to use it wisely and well for the benefit of others as well as one's self. "If your riches are yours," asked Poor Richard wryly, "why don't you take them with you to t'other world?" Defoe's *Essays Upon Several Projects*, which Franklin also mentioned as influential on his ideal of service, taught him that "God Almighty has commanded us to relieve and help one another in distress." So Franklin's endowments, financial and otherwise, carried for him a sense of stewardship for the less fortunate or gifted. "I would rather have it said," he wrote, " '*He lived usefully*,' than 'He died rich.' "

Service to others was ingrained in Franklin's religious creed. "To relieve the misfortunes of our fellow creatures," he once wrote, "is concurring with the Deity." It is noteworthy that the questions he asked himself as he marked his little book of self-improvement, morning and night, were "What good shall I do this day?" and "What good have I done this day?" The young men of the Junto asked at their meetings, "Do you

think of anything at present, in which the Junto may be serviceable to mankind, to their country, to their friends, or to themselves?" Franklin's belief that "the most acceptable service to
God is service to man" led him to devote much of his time and
restless energy to those projects — hospitals, fire companies, a
school for free Negroes, a subscription library, an academy, fund-
raising, and so on — the figure in his *Autobiography*. His feeling
of relationship to his fellowmen was colored neither by condescension nor do-goodism. He had little consciousness of class,
and was inclined to jest at social pretension, saying that he
preferred "hereditary professors of mathematics" far above
hereditary nobility. (He was human enough, though, to confess
with a little vanity that he, a poor printer, had "known five kings
and supped with one.") He was never accepted into Philadelphia's topmost social stratum, even after he became the city's
most famous citizen, nor did he ever express any interest in belonging to it. The product of a lower-middle-class family
himself, and essentially a skilled artisan by vocation, Franklin
spoke of "laborers" or "workmen" without patronizing. He
simply felt a strong kinship with his fellowmen and a strong
humanitarian sympathy toward them as part of the responsibility
of belonging to the human race. In helping others, he told
Joseph Huey in 1753, "I do not look upon myself as conferring
favors, but as paying debts. . . . I can only show my gratitude
for these mercies from God by a readiness to help his other
children and my brethren." At practically no time in Franklin's
life was he not connected in some way with a humanitarian
project or service organization. The last public act of his
life was signing a protest against slavery to Congress in his
capacity as President of the Anti-Slavery Society of Pennsylvania.

Franklin's pragmatic approach to religion in the *Autobiography*
has bothered some readers, who find in it signs of spiritual in-
sensitivity and of a faith bounded by convenience. Franklin,
by his own admission, was neither much interested in theological
doctrines nor concerned with religious disputation. "Metaphysical reasonings," he told Benjamin Vaughan, caused him
"great uncertainty," so he "quitted that kind of reading and
study for others more satisfactory." There were questions no
one could answer, he believed, and therefore one might as well
dismiss them. Yet no man held his religious views more firmly

than Franklin, or practiced them with greater sincerity and con-
sistency. As a youth he concluded that the Calvinism of his
fathers was not for him. The materialistic religion he substituted,
he soon found, might be true but was "not very useful." Therefore he evolved a set of religious principles that served to satisfy
him and which stood the test of utility. Ever after he avoided
controversy; he imposed his views on no one, and allowed none
to be imposed on him.

Franklin believed in a Christianity that produced results, a
faith that could be translated into life. As he once wrote a
friend:

> The worship of God is a duty; the hearing and reading of
> sermons may be useful; but, if men rest in hearing and praying,
> as many do, it is as if a tree should value itself on being
> watered and putting forth leaves, tho' it never produced any
> fruit.

Since Sunday was his "studying day," Franklin as a young apprentice did not attend church. Later, however, he agreed that
church attendance might have certain salutary influences on
one's character, and he showed more willingness to observe the
socially-acceptable religious amenities. He attacked no sect and
praised none, contributed to both a Protestant church and a
Jewish synagogue, and helped his friend John Carroll to become
the first Catholic Archbishop in America. His Junto, his
"projects," his humanitarian services, his interest in Freemasonry,
and his experiments in "moral perfection" apparently served him
as adequate substitutes for any formal religion. His ethical
system was founded on the simple belief that "truth, sincerity,
and integrity, in dealings between man and man, were of the
utmost importance to the felicity of life." He refused to think
deeply about morality, arriving early at the utilitarian conclusion
that acts which were bad were so "*because* they were bad for us,"
and those good "commanded *because* they were beneficial to us,
in their own natures, all the circumstances of things considered."

III

Franklin's essay on the paper money issue, written in 1729,
was the first step of a political career that ended almost sixty
years later at the Constitutional Convention. Because of his

sympathy for the causes of farmer and artisan, he was generally regarded in Pennsylvania, one of the Penns wrote, "as a sort of tribune of the people." Franklin played a prominent part in the formation of a successful coalition of Scotch-Irish farmers and city mechanics against the colonial proprietors and the Quaker merchant-bankers, and was one of the leaders in the effort to erase the last vestiges of feudalism from Pennsylvania's government. The Philadelphia aristocracy did not trust his political liberalism; Penn thought him "a dangerous man . . . , of uneasy spirit." It would be hard, however, to construe Franklin as a radical. He had seen too much of mankind to indulge in much bland optimism about its political sagacity, and he had at times, he told his friend Joseph Priestley, uneasy feelings that men were "a sort of Beings very badly constructed." He spoke out against those who saw "popular Liberty compatible only with a tendency toward anarchy," for he respected efficiency and authority too much to countenance untidiness or confusion in government. His ideal government, no doubt, was that which, as he told Le Veillard, suffered neither from "too much power to our *governors* nor too little obedience in the *governed*."

Franklin wrote little about his political theories, preferring to deal in practicalities. Unlike many of the leading figures of the Revolutionary generation, he was neither lawyer, philosopher, nor merchant. He was a scientist who based his speculations about political processes and institutions on experience, experiment, reading, and reasoning. He was not comfortable with abstractions, and he could express himself best when examining a specific problem or advocating a course of action. In the controversy over independence he seldom quoted Blackstone or Locke, spoke rarely of natural rights, and would have found it quite impossible to have written the glowing generalities of the opening paragraphs of the Declaration of Independence. Yet he believed as deeply as Jefferson did in much the same principles. He had a great respect for human values; at least a qualified faith in the potentialities of the average man; a belief in the ability of responsible men, properly educated and checked, to govern themselves; and a great hope for a better future that he felt sure was bound to come "from improvements in philosophy, morals, politics, and even the conveniences of common living." "God grant," he wrote in 1789, in one of his last comments on politics, "that not only the love of liberty, but a thorough knowledge of the rights of man, may pervade the nations of the earth, so that a philosopher may set his foot anywhere on its surface, and say, 'This is my country.'"

Franklin's career as a statesman and diplomat came primarily after 1757, the point at which his memoirs end. After his retirement from business, had he so desired, he could undoubtedly have obtained a lucrative Crown office. Instead he served for nearly twenty years as colonial agent in London, an especially unpleasant and taxing job as tensions mounted after 1765. At sixty-nine, instead of preparing to enjoy a peaceful old age, Franklin willingly joined a shaky revolution against the world's greatest military and naval power. There was good reason for him to turn Tory, as his son did, for he had valuable investments, powerful London friends, and a secure colonial position. Yet Franklin did not hesitate. When he might have retired to his study, he instead assumed management of the American postal system, accepted the chairmanship of the Pennsylvania Committee of Safety, and served as delegate to the Second Continental Congress, member of the Committee of Secret Correspondence, and delegate to Canada. After the signing of the Declaration of Independence he spent nine more years of the twilight of his life in the service of the new nation, charged with one of the most difficult and delicate diplomatic assignments in its history. (Characteristically, before he left for France he lent Congress between three and four thousand pounds out of his own pocket for expenses.) On his return he served two terms as President of his state, and finally, at eighty-one, he sat in convention with men forty years his junior to write a new Constitution, closing the debates with a brief admonition to the delegates that is still a classic bit of political wisdom.

IV

Franklin crossed the Atlantic eight times, spent twenty-six years in Europe, and was equally at home on The Strand, the Rue Royale, and Market Street. A cosmopolitan citizen of the world, he enjoyed England so much that he once thought of living there, and he loved equally well the grace and brilliance of French society. But he was, as Carlyle called him, the "Father of all the Yankees." He was "too much of an American," he said of himself, "with an indelible affection" for his country, ever to leave it permanently. Its "good climate, fertile soil, wholesome air, free governments, wise laws, and liberty" meant too much to him. Because he was so thoroughly an American, the Boston's candle-maker's son could serve his country in Europe without arrogance or timidity, walking among crowns and court intrigues with calm confidence of his own and his country's status.

Franklin was one of those rare men who attain distinction by incorporating in themselves the spirit of their time and place. There was no discord in him with his era, no lack of harmony with his society. His temperament suited the times, and the times encouraged the fullest development of his powers. He spoke the language of the Enlightenment (though with a native American accent) as clearly as Addison or Pope or Defoe, and like them was its true son. The qualities of mind displayed in his life and writings are distinctively those of the Age of Reason — tolerance, serenity, assurance, goodwill, intelligent skepticism, common sense, wit, belief in man's rationality, hope for his betterment, and faith in his progress. Franklin symbolized and confirmed the ideals of his age by being an eminently successful human being within its spiritual and intellectual framework. For those who wish to know what life was like in eighteenth-century America, Franklin's *Autobiography* contains its essence, recorded in the clear and steady prose of one of its greatest men.

A NOTE ON THE TEXT

FRANKLIN long hoped to write his memoirs, but the press of a busy life prevented him from beginning them until 1771, when he spent a long holiday with his friend Jonathan Shipley, Bishop of St. Asaph, at Twyford in Hampshire, England. After first sketching out a three-page outline, Franklin wrote eighty-six pages at Twyford, carrying his life down to 1730, or about one-third of his outline, before he left for London and his business as colonial agent. At the close of the Revolutionary War the manuscript came into the hands of Abel James, a Philadelphia publisher, who sent Franklin a copy with a plea for its completion and publication. In 1784, during his residence at Passy near Paris, he once more began work on the project, but when he returned to America in 1785 he had added only about twenty-six pages to the Twyford manuscript, which James had kindly returned to him. After making his will in July, 1788, Franklin again turned to his task, completing within the year more than a hundred additional pages. In 1789, aware that he would never live to finish his narrative, Franklin requested his grandson, Benjamin Franklin Bache, to make two "fair copies" of the manuscript for his friends Benjamin Vaughan and Guillaume Le Veillard, the Mayor of Passy, so that he might receive their advice. The original manuscript was by now interlined, corrected, and written over, and in making the copies Bache included some of these changes and made others, perhaps with his grandfather's approval. Shortly after this Franklin himself wrote seven and a half additional pages which Bache did not copy.

An alert reader thus may detect differences of spirit and attitude in the different portions of the memoirs. At Twyford, Franklin, in his mid-sixties, enjoying good health and obviously pleased at the opportunity to relive his youth, wrote with quiet satisfaction of his upward climb from runaway apprentice to man of fortune and reputation. When he resumed his task at Passy in 1784, however, he was one of the world's most honored men, writing not only the story of his life for his son and family, but a much more formal account for posterity of how he attained virtue, eminence, knowledge, and wealth. Here he treats more of his career as businessman, civic leader, and scientist than of his personal life, with more of the public record than of the inner man. In 1788, when he began writing the third major portion of the text, he was eighty-three, ill, completely retired from public life, and as he wrote Le Veillard a few months later, "afflicted with almost constant and grievous pain." Nevertheless his narrative, while it displays less of the zest and energy of the earlier portions, still shows remarkable force and swiftness. Finally, between bouts of illness and opium-induced relief, Franklin drew upon some reserve of strength to complete the last few pages of the fourth part only a few months before his death.

After Franklin's death in 1790 another of his grandsons, William Temple Franklin, who served as his literary executor, discovered the original manuscript of the *Autobiography* among his grandfather's papers and took it with him to Paris. A year later he saw Le Veillard's "fair copy," and since it was much easier to read, traded the original for it. Le Veillard, however, had also made a French translation of his copy. At about the same time an edition of the first portion of the *Autobiography* appeared in French, published by Buisson of Paris, based apparently on one of the "fair copies." William Franklin's edition of Franklin's *Works* did not appear until 1817–1818, including the autobiography as edited from Le Veillard's copy, not including the final few pages. John Bigelow, the American minister to France, found and purchased the original manuscript in 1865, and in 1868 edited and published it. Four source texts of the *Autobiography* now exist: the original manuscript (in the Huntington Library); Le Veillard's translation (in the Library of Congress); William Temple Franklin's version, prepared from Le Veillard's "fair copy"; and Buisson's French edition of 1791.

Dr. Max Farrand of the Huntington Library, after years of work with the four texts, prepared a "restored" copy of the *Autobiography* which is probably the nearest approach to Franklin's intended final version that readers will ever know. The text of this volume follows, with a few minor changes, that of Farrand's *Autobiography of Benjamin Franklin*, published by the University of California Press in cooperation with the Huntington Library, San Marino, California, 1949, reprinted here with the permission of the publishers.

The selections other than the *Autobiography* follow, for the most part, the text of Albert Henry Smyth, *The Writings of Benjamin Franklin* (ten volumes, New York, 1905–07).

FRANKLIN'S LIFE

1706   Born in Boston, January 12 (January 6, 1705, Old Style) on Milk Street, near Old South Church, where he was baptized.

1714   Enters Boston Grammar School, and after a year is sent to private school.

1716   Assists his father, a candlemaker.

1718   Apprenticed to his brother James as printer's assistant.

1723   Breaks his indenture and travels to Philadelphia, where he finds employment with Samuel Keimer, a printer.

1724   At the urging of Governor Keith, leaves for London in November with James Ralph.

1725–26   Employed in London at Palmer's and at Watts' printing houses.

1726   Leaves for Philadelphia July 21, with Mr. Denham, a Philadelphia merchant, who later employs Franklin in his shop.

1727   Returns to Keimer's shop, forms the Junto Club with his friends.

1729   Purchases Keimer's paper, *The Universal Instructor*, begins its publication as *The Pennsylvania Gazette*, and opens a stationer's shop.

1730   Marries Deborah Read (Mrs. Rogers). Appointed Public Printer by Assembly of Pennsylvania.

1732   Begins *Poor Richard's Almanac*.

1733–44   Years of public service as "first citizen" of Philadelphia — founds the Union Fire Company, proposes an Academy, is appointed colonial Deputy Postmaster-General, invents the "Franklin stove," plans city police, is chosen clerk of the General Assembly, and establishes the American Philosophical Society.

1746   Begins researches in electricity.

1748–49   Retires from active participation in printing and publishing.

1751   His Academy opens. Chosen Member of Pennsylvania Assembly.

1753   Awarded the Copley Medal of the Royal Society of London for his research into the nature of lightning and other experiments in electricity.

1754   Serves as a Commissioner from Pennsylvania to the Albany Colonial Congress, where he proposes a plan for uniting the colonies.

1755–56   Assists in raising supplies for Braddock's expedition, supervises construction of forts in Pennsylvania, and serves in the field as a colonel of militia.

1757   Appointed colonial agent for the Province of Pennsylvania, sails for London.

1762   Returns to Pennsylvania.

1764   Again sails for London as agent of Province of Pennsylvania, charged with obtaining change from proprietary to royal government.

1765–70   In London, lobbies against the Stamp Act. Visits Germany and France, and is appointed agent for Georgia, New Jersey and Massachusetts.

1771   Begins writing his autobiography.

1774   Deborah Franklin dies, December.

1775   Returns to America. Member of Philadelphia Committee of Safety, one of Pennsylvania's delegates to the Second Continental Congress, and member of the Committee of Secret Correspondence.

1776   President of Pennsylvania's Constitutional Convention; commissioner to Canada; member of committee to draft the Declaration of Independence; one of three commissioners to France from the new United States of America. Arrives in Paris in December.

1778   Signs treaty for French alliance with United States.

1779   Appointed U.S. Minister Plenipotentiary to France.

1783   With John Jay and John Adams, signs the Treaty of Paris, ending the American Revolution.

1784   In retirement at Passy, resumes his scientific interests and the writing of his autobiography.

1785   Resigns his diplomatic post and returns to Philadelphia, where he is chosen President of the Council of Pennsylvania; re-elected in 1786 and 1787.

1787   Member of Pennsylvania delegation to the Constitutional Convention.

1788   Retires from public life.

1790   Dies April 17. On April 21, is buried in the yard of Christ Church at Fifth and Arch Streets, Philadelphia, after a funeral procession witnessed by the largest crowd of private citizens ever assembled in the United States up to that time.

Benjamin Franklin

AUTOBIOGRAPHY

AND OTHER WRITINGS

Autobiography

DEAR SON,

I HAVE ever had a pleasure in obtaining any little anecdotes
of my ancestors. You may remember the enquiries I made among
the remains of my relations when you were with me in England
and the journey I undertook for that purpose. Imagining it may
be equally agreeable to you to know the circumstances of *my*
life — many of which you are yet unacquainted with — and
expecting a week's uninterrupted leisure in my present country
retirement, I sit down to write them for you. Besides, there
are some other inducements that excite me to this undertaking.
From the poverty and obscurity in which I was born and in which
I passed my earliest years, I have raised myself to a state of
affluence and some degree of celebrity in the world. As constant
good fortune has accompanied me even to an advanced period of
life, my posterity will perhaps be desirous of learning the means,
which I employed, and which, thanks to Providence, so well
succeeded with me. They may also deem them fit to be imitated,
should any of them find themselves in similar circumstances. That
good fortune, when I reflected on it, which is frequently the
case, has induced me sometimes to say that were it left to my
choice, I should have no objection to go over the same life from
its beginning to the end, only asking the advantage authors have
of correcting in a second edition some faults of the first. So
would I also wish to change some incidents of it for others more
favourable. Notwithstanding, if this condition were denied, I
should still accept the offer. But as this repetition is not to be
expected, that which resembles most living one's life over
again, seems to be to recall all the circumstances of it; and, to
render this remembrance more durable, to record them in writing. In thus employing myself I shall yield to the inclination so
natural to old men of talking of themselves and their own actions,
and I shall indulge it, without being tiresome to those who,

from respect to my age, might conceive themselves obliged to
listen to me, since they will be always free to read me or not.
And lastly (I may as well confess it, as the denial of it would be
believed by nobody) I shall perhaps not a little gratify my own
vanity. Indeed, I never heard or saw the introductory words,
"Without Vanity I may say," etc., but some vain thing immediately followed. Most people dislike vanity in others whatever
share they have of it themselves, but I give it fair quarter wherever I meet with it, being persuaded that it is often productive of
good to the possessor and to others who are within his sphere of
action. And therefore, in many cases it would not be altogether
absurd if a man were to thank God for his vanity among the
other comforts of life.

And now I speak of thanking God, I desire with all humility
to acknowledge that I owe the mentioned happiness of my past
life to his divine providence, which led me to the means I used
and gave them success. My belief of this induces me to *hope*,
though I must not *presume*, that the same goodness will still
be exercised towards me in continuing that happiness or in enabling me to bear a fatal reverse, which I may experience as others
have done — the complexion of my future fortune being known
to him only, and in whose power it is to bless to us even our
afflictions.

Some notes one of my uncles (who had the same curiosity in
collecting family anecdotes) once put into my hands furnished
me with several particulars relating to our ancestors. From these
notes I learned that they had lived in the same village, Ecton
in Northamptonshire, on a freehold of about thirty acres, for
at least three hundred years, and how much longer he knew not.
Perhaps from the time when the name of Franklin, which before
was the name of an order of people,[1] was assumed by them as a
surname, when others took surnames all over the kingdom.

This small estate would not have sufficed for their maintenance
without the business of a smith, which had continued in the
family down to my uncle's time, the eldest son being always
brought up to that business — a custom which he and my father
followed with regard to their eldest sons. When I searched the
register at Ecton, I found an account of their births, marriages,

[1] In fifteenth-century England, those who owned land or property,
freeholders.

and burials from the year 1555 only, there being no register kept in that parish previous thereto. By that register I learned that I was the youngest son of the youngest son for five generations back. My grandfather Thomas, who was born in 1598, lived at Ecton till he was too old to continue his business, when he retired to Banbury in Oxfordshire to the house of his son John, a dyer, with whom my father served an apprenticeship. There my grandfather died and lies buried. We saw his gravestone in 1758. His eldest son Thomas lived in the house at Ecton and left it with the land to his only daughter, who with her husband, one Fisher of Wallingborough, sold it to Mr. Isted, now lord of the manor there. My grandfather had four sons that grew up; viz., Thomas, John, Benjamin, and Josiah. Being at a distance from my papers, I will give you what account I can of them from memory, and if they are not lost in my absence, you will find among them many more particulars.

Thomas was bred a smith under his father, but being ingenious and encouraged in learning (as all his brothers were) by an Esquire Palmer, then the principal inhabitant of that parish, he qualified himself for the business of scrivener,[1] became a considerable man in the county affairs, was a chief mover of all public-spirited enterprizes for the county or town of Northampton and his own village, of which many instances were told us at Ecton, and he was much taken notice of and patronized by Lord Halifax. He died in 1702, the 6th of January, four years to a day before I was born. The recital which elderly people made to us of his life and character, I remember, struck you as something extraordinary from its similarity with what you knew of me. "Had he died," said you, "four years later, on the same day, one might have supposed a transmigration." John was bred a dyer, I believe of wool. Benjamin was bred a silk dyer, serving an apprenticeship at London. He was an ingenious man. I remember him well, for when I was a boy he came to my father's in Boston and lived in the house with us some years. There was always a particular affection between my father and him, and I was his godson. He lived to a great age. He left behind him two quarto volumes of manuscript of his own poetry, consisting of fugitive pieces addressed to his friends and relations, of which the following, sent to me, is a specimen.

[1] Professional writer or copyist.

To my Namesake upon a Report of his Inclination to Martial Affairs, July 7th, 1710

Believe me, Ben, war is a dangerous trade.
The sword has many marred as well as made;
By it do many fall, not many rise —
Makes many poor, few rich, and fewer wise;
Fills towns with ruin, fields with blood; beside
'Tis Sloth's maintainer and the shield of Pride.
Fair cities, rich today in plenty flow,
War fills with want tomorrow, and with woe.
Ruined estates, vice, broken limbs, and scars
Are the effects of desolating wars.

ACROSTIC

B-e to thy parents an obedient son,
E-ach day let duty constantly be done.
N-ever give way to sloth or lust or pride,
I-f free you'd be from thousand ills beside;
A-bove all ills, be sure avoid the shelf;[1]
M-an's danger lies in Satan, sin, and self.
I-n virtue, learning, wisdom progress make,
N-e'er shrink at suffering for thy Saviour's sake.
F-raud and all falsehood in thy dealings flee,
R-eligious always in thy station be,
A-dore the maker of thy inward part.
N-ow's the accepted time; give God thy heart.
K-eep a good conscience, 'tis a constant friend;
L-ike judge and witness this thy act attend.
I-n heart, with bended knee, alone, adore
N-one but the Three-in-One forevermore.

He had invented a shorthand of his own, which he taught me, but not having practised it, I have now forgot it. He was very pious, an assiduous attendant at the sermons of the best preachers, which he reduced to writing according to his method, and had thus collected several volumes of them. He was also a good deal of a politician — too much so, perhaps, for his station. There fell lately into my hands in London a collection he had made of all the principal pamphlets relating to public affairs from 1641 to 1717. Many of the volumes are wanting, as appears by the numbering, eight volumes in folio, and twenty-four in quarto

[1] Pawnshop.

and in octavo. A dealer in old books met with them, and knowing me by my sometimes buying books of him, he brought them to me. It would appear that my uncle must have left them here when he went to America, which was about fifty years ago. I have found many of his notes in the margins. His grandson, Samuel Franklin, is still living in Boston.

Our humble family early embraced the Reformation. Our forefathers continued Protestants through the rein of Mary, when they were sometimes in danger of persecution on account of their zeal against popery. They had an English Bible, and to conceal it and place it in safety, it was fastened open with tapes under and within the cover of a joint stool. When my great-great-grandfather wished to read it to his family, he turned up the joint stool upon his knees and then turned over the leaves under the tapes. One of the children stood at the door to give notice if he saw the apparitor coming, who was an officer of the spiritual court. In that case the stool was turned down again upon its feet, when the Bible remained concealed under it as before. This anecdote I had from my uncle Benjamin. The family continued all of the Church of England, till about the end of Charles the Second's reign, when some of the ministers that had been outed for nonconformity holding conventicles [1] in Northamptonshire, Benjamin and Josiah adhered to them and so continued all their lives. The rest of the family remained with the Episcopal church.

Josiah, my father, married young and carried his wife with three children to New England about 1682. The conventicles being at that time forbidden by law and frequently disturbed, some considerable men of his acquaintance determined to go to that country; and he was prevailed with to accompany them thither, where they expected to enjoy the exercise of their religion with freedom. By the same wife, my father had four children more born there, and by a second wife ten others — in all seventeen, of which I remember often to have seen thirteen sitting together at his table, who all grew up to years of maturity and married. I was the youngest son and the youngest of all the children except two daughters. I was born in Boston, in New England.

[1] Meetings of dissenters (here Presbyterians) outlawed by the 1662 Act of Uniformity.

My mother, the second wife, was Abiah Folger, daughter of Peter Folger, one of the first settlers of New England, of whom honourable mention is made by Cotton Mather in his ecclesiastical history of that country, entitled *Magnalia Christi Americana,* as a "godly and learned Englishman," if I remember the words rightly. I have heard that he wrote several small occasional pieces, but only one of them was printed, which I saw many years since. It was written in 1675, in familiar verse according to the taste of the time and people, and addressed to those then concerned in the government there. It asserts the liberty of conscience, and in behalf of the Anabaptists, Quakers, and other sectaries that had been persecuted. He attributes to this persecution the Indian Wars and other calamities that had befallen the country, regarding them as so many judgments of God to punish so heinous an offence, and exhorting a repeal of those laws, so contrary to charity. This piece appeared to me as written with manly freedom and a pleasing simplicity. The six last lines I remember, though I have forgotten the two first; the purport of them was that his censures proceeded from good will, and therefore he would be known to be the author.

> Because to be a libeller (says he),
> I hate it with my heart.
> From Sherburne Town [1] where now I dwell,
> My name I do put here,
> Without offence, your real friend,
> It is Peter Folgier.

My elder brothers were all put apprentices to different trades. I was put to the grammar school at eight years of age, my father intending to devote me as the tithe [2] of his sons to the service of the church. My early readiness in learning to read (which must have been very early, as I do not remember when I could not read) and the opinion of all his friends that I should certainly make a good scholar, encouraged him in this purpose of his. My uncle Benjamin, too, approved of it and proposed to give me all his shorthand volumes of sermons to set up with, if I would learn his shorthand. I continued, however, at the grammar school rather less than a year, though in that time I had risen gradually

[1] In the island of Nantucket. [*Franklin's note*]
[2] The tenth part of income set aside for the church; hence, gift or contribution.

from the middle of the class of that year to be at the head of the same class, and was removed into the next class, whence I was to be placed in the third at the end of the year. But my father, burdened with a numerous family, was unable without inconvenience to support the expence of a college education, considering, moreover, as he said to one of his friends in my presence, the little encouragement that line of life afforded to those educated for it. He gave up his first intentions, took me from the grammar school, and sent me to a school for writing and arithmetic kept by a then famous man, Mr. Geo. Brownell. He was a skillful master, and successful in his profession, employing the mildest and most encouraging methods. Under him I learned to write a good hand pretty soon, but I failed in the arithmetic and made no progress in it. At ten years old, I was taken home to help my father in his business, which was that of a tallow chandler and soap boiler — a business he was not bred to but had assumed on his arrival in New England, because he found his dyeing trade, being in little request, would not maintain his family. Accordingly, I was employed in cutting wick for the candles, filling the molds for cast candles, attending the shop, going of errands, etc.

I disliked the trade and had a strong inclination to go to sea, but my father declared against it; however, living near the water, I was much in it and on it. I learned early to swim well and to manage boats; and when embarked with other boys, I was commonly allowed to govern, especially in any case of difficulty; and upon other occasions I was generally the leader among the boys and sometimes led them into scrapes, of which I will mention one instance as it shows an early projecting public spirit, tho' not then justly conducted.

There was a salt marsh that bounded part of the mill pond, on the edge of which at high water, we used to stand to fish for minnows. By much trampling we had made it a mere quagmire. My proposal was to build a wharf there for us to stand upon, and I showed my comrades a large heap of stones which were intended for a new house near the marsh and which would very well suit our purpose. Accordingly, in the evening when the workmen were gone home, I assembled a number of my playfellows, and we worked diligently like so many emmets,[1] sometimes two or three to a stone, 'till we brought them all to make

[1] Ants.

our little wharf. The next morning the workmen were surprised at missing the stones, which had formed our wharf; enquiry was made after the authors of this transfer; we were discovered, complained of; several of us were corrected by our fathers, and tho' I demonstrated the utility of our work, mine convinced me that that which was not honest could not be truly useful.

I suppose you may like to know what kind of a man my father was. He had an excellent constitution, was of middle stature, but well set and very strong. He was ingenious, could draw prettily, was skilled a little in music; his voice was sonorous and agreeable, so that when he played Psalm tunes on his violin and sung withal as he sometimes did in an evening after the business of the day was over, it was extremely agreeable to hear. He had some knowledge of mechanics, too, and on occasion was very handy with other tradesmen's tools. But his great excellence was a sound understanding and a solid judgment in prudential matters, both in private and public affairs. It is true he was never employed in the latter, the numerous family he had to educate and the straitness of his circumstances keeping him close to his trade; but I remember well his being frequently visited by leading men who consulted him for his opinion in affairs of the town or of the church he belonged to, and who showed a good deal of respect for his judgment and advice. He was also much consulted by private persons about their affairs when any difficulty occurred, and frequently chosen an arbitrator between contending parties. At his table he liked to have, as often as he could, some sensible friend or neighbour to converse with, and always took care to start some ingenious or useful topic for discourse which might tend to improve the minds of his children. By this means he turned our attention to what was good, just, and prudent in the conduct of life; and little or no notice was ever taken of what related to the victuals on the table — whether it was well or ill dressed, in or out of season, of good or bad flavour, preferable or inferior to this or that other thing of the kind; so that I was brought up in such a perfect inattention to those matters as to be quite indifferent what kind of food was set before me, and so unobservant of it, that to this day I can scarce tell a few hours after dinner of what dishes it consisted. This has been a great convenience to me in travelling, where my companions have been sometimes very unhappy for want of a suitable gratification of their more delicate, because better instructed, tastes and appetites. My mother had likewise an excellent constitution. She suckled all her ten children. I never knew either my father or mother to have any sickness but that of which they died, he at eighty-nine and she at eighty-five years of age. They lie buried together at Boston, where I some years since placed a marble stone over their grave with this inscription:

Josiah Franklin
And Abiah his wife
Lie here interred.
They lived lovingly together in wedlock
Fifty-five years.
Without an estate or any gainful employment,
By constant labour and industry,
With God's blessing,
They maintained a large family
Comfortably;
And brought up thirteen children,
And seven grandchildren
Reputably.
From this instance, Reader,
Be encouraged to diligence in thy calling,
And distrust not Providence.
He was a pious and prudent man,
She a discreet and virtuous woman.
Their youngest son,
In filial regard to their memory,
Places this stone.
J. F. born 1655 — Died 1744 — AEtat. 89.
A. F. born 1667 — Died 1752 —— 85.

By my rambling digressions I perceive myself to be grown old. I used to write more methodically. But one does not dress for private company as for a public ball. Perhaps 'tis only negligence.

To return: I continued thus employed in my father's business for two years, that is, till I was twelve years old; and my brother John, who was bred to that business, having left my father, married and set up for himself at Rhode Island, there was every appearance that I was destined to supply his place and be a tallow chandler. But my dislike to the trade continuing, my father had apprehensions that if he did not put me to one more agreeable, I should break loose and go to sea, as my brother Josiah had done.

to his great vexation. In consequence he sometimes took me to walk with him and see joiners, bricklayers, turners, braziers, etc., at their work that he might observe my inclination and endeavour to fix it on some trade that would keep me on land. It has ever since been a pleasure to me to see good workmen handle their tools; and it has been useful to me to have learned so much by it as to be able to do little jobs myself in my house, when a workman could not readily be got, and to construct little machines for my experiments when the intention of making these was warm in my mind. My father determined at last for the cutler's trade, and placed me for some days on trial with Samuel, son of my uncle Benjamin, who was bred to that trade in London and had just established him in Boston. But the sum he exacted as a fee for my apprenticeship displeased my father, and I was taken home again.

From my infancy I was passionately fond of reading, and all the little money that came into my hands was laid out in the purchasing of books. I was very fond of voyages. My first acquisition was Bunyan's works in separate little volumes. I afterwards sold them to enable me to buy R. Burton's historical collections; they were small chapmen's books [1] and cheap, forty or fifty in all. My father's little library consisted chiefly of books in polemic divinity, most of which I read. I have since often regretted that at a time when I had such a thirst for knowledge, more proper books had not fallen in my way, since it was now resolved I should not be bred to divinity. There was among them Plutarch's *Lives*, in which I read abundantly, and I still think that time spent to great advantage. There was also a book of Defoe's called an *Essay on Projects* and another of Dr. Mather's called *Essays to do Good*,[2] which perhaps gave me a turn of thinking that had an influence on some of the principal future events of my life.

This bookish inclination at length determined my father to make me a printer, though he had already one son (James) of that profession. In 1717 my brother, James, returned from England with a press and letters to set up his business in Boston. I liked it much better than that of my father, but still had a hankering for

---

[1] Paper books sold by street peddlers.
[2] Daniel Defoe's *Essay on Projects* appeared in 1697, the Reverend Cotton Mather's *Essays to do Good* in 1710.

the sea. To prevent the apprehended effect of such an inclination, my father was impatient to have me bound [1] to my brother. I stood out some time, but at last was persuaded and signed the indenture, when I was yet but twelve years old. I was to serve as apprentice till I was twenty-one years of age, only I was to be allowed journeyman's wages during the last year. In a little time I made a great progress in the business and became a useful hand to my brother. I now had access to better books. An acquaintance with the apprentices of booksellers enabled me sometimes to borrow a small one, which I was careful to return soon and clean. Often I sat up in my room reading the greatest part of the night, when the book was borrowed in the evening and to be returned early in the morning, lest it should be found missing or wanted.

After some time a merchant, an ingenious, sensible man, Mr. Matthew Adams, who had a pretty collection of books and who frequented our printing house, took notice of me, invited me to see his library, and very kindly proposed to lend me such books as I chose to read. I now took a fancy to poetry and made some little pieces. My brother, supposing it might turn to account, encouraged me and induced me to compose two occasional ballads. One was called the "Lighthouse Tragedy," and contained an account of the shipwreck of Capt. Worthilake with his two daughters; the other was a "Sailor's Song on the Taking of the Famous *Teach*, or Blackbeard, the Pirate." They were wretched stuff, in street ballad style; and when they were printed, he sent me about the town to sell them. The first sold prodigiously, the event being recent and having made a great noise. This success flattered my vanity, but my father discouraged me by ridiculing my performances and telling me verse-makers were generally beggars. Thus I escaped being a poet and probably a very bad one. But as prose writing has been of great use to me in the course of my life and was a principal means of my advancement, I shall tell you how in such a situation I acquired what little ability I may be supposed to have in that way.

There was another bookish lad in the town, John Collins by name, with whom I was intimately acquainted. We sometimes disputed, and very fond we were of argument, and very desirous of confuting one another — which disputatious turn, by the way, is apt to become a very bad habit, making people often extremely

[1] Apprenticed.

disagreeable in company, by the contradiction that is necessary to bring it into practice; and thence besides souring and spoiling the conversation, it is productive of disgusts and perhaps enmities where you may have occasion for friendship. I had caught it by reading my father's books of dispute on religion. Persons of good sense, I have since observed, seldom fall into it, except lawyers, university men, and men of all sorts who have been bred at Edinburgh. A question was once somehow or other started between Collins and me on the propriety of educating the female sex in learning and their abilities for study. He was of opinion that it was improper and that they were naturally unequal to it. I took the contrary side, perhaps a little for dispute sake. He was naturally more eloquent, having a greater plenty of words, and sometimes, as I thought, I was vanquished more by his fluency than by the strength of his reasons. As we parted without settling the point and were not to see one another again for some time, I sat down to put my arguments in writing, which I copied fair and sent to him. He answered and I replied. Three or four letters on a side had passed, when my father happened to find my papers and read them. Without entering into the subject in dispute, he took occasion to talk with me about my manner of writing, observed that though I had the advantage of my antagonist in correct spelling and pointing [1] (which I owed to the printing house) I fell far short in elegance of expression, in method, and in perspicuity — of which he convinced me by several instances. I saw the justice of his remarks and thence grew more attentive to my manner of writing, and determined to endeavour to improve my style.

About this time I met with an odd volume of the *Spectator*.[2] It was the third. I had never before seen any of them. I bought it, read it over and over, and was much delighted with it. I thought the writing excellent and wished if possible to imitate it. With that view, I took some of the papers, and making short hints of the sentiment in each sentence, laid them by a few days, and then without looking at the book, tried to complete the papers again by expressing each hinted sentiment at length and as fully as it had been expressed before, in any suitable words that

[1] Punctuation.
[2] Joseph Addison's and Richard Steele's celebrated London periodical, published 1711–1712.

should occur to me. Then I compared my *Spectator* with the original, discovered some of my faults, and corrected them. But I found I wanted a stock of words or a readiness in recollecting and using them, which I thought I should have acquired before that time if I had gone on making verses; since the continual search for words of the same import but of different length to suit the measure, or of different sound for the rhyme would have laid me under a constant necessity of searching for variety, and also have tended to fix that variety in my mind, and make me master of it. Therefore I took some of the tales in the *Spectator* and turned them into verse, and after a time, when I had pretty well forgotten the prose, turned them back again. I also sometimes jumbled my collections of hints into confusion, and after some weeks endeavoured to reduce them into the best order before I began to form the full sentences and complete the paper. This was to teach me method in the arrangement of the thoughts. By comparing my work afterwards with the original, I discovered many faults and corrected them; but I sometimes had the pleasure of fancying that in certain particulars of small import I had been lucky enough to improve the method or the language, and this encouraged me to think that I might possibly in time come to be a tolerable English writer, of which I was extremely ambitious.

The time I allotted for these exercises and for reading, was at night after work, or before it began in the morning, or on Sundays, when I contrived to be in the printing house alone, avoiding as much as I could the common attendance on public worship which my father used to exact of me, when I was under his care — and which, indeed, I still thought a duty, though I could not, as it seemed to me, afford the time to practise it.

When about sixteen years of age I happened to meet with a book written by one Tryon, recommending a vegetable diet.[1] I determined to go into it. My brother, being yet unmarried, did not keep house but boarded himself and his apprentices in another family. My refusing to eat flesh occasioned an inconveniency, and I was frequently chid for my singularity. I made myself acquainted with Tryon's manner of preparing some of his dishes, such as boiling potatoes or rice, making hasty pudding, and a few others; and then proposed to my brother that

[1] Thomas Tryon (1634–1703) published various pamphlets on health.

if he would give me weekly half the money he paid for my board, I would board myself. He instantly agreed to it, and I presently found that I could save half what he paid me. This was an additional fund for buying of books. But I had another advantage in it. My brother and the rest going from the printing house to their meals, I remained there alone, and dispatching presently my light repast (which often was no more than a biscuit or a slice of bread, a handful of raisins or a tart from the pastry cook's, and a glass of water) had the rest of the time till their return for study, in which I made the greater progress from that greater clearness of head and quicker apprehension which generally attend temperance in eating and drinking. Now it was that being on some occasion made ashamed of my ignorance in figures, which I had twice failed in learning when at school, I took Cocker's book of arithmetic, and went through the whole by myself with the greatest ease. I also read Seller's and Sturmy's book on navigation and became acquainted with the little geometry it contains, but I never proceeded far in that science. I read about this time Locke *On Human Understanding*, and *The Art of Thinking* by Messrs. du Port Royal.[1]

While I was intent on improving my language, I met with an English grammar (I think it was Greenwood's) at the end of which there were two little sketches on the arts of rhetoric and logic, the latter finishing with a dispute in the Socratic method. And soon after I procured Xenophon's *Memorable Things of Socrates*, wherein there are many examples of the same method. I was charmed with it, adopted it, dropped my abrupt contradiction and positive argumentation, and put on the humble enquirer. And being then, from reading Shaftsbury and Collins,[2] made a doubter, as I already was in many points of our religious doctrines, I found this method the safest for myself and very embarrassing to those against whom I used it; therefore, I took a delight in it, practised it continually, and grew very artful and expert in drawing people, even of superior knowledge, into concessions the consequences of which they did not foresee, entangling them in difficulties out of which they could not extricate

---

[1] John Locke's essay appeared in 1690. *The Art of Thinking* was a collection of essays published in 1662 by French followers of Descartes.

[2] The Earl of Shaftesbury's *Characteristics* (1712, 1714), and Anthony Collins' *Discourse* (1713) were liberal, rational theological treatises.

themselves, and so obtaining victories that neither myself nor my cause always deserved. I continued this method some few years but gradually left it, retaining only the habit of expressing myself in terms of modest diffidence, never using when I advance anything that may possibly be disputed the words, "certainly," "undoubtedly," or any other that give the air of positiveness to an opinion; but rather say, "I conceive or apprehend a thing to be so or so," "It appears to me," or "I should think it so or so, for such and such reasons," or "I imagine it to be so," or "It is so if I am not mistaken." This habit, I believe, has been of great advantage to me when I have had occasion to inculcate my opinions and persuade men into measures that I have been from time to time engaged in promoting. And as the chief ends of conversation are to *inform*, or to *be informed*, to *please* or to *persuade*, I wish well-meaning and sensible men would not lessen their power of doing good by a positive, assuming manner that seldom fails to disgust, tends to create opposition, and to defeat every one of those purposes for which speech was given to us. In fact, if you wish to instruct others, a positive, dogmatical manner in advancing your sentiments may provoke contradiction and prevent a candid attention. If you desire instruction and improvement from the knowledge of others, you should not at the same time express yourself as firmly fixed in your present opinions; modest and sensible men, who do not love disputation, will probably leave you undisturbed in the possession of your error. In adopting such a manner you can seldom expect to please your hearers, or to persuade those whose concurrence you desire. Pope judiciously observes,

> Men must be taught as if you taught them not,
> And things unknown propos'd as things forgot.

He also recommends it to us,

> To speak, though sure, with seeming diffidence.

And he might have joined with this line that which he has coupled with another, I think less properly,

> For want of modesty is want of sense.

If you ask why *less properly*, I must repeat the lines,

> Immodest words admit of *no defence*,
> *For* want of modesty is want of sense.

Now is not the "want of sense" (where a man is so unfortunate as to want it) some apology for his "want of modesty"? and would not the lines stand more justly thus?

> Immodest words admit *but* this defense
> That want of modesty is want of sense.

This, however, I should submit to better judgments.

My brother had in 1720 or '21 begun to print a newspaper. It was the second that appeared in America and was called *The New England Courant.*[1] The only one before it was *The Boston Newsletter.* I remember his being dissuaded by some of his friends from the undertaking as not likely to succeed, one newspaper being in their judgment enough for America. At this time, 1771, there are not less than five-and-twenty. He went on, however, with the undertaking; I was employed to carry the papers to the customers, after having worked in composing the types and printing off the sheets. He had some ingenious men among his friends who amused themselves by writing little pieces for this paper, which gained it credit and made it more in demand; and these gentlemen often visited us. Hearing their conversations and their accounts of the approbation their papers were received with, I was excited to try my hand among them. But being still a boy and suspecting that my brother would object to printing anything of mine in his paper if he knew it to be mine, I contrived to disguise my hand; and writing an anonymous paper, I put it at night under the door of the printing house. It was found in the morning and communicated to his writing friends when they called in as usual. They read it, commented on it in my hearing, and I had the exquisite pleasure of finding it met with their approbation, and that in their different guesses at the author, none were named but men of some character among us for learning and ingenuity. I suppose now that I was rather lucky in my judges and that perhaps they were not really so very good as I then believed them to be. Encouraged, however, by this attempt, I wrote and sent in the same way to the press several other pieces, which were equally approved, and I kept my secret till my small fund of sense for such performances was pretty well exhausted, and then I discovered it,[2] when I began to be con-

---

[1] First published August 21, 1721. However, it was actually the fifth.
[2] Revealed.

sidered a little more by my brother's acquaintance. However, that did not quite please him as he thought that it tended to make me too vain.

This might be one occasion of the differences we began to have about this time. Though a brother, he considered himself as my master and me as his apprentice, and accordingly expected the same services from me as he would from another; while I thought he degraded me too much in some he required of me, who from a brother expected more indulgence. Our disputes were often brought before our father, and I fancy I was either generally in the right or else a better pleader, because the judgment was generally in my favour. But my brother was passionate and had often beaten me, which I took extremely amiss. I fancy his harsh and tyrannical treatment of me might be a means of impressing me with that aversion to arbitrary power that has stuck to me through my whole life. Thinking my apprenticeship very tedious, I was continually wishing for some opportunity of shortening it, which at length offered in a manner unexpected.

One of the pieces in our newspaper on some political point which I have now forgotten, gave offence to the Assembly. He was taken up, censured, and imprisoned for a month by the Speaker's warrant, I suppose because he would not discover the author. I, too, was taken up and examined before the Council; but though I did not give them any satisfaction, they contented themselves with admonishing me and dismissed me, considering me, perhaps, as an apprentice who was bound to keep his master's secrets. During my brother's confinement, which I resented a good deal notwithstanding our private differences, I had the management of the paper, and I made bold to give our rulers some rubs in it, which my brother took very kindly, while others began to consider me in an unfavourable light as a young genius that had a turn for libelling and satire. My brother's discharge was accompanied with an order from the House (a very odd one) that "James Franklin should no longer print the paper called the *New England Courant*." There was a consultation held in our printing house amongst his friends in this conjuncture. Some proposed to elude the order by changing the name of the paper; but my brother seeing inconveniences in that, it was finally concluded on as a better way to let it be printed for the future under the name of "Benjamin Franklin"; and to avoid the censure of the Assembly that might fall on him as still printing it by his apprentice, the contrivance was that my old indenture should be returned to me with a full discharge on the back of it, to show in case of necessity; but to secure to him the benefit of my service, I should sign new indentures for the remainder of the term, which were to be kept private. A very flimsy scheme it was, but, however, it was immediately executed, and the paper went on accordingly under my name for several months. At length a fresh difference arising between my brother and me, I took upon me to assert my freedom, presuming that he would not venture to produce the new indentures. It was not fair in me to take this advantage, and this I therefore reckon one of the first errata of my life. But the unfairness of it weighed little with me, when under the impressions of resentment for the blows his passion too often urged him to bestow upon me, though he was otherwise not an ill-natured man. Perhaps I was too saucy and provoking.

When he found I would leave him, he took care to prevent my getting employment in any other printing house of the town by going round and speaking to every master, who accordingly refused to give me work. I then thought of going to New York as the nearest place where there was a printer; and I was the rather inclined to leave Boston when I reflected that I had already made myself a little obnoxious to the governing party; and from the arbitrary proceedings of the Assembly in my brother's case, it was likely I might if I stayed soon bring myself into scrapes, and further that my indiscreet disputations about religion began to make me pointed at with horror by good people as an infidel or atheist. I determined on the point, but my father now siding with my brother, I was sensible that if I attempted to go openly, means would be used to prevent me. My friend Collins therefore undertook to manage my flight. He agreed with the captain of a New York sloop for my passage, under pretence of my being a young man of his acquaintance that had had an intrigue with a girl of bad character,[1] whose parents would compel me to marry her and therefore I could not appear or come away publicly. I sold some of my books to raise a little money, was taken on board the sloop privately, had a fair wind, and in three days found myself at New York, near three hundred miles from my home, at

[1] Franklin originally wrote: "that had got a naughty girl with child." [*Farrand's note*]

the age of seventeen, without the least recommendation to or knowledge of any person in the place, and with very little money in my pocket.

The inclination I had had for the sea was by this time done away, or I might now have gratified it. But having another profession and conceiving myself a pretty good workman, I offered my services to the printer of the place, old Mr. Wm. Bradford (who had been the first printer in Pennsylvania, but had removed thence in consequence of a quarrel with the Governor, Geo. Keith). He could give me no employment, having little to do and hands enough already. "But," says he, "my son at Philadelphia has lately lost his principal hand, Aquila Rose, by death. If you go thither I believe he may employ you."

Philadelphia was a hundred miles farther. I set out, however, in a boat for Amboy, leaving my chest and things to follow me round by sea. In crossing the bay we met with a squall that tore our rotten sails to pieces, prevented our getting into the kill,[1] and drove us upon Long Island. In our way a drunken Dutchman, who was a passenger, too, fell overboard; when he was sinking, I reached through the water to his shock pate [2] and drew him up so that we got him in again. His ducking sobered him a little, and he went to sleep, taking first out of his pocket a book which he desired I would dry for him. It proved to be my old favourite author Bunyan's *Pilgrim's Progress* in Dutch, finely printed on good paper with copper cuts, a dress better than I had ever seen it wear in its own language. I have since found that it has been translated into most of the languages of Europe, and suppose it has been more generally read than any other book except, perhaps, the Bible. Honest John was the first that I know of who mixes narration and dialogue, a method of writing very engaging to the reader, who in the most interesting parts finds himself, as it were, admitted into the company and present at the conversation. Defoe has imitated him successfully in his *Robinson Crusoe,* in his *Moll Flanders,* and other pieces; and Richardson has done the same in his *Pamela,* etc.

On approaching the island, we found it was in a place where there could be no landing, there being a great surf on the stony beach. So we dropped anchor and swung out our cable towards

---

[1] The channel west of Staten Island.
[2] Bushy hair.

the shore. Some people came down to the water edge and hallooed to us, as we did to them, but the wind was so high and the surf so loud that we could not understand each other. There were some canoes on the shore, and we made signs and called to them to fetch us, but they either did not comprehend us or thought it impracticable, so they went off. Night approaching, we had no remedy but to have patience till the wind abated, and in the meantime the boatman and I concluded to sleep if we could, and so we crowded into the scuttle with the Dutchman who was still wet, and the spray breaking over the head of our boat leaked through to us, so that we were soon almost as wet as he. In this manner we lay all night with very little rest; but the wind abating the next day, we made a shift to reach Amboy before night, having been thirty hours on the water without victuals or any drink but a bottle of filthy rum, the water we sailed on being salt.

In the evening I found myself very feverish and went to bed; but having read somewhere that cold water drank plentifully was good for a fever, I followed the prescription, sweat plentifully most of the night, my fever left me, and in the morning crossing the ferry, I proceeded on my journey on foot, having fifty miles to Burlington, where I was told I should find boats that would carry me the rest of the way to Philadelphia.

It rained very hard all the day, I was thoroughly soaked and by noon a good deal tired, so I stopped at a poor inn, where I stayed all night, beginning now to wish I had never left home. I made so miserable a figure, too, that I found by the questions asked me I was suspected to be some runaway servant, and in danger of being taken up on that suspicion. However, I proceeded the next day, and got in the evening to an inn within eight or ten miles of Burlington, kept by one Dr. Brown.

He entered into conversation with me while I took some refreshment and, finding I had read a little, became very sociable and friendly. Our acquaintance continued all the rest of his life. He had been, I imagine, an itinerant doctor, for there was no town in England or any country in Europe of which he could not give a very particular account. He had some letters and was ingenious,[1] but he was an infidel and wickedly undertook some years after to travesty the Bible in doggerel verse as Cotton had

[1] I.e., he had some learning and was shrewd.

done with Virgil.[1] By this means he set many of the facts in a very ridiculous light and might have done mischief with weak minds if his work had been published, but it never was. At his house I lay that night, and the next morning reached Burlington, but had the mortification to find that the regular boats were gone a little before and no other expected to go before Tuesday, this being Saturday. Wherefore, I returned to an old woman in the town of whom I had bought some gingerbread to eat on the water and asked her advice; she invited me to lodge at her house till a passage by water should offer; and being tired with my foot travelling, I accepted the invitation. Understanding I was a printer, she would have had me remain in that town and follow my business, being ignorant of the stock necessary to begin with. She was very hospitable, gave me a dinner of ox cheek with great goodwill, accepting only of a pot of ale in return. And I thought myself fixed till Tuesday should come. However, walking in the evening by the side of the river, a boat came by, which I found was going towards Philadelphia with several people in her. They took me in, and as there was no wind, we rowed all the way; and about midnight, not having yet seen the city, some of the company were confident we must have passed it and would row no farther; the others knew not where we were, so we put towards the shore, got into a creek, landed near an old fence, with the rails of which we made a fire, the night being cold in October, and there we remained till daylight. Then one of the company knew the place to be Cooper's Creek, a little above Philadelphia, which we saw as soon as we got out of the creek, and arrived there about eight or nine o'clock, on the Sunday morning and landed at the Market Street wharf.

I have been the more particular in this description of my journey, and shall be so of my first entry into that city, that you may in your mind compare such unlikely beginnings with the figure I have since made there. I was in my working dress, my best clothes being to come round by sea. I was dirty from my journey; my pockets were stuffed out with shirts and stockings; I knew no soul, nor where to look for lodging. Fatigued with walking, rowing, and want of sleep, I was very hungry, and my whole stock of cash consisted of a Dutch dollar and about a shilling in copper coin, which I gave to the boatmen for my pas-

[1] The British poet Charles Cotton's parody of Vergil, 1664.

sage. At first they refused it on account of my having rowed, but I insisted on their taking it. A man is sometimes more generous when he has little money than when he has plenty, perhaps through fear of being thought to have but little. I walked towards the top of the street, gazing about till near Market Street, where I met a boy with bread. I have often made a meal of dry bread, and inquiring where he had bought it, I went immediately to the baker's he directed me to. I asked for biscuit, meaning such as we had in Boston, but that sort, it seems, was not made in Philadelphia. I then asked for a threepenny loaf and was told they had none such. Not knowing the different prices nor the names of the different sorts of any bread, I told him to give me three pennyworth of any sort. He gave me accordingly three great puffy rolls. I was surprized at the quantity but took it, and having no room in my pockets, walked off with a roll under each arm and eating the other. Thus I went up Market Street as far as Fourth Street, passing by the door of Mr. Read, my future wife's father, when she, standing at the door, saw me, and thought I made — as I certainly did — a most awkward, ridiculous appearance. Then I turned and went down Chestnut Street and part of Walnut Street, eating my roll all the way, and coming round, found myself again at Market Street wharf near the boat I came in, to which I went for a draught of the river water, and being filled with one of my rolls, gave the other two to a woman and her child that came down the river in the boat with us and were waiting to go farther. Thus refreshed, I walked again up the street, which by this time had many clean dressed people in it who were all walking the same way; I joined them, and thereby was led into the great meetinghouse of the Quakers near the market. I sat down among them, and after looking round awhile and hearing nothing said, being very drowsy through labour and want of rest the preceding night, I fell fast asleep and continued so till the meeting broke up, when someone was kind enough to rouse me. This was therefore the first house I was in or slept in, in Philadelphia.

I then walked down again towards the river and looking in the faces of everyone, I met a young Quaker man whose countenance pleased me, and accosting him requested he would tell me where a stranger could get a lodging. We were then near the Sign of the Three Mariners. "Here," says he, "is a house where they receive strangers, but it is not a reputable one; if thee wilt walk with me, I'll show thee a better one." He conducted me to the Crooked Billet in Water Street. There I got a dinner. And while I was eating, several sly questions were asked me, as from my youth and appearance I was suspected of being a runaway. After dinner my sleepiness returned; and being shown to a bed, I lay down without undressing and slept till six in the evening, when I was called to supper. I went to bed again very early and slept soundly till next morning. Then I dressed myself as neat as I could, and went to Andrew Bradford, the printer's. I found in the shop the old man his father, whom I had seen at New York, and who travelling on horseback, had got to Philadelphia before me. He introduced me to his son, who received me civilly, gave me a breakfast, but told me he did not at present want a hand, being lately supplied with one. But there was another printer in town lately set up, one Keimer, who perhaps might employ me; if not, I should be welcome to lodge at his house, and he would give me a little work to do now and then till fuller business should offer.

The old gentleman said he would go with me to the new printer. And when we found him, "Neighbour," says Bradford, "I have brought to see you a young man of your business; perhaps you may want such a one." He asked me a few questions, put a composing stick in my hand to see how I worked, and then said he would employ me soon, though he had just then nothing for me to do. And taking old Bradford, whom he had never seen before, to be one of the townspeople that had a good will for him, entered into a conversation on his present undertaking and prospects; while Bradford, not discovering [1] that he was the other printer's father, on Keimer's saying he expected soon to get the greatest part of the business into his own hands, drew him on by artful questions and starting little doubts to explain all his views, what influence he relied on, and in what manner he intended to proceed. I, who stood by and heard all, saw immediately that one of them was a crafty old sophister, and the other a true novice. Bradford left me with Keimer, who was greatly surprized when I told him who the old man was.

Keimer's printing house, I found, consisted of an old damaged press and a small worn-out fount of English types, which he was

[1] Disclosing.

then using himself, composing an elegy on Aquila Rose, before-mentioned, an ingenious young man of excellent character, much respected in the town, secretary to the Assembly, and a pretty poet. Keimer made verses, too, but very indifferently. He could not be said to write them, for his method was to compose them in the types directly out of his head; so there being no copy but one pair of cases,[1] and the elegy probably requiring all the letter, no one could help him. I endeavoured to put his press (which he had not yet used, and of which he understood nothing) into order fit to be worked with; and promising to come and print off his elegy as soon as he should have got it ready, I returned to Bradford's, who gave me a little job to do for the present, and there I lodged and dieted. A few days after Keimer sent for me to print off the elegy. And now he had got another pair of cases, and a pamphlet to reprint, on which he set me to work.

These two printers I found poorly qualified for their business. Bradford had not been bred to it and was very illiterate; and Keimer, though something of a scholar, was a mere compositor, knowing nothing of presswork. He had been one of the French prophets [2] and could act their enthusiastic agitations. At this time he did not profess any particular religion, but something of all on occasion, was very ignorant of the world, and had — as I afterwards found — a good deal of the knave in his composition. He did not like my lodging at Bradford's while I worked with him. He had a house, indeed, but without furniture, so he could not lodge me; but he got me a lodging at Mr. Read's, before-mentioned, who was the owner of his house. And my chest and clothes being come by this time, I made rather a more respectable appearance in the eyes of Miss Read than I had done when she first happened to see me eating my roll in the street.

I began now to have some acquaintance among the young people of the town that were lovers of reading, with whom I spent my evenings very pleasantly and gained money by my industry and frugality. I lived very contented, and forgot Boston as much as I could, and did not wish it should be known where I resided except to my friend Collins, who was in my secret and kept it when I wrote to him. At length an incident happened that sent me back again much sooner than I had intended.

[1] Shallow, divided trays for holding type.
[2] Camisards, a French evangelistic sect.

I had a brother-in-law, Robert Holmes,[1] master of a sloop that traded between Boston and Delaware. He being at New Castle, forty miles below Philadelphia, heard there of me and wrote me a letter mentioning the concern of my relations and friends in Boston at my abrupt departure, assuring me of their goodwill to me, and that every thing would be accommodated to my mind if I would return, to which he exhorted me very earnestly. I wrote an answer to his letter, thanked him for his advice, but stated my reasons for quitting Boston so fully and in such a light as to convince him that I was not so much in the wrong as he had apprehended.

Sir William Keith, Governor of the province,[2] was then at New Castle, and Captain Holmes happening to be in company with him when my letter came to hand, spoke to him of me, and showed him the letter. The Governor read it, and seemed surprized when he was told my age. He said I appeared a young man of promising parts and therefore should be encouraged. The printers at Philadelphia were wretched ones, and if I would set up there, he made no doubt I should succeed; for his part, he would procure me the public business, and do me every other service in his power. This my brother-in-law afterwards told me in Boston. But I knew as yet nothing of it; when one day Keimer and I being at work together near the window, we saw the Governor and another gentleman (who proved to be Colonel French of New Castle) finely dressed, come directly across the street to our house and heard them at the door. Keimer ran down immediately, thinking it a visit to him; but the Governor enquired for me, came up, and with a condescension and politeness I had been quite unused to, made me many compliments, desired to be acquainted with me, blamed me kindly for not having made myself known to him when I first came to the place, and would have me away with him to the tavern where he was going with Colonel French to taste, as he said, some excellent Madeira. I was not a little surprized, and Keimer stared with astonishment.[3] I went, however, with the Governor and Colonel French, to a tavern the corner of Third Street, and over the

---

[1] Franklin later spells the name correctly as "Homes."
[2] Governor of Pennsylvania 1717–1726.
[3] Franklin originally wrote: "Keimer stared like a pig poisoned." [*Farrand's note*]

Madeira he proposed my setting up my business. He stated the probabilities of success, and both he and Colonel French assured me I should have their interest and influence to obtain for me the public business of both governments.[1] On my doubting whether my father would assist me in it, Sir William said he would give me a letter to him in which he would set forth the advantages, and he did not doubt he should determine him to comply. So it was concluded I should return to Boston by the first vessel with the Governor's letter of recommendation to my father. In the meantime the intention was to be kept secret, and I went on working with Keimer as usual. The Governor sent for me now and then to dine with him, which I considered a great honour, more particularly as he conversed with me in the most affable, familiar, and friendly manner imaginable.

About the end of April, 1724, a little vessel offered for Boston. I took leave of Keimer as going to see my friends. The Governor gave me an ample letter, saying many flattering things of me to my father and strongly recommending the project of my setting up at Philadelphia as a thing that would make my fortune. We struck on a shoal in going down the bay and sprung a leak; we had a blustering time at sea and were obliged to pump almost continually, at which I took my turn. We arrived safe, however, at Boston in about a fortnight. I had been absent seven months, and my friends had heard nothing of me, for my brother Homes was not yet returned and had not written about me. My unexpected appearance surprized the family; all were, however, very glad to see me and made me welcome, except my brother. I went to see him at his printing house. I was better dressed than ever while in his service, having a genteel new suit from head to foot, a watch, and my pockets lined with near five pounds sterling in silver. He received me not very frankly, looked me all over, and turned to his work again. The journeymen were inquisitive where I had been, what sort of a country it was, and how I liked it. I praised it much and the happy life I led in it, expressing strongly my intention of returning to it; and one of them asking what kind of money we had there, I produced a handful of silver and spread it before them, which was a kind of raree show [2] they had not been used to, paper being the money

---

[1] Pennsylvania and Delaware.
[2] Peep show, usually carried in a box and displayed on the street.

of Boston. Then I took an opportunity of letting them see my watch, and lastly (my brother still grum and sullen) I gave them a piece of eight to drink [1] and took my leave. This visit of mine offended him extremely. For when my mother sometime after spoke to him of a reconciliation, and of her wish to see us on good terms together, and that we might live for the future as brothers, he said I had insulted him in such a manner before his people that he could never forget or forgive it. In this, however, he was mistaken.

My father received the Governor's letter with some surprize but said little of it to me for some days. Captain Homes returning, he showed it to him, and asked him if he knew Keith and what kind of a man he was, adding his opinion that he must be of small discretion to think of setting a boy up in business who wanted yet three years to arrive at man's estate. Homes said what he could in favour of the project; but my father was clear in the impropriety of it, and at last gave a flat denial. Then he wrote a civil letter to Sir William, thanking him for the patronage he had so kindly offered me, and declining to assist me as yet in setting up, I being in his opinion too young to be trusted with the management of an undertaking so important, and for which the preparation required a considerable expenditure.

My old companion Collins, who was a clerk in the post office, pleased with the account I gave him of my new country, determined to go thither also. And while I waited for my father's determination, he set out before me by land to Rhode Island, leaving his books, which were a pretty collection of mathematics and natural philosophy, to come with mine and me to New York, where he proposed to wait for me.

My father, though he did not approve Sir William's proposition, was yet pleased that I had been able to obtain so advantageous a character from a person of such note where I had resided, and that I had been so industrious and careful as to equip myself so handsomely in so short a time. Therefore, seeing no prospect of an accommodation between my brother and me, he gave his consent to my returning again to Philadelphia, advised me to behave respectfully to the people there, endeavour to obtain general esteem, and avoid lampooning and libelling, to which he thought I had too much inclination — telling me that by

[1] He gave a Spanish dollar to buy drinks.

steady industry and a prudent parsimony I might save enough by the time I was one-and-twenty to set me up, and that if I came near the matter he would help me out with the rest. This was all I could obtain, except some small gifts as tokens of his and my mother's love, when I embarked again for New York, now with their approbation and their blessing. The sloop putting in at Newport, Rhode Island, I visited my brother John, who had been married and settled there some years. He received me very affectionately, for he always loved me. A friend of his, one Vernon, having some money due to him in Pennsylvania, about thirty-five pounds currency, desired I would recover it for him, and keep it till I had his directions what to employ it in. Accordingly he gave me an order. This business afterwards occasioned me a good deal of uneasiness.

At Newport we took in a number of passengers — among which were two young women travelling together and a grave, sensible, matron-like Quaker lady with her servants. I had shown an obliging readiness to render her some little services, which impressed her, I suppose, with a degree of good-will towards me; for when she saw a daily growing familiarity between me and the two young women, which they appeared to encourage, she took me aside and said, "Young man, I am concerned for thee, as thou hast no friend with thee and seems not to know much of the world or of the snares youth is exposed to; depend upon it, those are very bad women; I can see it by all their actions; and if thee art not upon thy guard, they will draw thee into some danger; they are strangers to thee, and I advise thee, in a friendly concern for thy welfare, to have no acquaintance with them." As I seemed at first not to think so ill of them as she did, she mentioned some things she had observed and heard that had escaped my notice, but now convinced me she was right. I thanked her for her kind advice and promised to follow it. When we arrived at New York, they told me where they lived and invited me to come and see them; but I avoided it. And it was well I did; for the next day the captain missed a silver spoon and some other things that had been taken out of his cabin; and knowing that these were a couple of strumpets, he got a warrant to search their lodgings, found the stolen goods, and had the thieves punished. So though we escaped a sunken rock which we scraped upon in the passage, I thought this escape of rather more importance to me.

At New York I found my friend Collins, who had arrived there sometime before me. We had been intimate from children and had read the same books together, but he had the advantage of more time for reading and studying and a wonderful genius for mathematical learning, in which he far outstripped me. While I lived in Boston, most of my hours of leisure for conversation were spent with him; and he continued a sober as well as an industrious lad, was much respected for his learning by several of the clergy and other gentlemen, and seemed to promise making a good figure in life. But during my absence he had acquired a habit of sotting with brandy, and I found by his own account, as well as that of others, that he had been drunk every day since his arrival at New York, and behaved himself in a very extravagant manner. He had gamed, too, and lost his money, so that I was obliged to discharge [1] his lodgings and defray his expenses on the road and at Philadelphia — which proved a great burden to me. The then Governor of New York, Burnet, son of Bishop Burnet,[2] hearing from the captain that a young man, one of his passengers, had a great many books, desired him to bring me to see him. I waited upon him and should have taken Collins with me, had he been sober. The Governor received me with great civility, showed me his library, which was a very considerable one, and we had a good deal of conversation about books and authors. This was the second governor who had done me the honour to take notice of me, and for a poor boy like me was very pleasing.

We proceeded to Philadelphia. I received on the way Vernon's money, without which we could hardly have finished our journey. Collins wished to be employed in some counting-house; but whether they discovered his dramming by his breath or by his behaviour, though he had some recommendations, he met with no success in any application and continued lodging and boarding at the same house with me and at my expense. Knowing I had that money of Vernon's, he was continually borrow-

1 Pay for.
2 William Burnet, Governor of New York and New Jersey, 1720–1728 of Massachusetts 1728–1729, and son of the Bishop of Salisbury.

ing of me, still promising repayment as soon as he should be in business. At length he had got so much of it, that I was distressed to think what I should do in case of being called on to remit it. His drinking continued, about which we sometimes quarreled, for when a little intoxicated he was very fractious. Once in a boat on the Delaware with some other young men, he refused to row in his turn.

"I will be rowed home," says he.

"We will not row you," says I.

"You must," says he, "or stay all night on the water, just as you please."

The others said, "Let us row; what signifies it?"

But my mind being soured with his other conduct, I continued to refuse. So he swore he would make me row or throw me overboard; and coming along stepping on the thwarts towards me, when he came up and struck at me, I clapped my hand under his crutch and rising pitched him head-foremost into the river. I knew he was a good swimmer and so was under little concern about him; but before he could get round to lay hold of the boat, we had with a few strokes pulled her out of his reach. And ever when he drew near the boat, we asked if he would row, striking a few strokes to slide her away from him. He was ready to stifle with vexation, and obstinately would not promise to row; however, seeing him at last beginning to tire, we drew him into the boat and brought him home dripping wet in the evening. We hardly exchanged a civil word after this adventure. At length a West India captain who had a commission to procure a tutor for the sons of a gentleman at Barbadoes, happening to meet with him, proposed to carry him thither to fill that situation. He accepted and left me, promising to remit me what he owed me out of the first money he should receive, but I never heard of him after.

The violation of my trust respecting Vernon's money was one of the first great errata of my life, and this affair showed that my father was not much out in his judgment when he supposed me too young to manage business of importance. But Sir William, on reading his letter, said he was too prudent, that there was a great difference in persons, and discretion did not always accompany years, nor was youth always without it. "And since he will not set you up," says he, "I will do it myself. Give me an inventory of the things necessary to be had from England, and I will send for them. You shall repay me when you are able; I am resolved to have a good printer here, and I am sure you must succeed." This was spoken with such an appearance of cordiality that I had not the least doubt of his meaning what he said. I had hitherto kept the proposition of my setting up a secret in Philadelphia, and I still kept it. Had it been known that I depended on the Governor, probably some friend that knew him better would have advised me not to rely on him, as I afterwards heard it as his known character to be liberal of promises which he never meant to keep. Yet unsolicited as he was by me, how could I think his generous offers insincere? I believed him one of the best men in the world.

I presented him an inventory of a little printing house, amounting by my computation to about £100 sterling. He liked it but asked me if my being on the spot in England to choose the types and see that everything was good of the kind might not be of some advantage. "Then," says he, "when there you may make acquaintances and establish correspondences in the bookselling and stationery way." I agreed that this might be advantageous. "Then," says he, "get yourself ready to go with *Annis*," which was the annual ship and the only one at that time usually passing between London and Philadelphia. But it would be some months before *Annis* sailed, so I continued working with Keimer, fretting extremely about the money Collins had got from me, and in daily apprehensions of being called upon for it by Vernon — which, however, did not happen for some years after.

I believe I have omitted mentioning that in my first voyage from Boston to Philadelphia, being becalmed off Block Island, our crew employed themselves catching cod and hauled up a great number. 'Till then I had stuck to my resolution to eat nothing that had had life; and on this occasion I considered, according to my Master Tryon, the taking every fish as a kind of unprovoked murder, since none of them had or ever could do us any injury that might justify this massacre. All this seemed very reasonable. But I had formerly been a great lover of fish, and when this came hot out of the frying pan, it smelled admirably well. I balanced some time between principle and inclination till I recollected that when the fish were opened, I saw smaller fish taken out of their stomachs. "Then," thought I, "if you eat one another, I don't see why we mayn't eat you." So I dined upon cod very heartily and have since continued to eat as other people, returning only now and then occasionally to a vegetable diet. So convenient a thing it is to be a *reasonable creature*, since it enables one to find or make a reason for everything one has a mind to do.

Keimer and I lived on a pretty good familiar footing and agreed tolerably well, for he suspected nothing of my setting up. He retained a great deal of his old enthusiasm and loved argumentation. We therefore had many disputations. I used to work him so with my Socratic method and had trapanned [1] him so often by questions apparently so distant from any point we had in hand, and yet by degrees leading to the point and bringing him into difficulties and contradictions, that at last he grew ridiculously cautious and would hardly answer the most common question without asking first, "What do you intend to infer from that?" However, it gave him so high an opinion of my abilities in the confuting way that he seriously proposed my being his colleague in a project he had of setting up a new sect. He was to preach the doctrines, and I was to confound all opponents. When he came to explain with me upon the doctrines, I found several conundrums which I objected to, unless I might have my way a little, too, and introduce some of mine. Keimer wore his beard at full length, because somewhere in the Mosaic Law it is said, "Thou shalt nor mar the corners of thy beard." He likewise kept the seventh day Sabbath, and these two points were essentials with him. I disliked both but agreed to admit them upon condition of his adopting the doctrine of not using animal food. "I doubt," says he, "my constitution will bear it." I assured him it would and that he would be the better for it. He was usually a great glutton, and I wished to give myself some diversion in half-starving him. He consented to try the practice if I would keep him company; I did so, and we held it for three months. Our provisions were purchased, cooked, and brought to us regularly by a woman in the neighbourhood who had from me a list of forty dishes to be prepared for us at different times, in which there entered neither fish, flesh, nor fowl. This whim suited me better at this time from the cheapness of it, not costing us above eighteen pence sterling each per week. I have since

[1] Snared.

kept several Lents most strictly, leaving the common diet for that, and that for common, abruptly, without the least inconvenience, so that I think there is little in the advice of making those changes by easy gradations. I went on pleasantly, but poor Keimer suffered grievously, tired of the project, longed for the flesh pots of Egypt, and ordered a roast pig. He invited me and two women friends to dine with him, but it being brought too soon upon table, he could not resist the temptation and ate it all up before we came.

I had made some courtship during this time to Miss Read. I had a great respect and affection for her, and had some reasons to believe she had the same for me; but as I was about to take a long voyage and we were both very young, only a little above eighteen, it was thought most prudent by her mother to prevent our going too far at present, as a marriage, if it was to take place, would be more convenient after my return, when I should be as I hoped set up in my business. Perhaps, too, she thought my expectations not so well founded as I imagined them to be.

My chief acquaintances at this time were Charles Osborne, Joseph Watson, and James Ralph — all lovers of reading. The two first were clerks to an eminent scrivener or conveyancer [1] in the town, Charles Brogden; the other was clerk to a merchant. Watson was a pious, sensible young man of great integrity. The others [were] rather more lax in their principles of religion, particularly Ralph, who as well as Collins had been unsettled by me, for which they both made me suffer. Osborne was sensible, candid, frank — sincere and affectionate to his friends — but in literary matters too fond of criticism. Ralph was ingenious, genteel in his manners, and extremely eloquent; I think I never knew a prettier talker. Both were great admirers of poetry and began to try their hands in little pieces. Many pleasant walks we four had together on Sundays in the woods on the banks of the Schuylkill, when we read to one another and conferred on what we read. Ralph was inclined to give himself up entirely to poetry, not doubting but he might make great proficiency in it and even make his fortune by it. He pretended that the greatest poets must, when they first began to write, have committed as many faults as he did. Osborne endeavoured to dissuade him, as-

---

[1] One whose business is drawing deeds, leases, titles for transfers of property.

sured him he had no genius for poetry, and advised him to think of nothing beyond the business he was bred to: "That in the mercantile way, though he had no stock, he might by his diligence and punctuality recommend himself to employment as a factor [1] and in time acquire wherewith to trade on his own account." I approved for my part the amusing one's self with poetry now and then, so far as to improve one's language, but no farther. On this it was proposed that we should each of us at our next meeting produce a piece of our own composing in order to improve by our mutual observations, criticisms, and corrections. As language and expression was what we had in view, we excluded all considerations of invention, by agreeing that the task should be a version of the eighteenth Psalm, which describes the descent of a deity. When the time of our meeting drew nigh, Ralph called on me first and let me know his piece was ready; I told him I had been busy and, having little inclination, had done nothing. He then showed me his piece for my opinion; and I much approved it, as it appeared to have great merit. "Now," says he, "Osborne never will allow the least merit in anything of mine but makes a thousand criticisms out of mere envy. He is not so jealous of you. I wish therefore you would take this piece and produce it as yours. I will pretend not to have had time, and so produce nothing. We shall then see what he will say to it." It was agreed, and I immediately transcribed it that it might appear in my own hand. We met. Watson's performance was read; there were some beauties in it, but many defects. Osborne's was read; it was much better. Ralph did it justice, remarked some faults, but applauded the beauties. He himself had nothing to produce. I was backward, seemed desirous of being excused, had not had sufficient time to correct, etc.; but no excuse could be admitted, produce I must. It was read and repeated; Watson and Osborne gave up the contest and joined in applauding it. Ralph only made some criticisms and proposed some amendments, but I defended my text. Osborne was against Ralph, and told him he was no better able to criticise than compose verses. As these two were returning home together, Osborne expressed himself still more strongly in favour of what he thought my production, having before refrained, as he said, lest I should think he meant to flatter me. "But who would have imagined," says he, "that

[1] Business agent.

Franklin had been capable of such a performance — such painting, such force, such fire! He has even improved the original. In his common conversation, he seems to have no choice of words; he hesitates and blunders; and yet, good God, how he writes!" When we next met, Ralph discovered [1] the trick we had played him, and Osborne was a little laughed at. This transaction fixed Ralph in his resolution of becoming a poet. I did all I could to dissuade him from it, but he continued scribbling verses till Pope cured him.[2] He became, however, a pretty good prose writer. More of him hereafter. But as I may not have occasion to mention the other two, I shall just remark here that Watson died in my arms a few years after, much lamented, being the best of our set. Osborne went to the West Indies, where he became an eminent lawyer and made money but died young. He and I had made a serious agreement that the one who happened first to die should, if possible, make a friendly visit to the other and acquaint him how he found things in that separate state. But he never fulfilled his promise.

The Governor, seeming to like my company, had me frequently to his house; and his setting me up was always mentioned as a fixed thing. I was to take with me letters recommendatory to a number of his friends, besides the letter of credit, to furnish me with the necessary money for purchasing the press, types, paper, etc. For these letters I was appointed to call at different times, when they were to be ready, but a future time was still [3] named. Thus we went on till the ship (whose departure, too, had been several times postponed) was on the point of sailing. Then when I called to take my leave and receive the letters, his secretary, Dr. Bard, came out to me and said the Governor was extremely busy in writing but would be down at New Castle before the ship, and there the letters would be delivered to me.

Ralph, though married and having one child, had determined to accompany me in this voyage. It was thought he intended to establish a correspondence and obtain goods to sell on commission. But I found afterwards that having some cause of discontent with his wife's relations, he proposed to leave her on

---

[1] Revealed.

[2] "Silence ye wolves, while Ralph to Cynthia howls,
    And makes night hideous: — answer him ye owls!"
                                        (Pope's *Dunciad*)

[3] Always.

their hands and never to return to America. Having taken leave
of my friends and exchanged promises with Miss Read, I
quitted Philadelphia in the ship, which anchored at New Castle.
The Governor was there, but when I went to his lodging, his
secretary came to me from him with expressions of the greatest
regret that he could not then see me, being engaged in business
of the utmost importance, but that he would send the letters to
me on board, wished me heartily a good voyage and a speedy return, etc. I returned on board a little puzzled but still not
doubting.

Mr. Andrew Hamilton, a famous lawyer of Philadelphia, had
taken passage in the same ship for himself and son, and with Mr.
Denham, a Quaker merchant, and Messrs. Onion and Russel,
masters of an iron work in Maryland, had engaged the great
cabin, so that Ralph and I were forced to take up with a berth
in the steerage — and none on board knowing us, were considered as ordinary persons. But Mr. Hamilton and his son (it
was James, since Governor) returned from New Castle to Philadelphia, the father being recalled by a great fee to plead for a
seized ship. And just before we sailed Col. French coming on
board, and showing me great respect, I was more taken notice of
and with my friend Ralph invited by the other gentlemen to
come into the cabin, there being now room. Accordingly, we
removed thither.

Understanding that Col. French had brought on board the
Governor's dispatches, I asked the captain for those letters that
were to be under my care. He said all were put into the bag
together; and he could not then come at them, but before we
landed in England I should have an opportunity of picking them
out. So I was satisfied for the present, and we proceeded on our
voyage. We had a sociable company in the cabin and lived
uncommonly well, having the addition of all Mr. Hamilton's
stores, who had laid in plentifully. In this passage, Mr. Denham
contracted a friendship for me that continued during his life.
The voyage was otherwise not a pleasant one, as we had a great
deal of bad weather.

When we came into the channel, the captain kept his word
with me and gave me an opportunity of examining the bag for
the Governor's letters. I found none upon which my name was
put as under my care; I picked out six or seven that by the hand-
writing I thought might be the promised letters, especially as one

of them was addressed to Basket, the King's printer, another to some stationer. We arrived in London the 24th of December, 1724. I waited upon the stationer who came first in my way, delivering the letter as from Gov. Keith. "I don't know such a person," says he, but opening the letter, "Oh, this is from Riddlesden; I have lately found him to be a complete rascal, and I will have nothing to do with him, nor receive any letters from him." So putting the letter into my hand, he turned on his heel and left me to serve some customer. I was surprized to find these were not the Governor's letters; and after recollecting and comparing circumstances, I began to doubt his sincerity. I found my friend Denham and opened the whole affair to him. He let me into Keith's character, told me there was not the least probability that he had written any letters for me, that no one who knew him had the smallest dependence on him, and he laughed at the idea of the Governor's giving me a letter of credit, having, as he said, no credit to give. On my expressing some concern about what I should do, he advised me to endeavour getting some employment in the way of my business. "Among the printers here," says he, "you will improve yourself; and when you return to America, you will set up to greater advantage."

We both of us happened to know, as well as the stationer, that Riddlesden, the attorney, was a very knave. He had half ruined Miss Read's father by drawing him in to be bound [1] for him. By his letter it appeared there was a secret scheme on foot to the prejudice of Mr. Hamilton (supposed to be then coming over with us) and that Keith was concerned in it with Riddlesden. Denham, who was a friend of Hamilton's, thought he ought to be acquainted with it. So when he arrived in England, which was soon after, partly from resentment and ill-will to Keith and Riddlesden, and partly from good will to him, I waited on him and gave him the letter. He thanked me cordially, the information being of importance to him. And from that time he became my friend, greatly to my advantage afterwards on many occasions.

But what shall we think of a Governor playing such pitiful tricks and imposing so grossly on a poor ignorant boy! It was a habit he had acquired. He wished to please everybody; and having little to give, he gave expectations. He was otherwise an ingenious, sensible man, a pretty good writer, and a good governor for the people, tho' not for his constituents, the Proprie-

[1] As a co-signer of a bond.

taries, whose instructions he sometimes disregarded. Several of our best laws were of his planning and passed during his administration.

Ralph and I were inseparable companions. We took lodgings together in Little Britain [1] at 3 s. 6 d. per week, as much as we could then afford. He found some relations, but they were poor and unable to assist him. He now let me know his intentions of remaining in London and that he never meant to return to Philadelphia. He had brought no money with him, the whole he could muster having been expended in paying his passage. I had fifteen pistoles, [2] so he borrowed occasionally of me to subsist while he was looking out for business. He first endeavoured to get into the playhouse, believing himself qualified for an actor; but Wilkes to whom he applied, [3] advised him candidly not to think of that employment, as it was impossible he should succeed in it. Then he proposed to Roberts, a publisher in Paternoster Row, to write for him a weekly paper like the *Spectator*, on certain conditions which Roberts did not approve. Then he endeavoured to get employment as a hackney writer to copy for the stationers and lawyers about the Temple, but could find no vacancy.

For myself, I immediately got into work at Palmer's, then a famous printing house in Bartholomew Close, and here I continued near a year. I was pretty diligent, but I spent with Ralph a good deal of my earnings in going to plays and other places of amusement. We had together consumed all my pistoles, and now just rubbed on from hand to mouth. He seemed quite to have forgotten his wife and child, and I by degrees my engagements with Miss Read, to whom I never wrote more than one letter, and that was to let her know I was not likely soon to return. This was another of the great errata of my life which I should wish to correct if I were to live it over again. In fact, by our expenses, I was constantly kept unable to pay my passage.

At Palmer's I was employed in composing for the second edition of Wollaston's *Religion of Nature*. [4] Some of his reason-

---

[1] London street near St. Paul's.
[2] Spanish quarter doubloons, worth about four dollars each.
[3] Robert Wilks, of the Haymarket and Drury Lane theaters.
[4] William Wollaston (1660–1724), a moderate British deist.

ings not appearing to me well-founded, I wrote a little metaphysical piece in which I made remarks on them. It was entitled "A Dissertation on Liberty and Necessity, Pleasure and Pain." I inscribed it to my friend Ralph; I printed a small number. It occasioned my being more considered by Mr. Palmer as a young man of some ingenuity, tho' he seriously expostulated with me upon the principles of my pamphlet, which to him appeared abominable.[1] My printing this pamphlet was another erratum.

While I lodged in Little Britain I made an acquaintance with one Wilcox, a bookseller, whose shop was next door. He had an immense collection of second-hand books. Circulating libraries were not then in use; but we agreed that on certain reasonable terms, which I have now forgotten, I might take, read, and return any of his books. This I esteemed a great advantage, and I made as much use of it as I could.

My pamphlet by some means falling into the hands of one Lyons, a surgeon, author of a book entitled *The Infallibility of Human Judgment*, it occasioned an acquaintance between us; he took great notice of me, called on me often to converse on those subjects, carried me to the Horns, a pale ale house in —— Lane, Cheapside, and introduced me to Dr. Mandeville, author of *The Fable of the Bees* who had a club there, of which he was the soul, being a most facetious, entertaining companion. Lyons, too, introduced me to Dr. Pemberton [2] at Batson's Coffee House, who promised to give me an opportunity sometime or other of seeing Sir Isaac Newton, of which I was extremely desirous; but this never happened.

I had brought over a few curiosities, among which the principal was a purse made of the asbestos, which purifies by fire. Sir Hans Sloane heard of it, came to see me, and invited me to his house in Bloomsbury Square,[3] where he showed me all his

[1] Franklin's *Dissertation,* a reflection of his readings in Locke and the Newtonians, set out to "prove the doctrine of fate, from the supposed attributes of God. . . ."

[2] Bernard Mandeville's satiric *Fable of the Bees* appeared in 1714. Henry Pemberton, a friend of Newton's, published an exposition of Newtonian philosophy in 1728.

[3] Sir Hans Sloane, president of the Royal Society from 1727 to 1741, was a noted scientist whose collections and library formed part of the nucleus of the British Museum.

curiosities and persuaded me to add that to the number, for which he paid me handsomely.

In our house there lodged a young woman, a milliner, who, I think, had a shop in the cloisters. She had been genteelly bred, was sensible, lively, and of a most pleasing conversation. Ralph read plays to her in the evenings, they grew intimate, she took another lodging, and he followed her. They lived together some time, but he being still out of business, and her income not sufficient to maintain them with her child, he took a resolution of going from London, to try for a country school, which he thought himself well qualified to undertake, as he wrote an excellent hand and was a master of arithmetic and accounts. This, however, he deemed a business below him, and confident of future better fortune when he should be unwilling to have it known that he was once so meanly employed, he changed his name and did me the honour to assume mine. For I soon after had a letter from him, acquainting me that he was settled in a small village in Berkshire, I think it was, where he taught reading and writing to ten or a dozen boys at sixpence per week, recommending Mrs. T. to my care and desiring me to write to him, directing for Mr. Franklin, schoolmaster at such a place. He continued to write to me frequently, sending me large specimens of an epic poem which he was then composing, and desiring my remarks and corrections. These I gave him from time to time, but endeavoured rather to discourage his proceeding. One of Young's satires was then just published. I copied and sent him a great part of it, which set in a strong light the folly of pursuing the Muses with any hope of advancement by them. All was in vain; sheets of the poem continued to come by every post. In the meantime Mrs. T., having on his account lost her friends and business, was often in distresses and used to send for me and borrow what I could spare to help her out of them. I grew fond of her company, and being at this time under no religious restraint, and presuming on my importance to her, I attempted familiarities (another erratum), which she repulsed with a proper resentment. She wrote to Ralph and acquainted him with my conduct; this occasioned a breach between us. And when he returned to London, he let me know he considered all the obligations he had been under to me as annulled — from which I concluded I was never to expect his repaying the money I had lent him or that I had advanced for him. This, however, was of little consequence, as he was totally unable; and by the loss of his friendship, I found myself relieved from a heavy burthen. I now began to think of getting a little money before-hand, and expecting better employment, I left Palmer's to work at Watts's near Lincoln's Inn Fields, a still greater printing house. Here I continued all the rest of my stay in London.

At my first admission into this printing house, I took to work-ing at press, imagining I felt a want of the bodily exercise I had been used to in America, where presswork is mixed with the composing. I drank only water; the other workmen, near fifty in number, were great guzzlers of beer. On occasion I carried up and down stairs a large form of types in each hand, when others carried but one in both hands. They wondered to see from this and several instances that the "Water-American," as they called me, was *stronger* than themselves who drank *strong* beer. We had an alehouse boy who attended always in the house to supply the workmen. My companion at the press drank every day a pint before breakfast, a pint at breakfast with his bread and cheese, a pint between breakfast and dinner, a pint at dinner, a pint in the afternoon about six o'clock, and another when he had done his day's work. I thought it a detestable custom; but it was necessary, he supposed, to drink *strong* beer that he might be *strong* to labour. I endeavoured to convince him that the bodily strength afforded by beer could only be in proportion to the grain or flour of the barley dissolved in the water of which it was made, that there was more flour in a pennyworth of bread, and therefore if he would eat that with a pint of water, it would give him more strength than a quart of beer. He drank on, how-ever, and had four or five shillings to pay out of his wages every Saturday night for that muddling liquor; an expence I was free from. And thus these poor devils keep themselves always under.

Watts after some weeks desiring to have me in the composing room, I left the pressmen. A new *bienvenu* for drink, being five shillings, was demanded of me by the compositors. I thought it an imposition, as I had paid below. The master thought so, too, and forbad my paying it. I stood out two or three weeks, was accordingly considered as an excommunicate, and had so many

little pieces of private malice practised on me by mixing my
sorts,[1] transposing my pages, breaking by matter, etc., etc., if
ever I stepped out of the room — and all ascribed to the Chapel [2]
Ghost, which they said ever haunted those not regularly admitted — that notwithstanding the master's protection, I found
myself obliged to comply and pay the money, convinced of the
folly of being on ill terms with those one is to live with continually. I was now on a fair footing with them and soon acquired considerable influence. I proposed some reasonable alterations in their chapel laws, and carried them against all opposition. From my example, a great many of them left their
muddling breakfast of beer, bread, and cheese, finding they
could with me be supplied from a neighboring house with a
large porringer of hot water gruel, sprinkled with pepper,
crumbed with bread, and a bit of butter in it, for the price of a
pint of beer, viz., three halfpence. This was a more comfortable
as well as a cheaper breakfast and kept their heads clearer. Those
who continued sotting with beer all day were often, by not paying, out of credit at the alehouse and used to make interest with
me to get beer, their "light," as they phrased it, "being out." I
watched the paytable on Saturday night, and collected what I
stood engaged for them, having to pay sometimes near thirty
shillings a week on their accounts. This and my being esteemed
a pretty good "riggite"; that is, a jocular, verbal satirist, supported
my consequence in the society. My constant attendance (I never
making a St. Monday),[3] recommended me to the master; and my
uncommon quickness at composing occasioned my being put
upon all work of dispatch, which was generally better paid. So
I went on now very agreeably.

My lodging in Little Britain being too remote, I found another
in Duke Street opposite to the Romish chapel. It was up two
pair of stairs backwards, at an Italian warehouse. A widow lady
kept the house; she had a daughter and a maidservant and a
journeyman, who attended the warehouse but lodged abroad.
After sending to enquire my character at the house where I last
lodged, she agreed to take me in at the same rate 3 *s.* 6 *d.* per

[1] Type.

[2] A printing house was called a "chapel" by the workmen. Franklin, a
newcomer, was being hazed.

[3] Franklin did not make a holiday of Monday, as some workmen did
because of weekend dissipation.

week, cheaper, as she said, from the protection she expected in having a man lodge in the house. She was a widow, an elderly woman, and had been bred a Protestant, (being a clergyman's daughter), but was converted to the Catholic religion by her husband, whose memory she much revered; had lived much among people of distinction and knew a thousand anecdotes of them as far back as the times of Charles the Second. She was lame in her knees with the gout and therefore seldom stirred out of her room, so sometimes wanted company; and hers was so highly amusing to me that I was sure to spend an evening with her whenever she desired it. Our supper was only half an anchovy each, on a very little slice of bread and butter, and half a pint of ale between us; but the entertainment was in her conversation. My always keeping good hours and giving little trouble in the family made her unwilling to part with me so that when I talked of a lodging I had heard of nearer my business for 2 s. a week, which, intent as I now was on saving money, made some difference, she bid me not think of it, for she would abate me two shillings a week for the future; so I remained with her at 1 s. 6 d. as long as I stayed in London.

In a garret of her house there lived a maiden lady of seventy in the most retired manner, of whom my landlady gave me this account: that she was a Roman Catholic, had been sent abroad when young and lodged in a nunnery with an intent of becoming a nun; but the country not agreeing with her, she returned to England, where there being no nunnery, she had vowed to lead the life of a nun as near as might be done in those circumstances. Accordingly, she had given all her estate to charitable uses, reserving only twelve pounds a year to live on, and out of this sum she still gave a part in charity, living herself on water gruel only and using no fire but to boil it. She had lived many years in that garret, being permitted to remain there gratis by successive Catholic tenants of the house below, as they deemed it a blessing to have her there. A priest visited her, to confess her every day. "I have asked her," says my landlady, "how she, as she lived, could possibly find so much employment for a confessor." "O," says she, "it is impossible to avoid *vain thoughts*."

I was permitted once to visit her. She was cheerful and polite, and conversed pleasantly. The room was clean, but had no other furniture than a mattress, a table with a crucifix and book, a stool, which she gave me to sit on, and a picture over the chimney of St. Veronica, displaying her handkerchief, with the miraculous figure of Christ's bleeding face on it, which she explained to me with great seriousness. She looked pale but was never sick, and I give it as another instance on how small an income life and health may be supported.

At Watts's printing house I contracted an acquaintance with an ingenious young man, one Wygate, who having wealthy relations, had been better educated than most printers, was a tolerable Latinist, spoke French, and loved reading. I taught him, and a friend of his to swim, at twice going into the river, and they soon became good swimmers. They introduced me to some gentlemen from the country, who went to Chelsea by water to see the college and Don Saltero's curiosities.[1] In our return, at the request of the company, whose curiosity Wygate had excited, I stripped and leaped into the river and swam from near Chelsea to Blackfriar's, performing on the way many feats of activity, both upon and under water, that surprized and pleased those to whom they were novelties. I had from a child been ever delighted with this exercise, had studied and practised all Thevenot's motions and positions,[2] added some of my own, aiming at the graceful and easy as well as the useful. All these I took this occasion of exhibiting to the company and was much flattered by their admiration. And Wygate, who was desirous of becoming a master, grew more and more attached to me on that account, as well as from the similarity of our studies. He at length proposed to me travelling all over Europe together, supporting ourselves everywhere by working at our business. I was once inclined to it; but mentioning it to my good friend Mr. Denham, with whom I often spent an hour when I had leisure, he dissuaded me from it, advising me to think only of returning to Pennsylvania, which he was now about to do.

I must record one trait of this good man's character. He had formerly been in business at Bristol, but failed in debt to a number of people, compounded,[3] and went to America. There, by a close application to business as a merchant, he acquired a plenti-

---

[1] Chelsea Hospital, a home for military veterans. Don Saltero (James Salter) kept a museum and coffeehouse nearby.

[2] M. Thévenot's *Art of Swimming*, translated from the French in 1699. Franklin's Thames swim covered nearly three miles.

[3] Compromised on a settlement.

ful fortune in a few years. Returning to England in the ship with me, he invited his old creditors to an entertainment, at which he thanked them for the easy composition [1] they had favoured him with; and when they expected nothing but the treat, every man at the first remove [2] found under his plate an order on a banker for the full amount of the unpaid remainder with interest.

He now told me he was about to return to Philadelphia and should carry over a great quantity of goods in order to open a store there. He proposed to take me over as his clerk to keep his books (in which he would instruct me), copy his letters, and attend the store. He added that as soon as I should be acquainted with mercantile business he would promote me by sending me with a cargo of flour and bread, etc., to the West Indies, and procure me commissions from others which would be profitable, and if I managed well, would establish me handsomely. The thing pleased me, for I was grown tired of London, remembered with pleasure the happy months I had spent in Pennsylvania, and wished again to see it. Therefore, I immediately agreed on the terms of fifty pounds a year, Pennsylvania money — less, indeed, than my then present gettings as a compositor but affording a better prospect.

I now took leave of printing, as I thought, forever, and was daily employed in my new business — going about with Mr. Denham among the tradesmen to purchase various articles and see them packed up, delivering messages, calling upon workmen to dispatch, etc.; and when all was on board, I had a few days' leisure. On one of these days I was, to my surprise, sent for by a great man I knew only by name, a Sir William Wyndham, and I waited upon him. He had heard by some means or other of my swimming from Chelsea to Blackfriars and of my teaching Wygate and another young man to swim in a few hours. He had two sons about to set out on their travels; he wished to have them first taught swimming, and proposed to gratify me handsomely if I would teach them. They were not yet come to town, and my stay was uncertain, so I could not undertake it. But from this incident I thought it likely that if I were to remain in England and open a swimming school, I might get a good deal of money; and it struck me so strongly that, had the overture been

---

[1] Settlement or agreement.
[2] After the removal of the first course of the meal.

made me sooner, probably I should not so soon have returned to America. After many years, you and I had something of more importance to do with one of these sons of Sir William Wyndham, become Earl of Egremont, which I shall mention in its place.

Thus I passed about eighteen months in London. Most part of the time, I worked hard at my business, and spent but little upon myself except in seeing plays, and in books. My friend Ralph had kept me poor. He owed me about twenty-seven pounds, which I was now never likely to receive — a great sum out of my small earnings. I loved him notwithstanding, for he had many amiable qualities. I had improved my knowledge, however, though I had by no means improved my fortune. But I had made some very ingenious acquaintance, whose conversation was of great advantage to me, and I had read considerably.

We sailed from Gravesend on the 23rd of July, 1726. For the incidents of the voyage, I refer you to my Journal where you will find them all minutely related. Perhaps the most important part of that Journal is the *Plan* to be found in it, which I formed at sea, for regulating the future conduct of my life. It is the more remarkable as being formed when I was so young and yet being pretty faithfully adhered to quite thro' to old age.

We landed at Philadelphia the 11th of October, where I found sundry alterations. Keith was no longer Governor, being superceded by Major Gordon.[1] I met him walking the streets as a common citizen. He seemed a little ashamed at seeing me, but passed without saying anything. I should have been as much ashamed at seeing Miss Read, had not her friends, despairing with reason of my return after the receipt of my letter, persuaded her to marry another, one Rogers, a potter, which was done in my absence. With him, however, she was never happy, and soon parted from him, refusing to cohabit with him, or bear his name, it being now said he had another wife. He was a worthless fellow, though an excellent workman, which was the temptation to her friends. He got into debt and ran away in 1727 or '28, went to the West Indies, and died there. Keimer had got a better house, a shop well supplied with stationery, plenty of new types, and a number of hands, tho' none good, and seemed to have a great deal of business.

Mr. Denham took a store in Water Street, where we opened

[1] Patrick Gordon, Governor of Pennsylvania, 1726–1736.

our goods. I attended the business diligently, studied accounts, and grew in a little time expert at selling. We lodged and boarded together; he counselled me as a father, having a sincere regard for me. I respected and loved him, and we might have gone on together very happily; but in the beginning of February, 1727, when I had just passed my twenty-first year, we both were taken ill. My distemper was a pleurisy, which very nearly carried me off. I suffered a good deal, gave up the point in my own mind, and was rather disappointed when I found myself recovering, regretting in some degree that I must now sometime or other have all that disagreeable work to go over again. I forget what Mr. Denham's distemper was; it held him a long time and at length carried him off. He left me a small legacy in a nuncupative will,[1] as a token of his kindness for me, and he left me once more to the wide world; for the store was taken into the care of his executors, and my employment under him ended. My brother-in-law Homes, being now at Philadelphia, advised my return to my business; and Keimer tempted me with an offer of large wages by the year to come and take the management of his printing house, that he might better attend to his stationer's shop. I had heard a bad character of him in London, from his wife and her friends, and was not for having any more to do with him. I tried for further employment as a merchant's clerk, but not readily meeting with any, I closed again with Keimer.

I found in his house these hands: Hugh Meredith, a Welsh Pennsylvanian, thirty years of age, bred to country work; he was honest, sensible, a man of experience, and fond of reading, but addicted to drinking. Stephen Potts, a young country man of full age, bred to the same, of uncommon natural parts, and great wit and humour, but a little idle. These he had agreed with at extreme low wages per week, to be raised a shilling every three months, as they would deserve by improving in their business, and the expectation of these high wages to come on hereafter was what he had drawn them in with. Meredith was to work at press, Potts at bookbinding, which he by agreement was to teach them, though he knew neither one nor t'other. John —, a wild Irishman, brought up to no business, whose service for four years Keimer had purchased from the captain of a ship,[2] he too was

---

[1] Oral, not written.
[2] By paying the cost of his passage from Ireland.

to be made a pressman. George Webb, an Oxford scholar, whose time for four years he had likewise bought, intending him for a compositor (of whom more presently); and David Harry, a country boy, whom he had taken apprentice.

I soon perceived that the intention of engaging me at wages so much higher than he had been used to give was to have these raw, cheap hands formed thro' me, and as soon as I had instructed them, then, they being all articled [1] to him, he should be able to do without me. I went on, however, very cheerfully, put his printing house in order, which had been in great confusion, and brought his hands by degrees to mind their business and to do it better.

It was an odd thing to find an Oxford scholar in the situation of a bought servant. He was not more than eighteen years of age, and he gave me this account of himself: that he was born in Gloucester, educated at a grammar school there, and had been distinguished among the scholars for some apparent superiority in performing his part when they exhibited plays; belonged to the Witty Club there, and had written some pieces in prose and verse which were printed in the Gloucester newspapers; thence was sent to Oxford; there he continued about a year, but not well satisfied, wishing of all things to see London and become a player. At length receiving his quarterly allowance of fifteen guineas, instead of discharging his debts, he walked out of town, hid his gown in a furze bush, and footed it to London; where having no friend to advise him, he fell into bad company, soon spent his guineas, found no means of being introduced among the players, grew necessitous, pawned his clothes, and wanted bread. Walking the street very hungry and not knowing what to do with himself, a crimp's bill [2] was put into his hand, offering immediate entertainment and encouragement to such as would bind themselves to serve in America. He went directly, signed the indentures, was put into the ship, and came over, never writing a line to acquaint his friends what was become of him. He was lively, witty, good-natured, and a pleasant companion; but idle, thoughtless, and imprudent to the last degree.

John, the Irishman, soon ran away. With the rest I began to

---

[1] Apprenticed.
[2] A printed circular designed to attract emigrants to the American labor market.

live very agreeably; for they all respected me, the more as they found Keimer incapable of instructing them and that from me they learned something daily. We never worked on a Saturday, that being Keimer's Sabbath. So I had two days for reading. My acquaintance with ingenious people in the town increased. Keimer himself treated me with great civility and apparent regard; and nothing now made me uneasy but my debt to Vernon, which I was yet unable to pay, being hitherto but a poor economist. He, however, kindly made no demand of it.

Our printing house often wanted sorts,[1] and there was no letter founder in America. I had seen types cast at James's in London, but without much attention to the manner. However, I now contrived a mould, made use of the letters we had, as puncheons, struck the matrices in lead, and thus supplied in a pretty tolerable way all deficiencies. I also engraved several things on occasion. I made the ink, I was warehouse man, and in short quite a factotum.

But however serviceable I might be, I found that my services became every day of less importance as the other hands improved in the business; and when Keimer paid me a second quarter's wages, he let me know that he felt them too heavy and thought I should make an abatement. He grew by degrees less civil, put on more the airs of master, frequently found fault, was captious, and seemed ready for an outbreaking. I went on, nevertheless, with a good deal of patience, thinking that his incumbered circumstances were partly the cause. At length a trifle snapped our connection; for a great noise happening near the courthouse, I put my head out of the window to see what was the matter. Keimer being in the street, looked up and saw me, called out to me in a loud voice and angry tone to mind my business, adding some reproachful words that nettled me the more for their publicity, all the neighbours who were looking out on the same occasion being witnesses how I was treated. He came up immediately into the printing house, continued the quarrel; high words passed on both sides, he gave me the quarter's warning we had stipulated, expressing a wish that he had not been obliged to so long a warning. I told him his wish was unnecessary for I would leave him that instant, and so taking my hat, walked out of doors, desiring Meredith, whom I saw below,

[1] Type characters.

to take care of some things I left, and bring them to my lodging. Meredith came accordingly in the evening, when we talked my affair over. He had conceived a great regard for me and was very unwilling that I should leave the house while he remained in it. He dissuaded me from returning to my native country, which I began to think of. He reminded me that Keimer was in debt for all he possessed, that his creditors began to be uneasy, that he kept his shop miserably, sold often without profit for ready money, and often trusted without keeping accounts; that he must therefore fail, which would make a vacancy I might profit of. I objected my want of money. He then let me know that his father had a high opinion of me, and from some discourse that had passed between them, he was sure would advance money to set us up, if I would enter into partnership with him. "My time," says he, "will be out with Keimer in the spring; by that time we may have our press and types in from London. I am sensible I am no workman. If you like it, your skill in the business shall be set against the stock I furnish; and we will share the profits equally." The proposal was agreeable to me, and I consented. His father was in town and approved of it — the more as he saw I had great influence with his son, had prevailed on him to abstain long from dramdrinking, and he hoped might break him of that wretched habit entirely, when we came to be so closely connected. I gave an inventory to the father, who carried it to a merchant; the things were sent for; the secret was to be kept till they should arrive, and in the meantime I was to get work if I could at the other printing house. But I found no vacancy there and so remained idle a few days, when Keimer, on a prospect of being employed to print some paper money in New Jersey which would require cuts and various types that I only could supply, and apprehending Bradford might engage me and get the job from him, sent me a very civil message that old friends should not part for a few words, the effect of sudden passion, and wishing me to return. Meredith persuaded me to comply, as it would give more opportunity for his improvement under my daily instructions. So I returned, and we went on more smoothly than for some time before. The New Jersey job was obtained. I contrived a copper-plate press for it, the first that had been seen in the country. I cut several ornaments and checks for the bills. We went together to Burlington, where

I executed the whole to satisfaction; and he received so large a sum for the work as to be enabled thereby to keep his head much longer above water.

At Burlington I made an acquaintance with many principal people of the province. Several of them had been appointed by the Assembly a committee to attend the press and take care that no more bills were printed than the law directed. They were therefore by turns constantly with us, and generally he who attended brought with him a friend or two for company. My mind having been much more improved by reading than Keimer's, I suppose it was for that reason my conversation seemed to be more valued. They had me to their houses, introduced me to their friends, and showed me much civility; while he, tho' the master, was a little neglected. In truth he was an odd fish, ignorant of common life, fond of rudely opposing received opinions, slovenly to extreme dirtiness, enthusiastic [1] in some points of religion, and a little knavish withal.

We continued there near three months, and by that time I could reckon among my acquired friends Judge Allen, Samuel Bustill, the Secretary of the province, Isaac Pearson, Joseph Cooper, and several of the Smiths, members of Assembly, and Isaac Decow, the Surveyor-General. The latter was a shrewd, sagacious, old man, who told me that he began for himself when young by wheeling clay for the brickmakers, learned to write after he was of age, carried the chain for surveyors, who taught him surveying, and he had now by his industry acquired a good estate; and says he, "I foresee that you will soon work this man out of business and make a fortune in it at Philadelphia." He had not then the least intimation of my intention to set up there or anywhere. These friends were afterwards of great use to me, as I occasionally was to some of them. They all continued their regard for me as long as they lived.

Before I enter upon my public appearance in business, it may be well to let you know the then state of my mind with regard to my principles and morals, that you may see how far those influenced the future events of my life. My parents had early given me religious impressions, and brought me through my childhood piously in the dissenting way. But I was scarce fifteen when, after doubting by turns of several points, as I found them

[1] Over-emotional.

disputed in the different books I read, I began to doubt of revelation [1] itself. Some books against deism fell into my hands; they were said to be the substance of the sermons which had been preached at Boyle's lectures.[2] It happened that they wrought an effect on me quite contrary to what was intended by them, for the arguments of the deists which were quoted to be refuted appeared to me much stronger than the refutations. In short, I soon became a thorough deist. My arguments perverted some others, particularly Collins and Ralph; but each of them having afterwards wronged me greatly without the least compunction, and recollecting Keith's conduct towards me (who was another freethinker) and my own towards Vernon and Miss Reed (which at times gave me great trouble), I began to suspect that this doctrine, tho' it might be true, was not very useful. My London pamphlet, which had for its motto these lines of Dryden

> Whatever is, is right
> Tho' purblind man
> Sees but a part of the chain, the nearest link,
> His eyes not carrying to the equal beam,
> That poizes all above.

And which from the attributes of God, his infinite wisdom, goodness, and power, concludes that nothing could possibly be wrong in the world and that vice and virtue were empty distinctions, no such things existing, appeared now not so clever a performance as I once thought it; and I doubted whether some error had not insinuated itself unperceived into my argument so as to infect all that followed, as is common in metaphysical reasonings. I grew convinced that *truth, sincerity* and *integrity* in dealings between man and man were of the utmost importance to the felicity of life, and I formed written resolutions (which still remain in my Journal book) to practise them ever while I lived. Revelation had indeed no weight with me as such; but I entertained an opinion that tho' certain actions might not be bad *because* they were forbidden by it, or good *because* it commanded them, yet probably those actions might be forbidden *because* they were bad for us or commanded *because* they were

---

[1] I.e., of the Bible as a source of divine revelation.
[2] Robert Boyle, British scientist who endowed a series of lectures in 1692 "to prove the truth of the Christian religion" against unorthodoxy.

beneficial to us, in their own natures, all the circumstances of things considered. And this persuasion, with the kind hand of Providence, or some guardian angel, or accidental favourable circumstances and situations, or all together, preserved me (thro' this dangerous time of youth and the hazardous situations I was sometimes in among strangers, remote from the eye and advice of my father) without any *wilful*, gross immorality or injustice that might have been expected from my want of religion. I say *wilful* because the instances I have mentioned had something of necessity in them, from my youth, inexperience, and the knavery of others. I had, therefore, a tolerable character to begin the world with; I valued it properly and determined to preserve it.

We had not been long returned to Philadelphia, before the new types arrived from London. We settled with Keimer and left him by his consent before he heard of it. We found a house to hire near the market and took it. To lessen the rent (which was then but £24 a year, tho' I have since known it let for seventy) we took in Thomas Godfrey, a glazier,[1] and his family, who were to pay a considerable part of it to us, and we to board with them. We had scarce opened our letters and put our press in order before George House, an acquaintance of mine, brought a country man to us whom he had met in the street enquiring for a printer. All our cash was now expended in the variety of particulars we had been obliged to procure, and this country man's five shillings, being our first fruits and coming so seasonably, gave me more pleasure than any crown I have since earned, and from the gratitude I felt towards House, has made me often more ready than perhaps I should otherwise have been to assist young beginners.

There are croakers in every country always boding its ruin. Such a one then lived in Philadelphia, a person of note, an elderly man with a wise look and very grave manner of speaking. His name was Samuel Mickle. This gentleman, a stranger to me, stopped one day at my door and asked me if I was the young man who had lately opened a new printing house. Being answered in the affirmative, he said he was sorry for me because it was an expensive undertaking and the expence would be lost, for Philadelphia was a sinking place, the people already half bankrupts or

[1] Godfrey, a brilliant mathematician, invented a navigator's quadrant, while his son, Thomas junior, became one of the first American dramatists.

near being so — all appearances of the contrary, such as new buildings and the rise of rents, being to his certain knowledge fallacious, for they were in fact among the things that would soon ruin us. And he gave me such a detail of misfortunes now existing, or that were soon to exist, that he left me half-melancholy. Had I known him before I engaged in this business, probably I never should have done it. This man continued to live in this decaying place and to declaim in the same strain, refusing for many years to buy a house there because all was going to destruction, and at last I had the pleasure of seeing him give five times as much for one as he might have bought it for when he first began his croaking.

I should have mentioned before that in the autumn of the preceding year I had formed most of my ingenious acquaintance into a club for mutual improvement which we called the Junto. We met on Friday evenings. The rules I drew up required that every member in his turn should produce one or more queries on any point of morals, politics, or natural philosophy, to be discussed by the company, and once in three months produce and read an essay of his own writing on any subject he pleased. Our debates were to be under the direction of a president, and to be conducted in the sincere spirit of enquiry after truth, without fondness for dispute or desire of victory; and to prevent warmth, all expressions of positiveness in opinion or of direct contradiction were after some time made contraband and prohibited under small pecuniary penalties.

The first members were, Joseph Breintnal, a copier of deeds for the scriveners, a good-natured, friendly, middle-aged man, a great lover of poetry — reading all he could meet with and writing some that was tolerable — very ingenious in many little nicknackeries, and of sensible conversation.

Thomas Godfrey, a self-taught mathematician, great in his way, and afterwards inventor of what is now called Hadley's Quadrant. But he knew little out of his way and was not a pleasing companion, as like most great mathematicians I have met with, he expected unusual precision in everything said, or was forever denying or distinguishing upon trifles to the disturbance of all conversation. He soon left us.

Nicholas Scull, a surveyor, afterwards Surveyor-General, who loved books, and sometimes made a few verses.

William Parsons, bred a shoemaker, but loving reading, had

acquired a considerable share of mathematics, which he first studied with a view to astrology that he afterwards laughed at. He also became Surveyor-General.

William Maugridge, a joiner, but a most exquisite mechanic, and a solid, sensible man.

Hugh Meredith, Stephen Potts, and George Webb I have characterised before.

Robert Grace, a young gentleman of some fortune, generous, lively, and witty, a lover of punning and of his friends.

Lastly, William Coleman, then a merchant's clerk, about my age, who had the coolest, clearest head, the best heart, and the exactest morals of almost any man I ever met with. He became afterwards a merchant of great note, and one of our provincial judges. Our friendship continued without interruption to his death, upwards of forty years. And the club continued almost as long and was the best school of philosophy, and politics that then existed in the province; for our queries which were read the week preceding their discussion, put us on reading with attention upon the several subjects that we might speak more to the purpose; and here, too, we acquired better habits of conversation, everything being studied in our rules which might prevent our disgusting each other — from hence the long continuance of the club, which I shall have frequent occasion to speak further of hereafter. But my giving this account of it here is to show something of the interest I had, every one of these exerting themselves in recommending business to us. Breintnal particularly procured us from the Quakers the printing forty sheets of their history, the rest being to be done by Keimer; and upon this we worked exceeding hard, for the price was low. It was a folio, *pro patria* size, in pica with long primer notes. I composed of it a sheet a day, and Meredith worked it off at press. It was often eleven at night, and sometimes later, before I had finished my distribution for the next day's work. For the little jobs sent in by our other friends now and then put us back. But so determined I was to continue doing a sheet a day of the folio, that one night when having imposed my forms I thought my day's work over, one of them by accident was broken and two pages reduced to pie,[1] I immediately distributed and composed it over again before I went to bed. And this industry visible to our

[1] Franklin had set up his forms for printing, but by accident the type for two pages was scrambled.

neighbours began to give us character and credit — particularly, I was told, that mention being made of the new printing office at the merchants' Every-night Club, the general opinion was that it must fail, there being already two printers in the place, Keimer and Bradford; but Doctor Baird (whom you and I saw many years after at his native place, St. Andrew's in Scotland) gave a contrary opinion: "For the industry of that Franklin," says he, "is superior to anything I ever saw of the kind; I see him still at work when I go home from club, and he is at work again before his neighbours are out of bed." This struck the rest, and we soon after had offers from one of them to supply us with stationery; but as yet we did not choose to engage in shop business.

I mention this industry the more particularly and the more freely, tho' it seems to be talking in my own praise, that those of my posterity who shall read it may know the use of that virtue, when they see its effects in my favour throughout this relation.

George Webb, who had found a female friend that lent him wherewith to purchase his time of Keimer, now came to offer himself as a journeyman to us. We could not then employ him, but I foolishly let him know, as a secret, that I soon intended to begin a newspaper and might then have work for him. My hopes of success, as I told him, were founded on this: that the then only newspaper, printed by Bradford, was a paltry thing, wretchedly managed, no way entertaining, and yet was profitable to him. I therefore thought a good paper could scarcely fail of good encouragement. I requested Webb not to mention it, but he told it to Keimer, who immediately, to be beforehand with me, published proposals for printing one himself, on which Webb was to be employed. I was vexed at this, and to counteract them, not being able to commence our paper, I wrote several amusing pieces for Bradford's paper under the title of the "Busybody," which Breintnal continued some months.[1] By this means the attention of the public was fixed on that paper, and Keimer's proposals, which we burlesqued and ridiculed, were disregarded. He began his paper, however, and after carrying it on three-quarters of a year with at most only ninety subscribers, he offered it to me for a trifle; and I, having been ready some time to go on with it, took it in

---

[1] These appeared in Bradford's *American Weekly Mercury* in 1729.

hand directly, and it proved in a few years extremely profitable to me.[1]

I perceive that I am apt to speak in the singular number, though our partnership still continued; it may be that in fact the whole management of the business lay upon me. Meredith was no compositor, a poor pressman, and seldom sober. My friends lamented my connection with him, but I was to make the best of it.

Our first papers made a quite different appearance from any before in the province, a better type and better printed; but some spirited remarks of my writing on the dispute then going on between Governor Burnet and the Massachusetts Assembly struck the principal people, occasioned the paper and the manager of it to be much talked of, and in a few weeks brought them all to be our subscribers. Their example was followed by many, and our number went on growing continually. This was one of the first good effects of my having learned a little to scribble. Another was that the leading men, seeing a newspaper now in the hands of one who could also handle a pen, thought it convenient to oblige and encourage me. Bradford still printed the votes and laws and other public business. He had printed an address of the House to the Governor in a coarse blundering manner. We reprinted it elegantly and correctly, and sent one to every member. They were sensible of the difference, it strengthened the hands of our friends in the House, and they voted us their printers for the year ensuing.

Among my friends in the House I must not forget Mr. Hamilton before-mentioned, who was then returned from England and had a seat in it. He interested himself for me strongly in that instance, as he did in many others afterwards, continuing his patronage till his death.

Mr. Vernon, about this time, put me in mind of the debt I owed him, but did not press me. I wrote him an ingenuous letter of acknowledgments, craved his forbearance a little longer, which he allowed me; and as soon as I was able, I paid the prin-

[1] Keimer's journal was named *The Universal Instructor in All Arts and Sciences: and Pennsylvania Gazette.* Franklin shortened the name to *The Pennsylvania Gazette,* publishing his first number in October, 1729. After amassing a small fortune from it, he sold the paper to David Hall in 1766.

cipal with interest and many thanks; so that erratum was in some degree corrected.

But now another difficulty came upon me which I had never the least reason to expect. Mr. Meredith's father, who was to have paid for our printing house according to the expectations given me, was able to advance only one hundred pounds currency, which had been paid; and a hundred more was due to the merchant, who grew impatient and sued us all. We gave bail but saw that if the money could not be raised in time, the suit must come to a judgment and execution, and our hopeful prospects must with us be ruined, as the press and letters must be sold for payment, perhaps at half price. In this distress two true friends, whose kindness I have never forgotten nor ever shall forget while I can remember anything, came to me separately, unknown to each other, and without any application from me, offered each of them to advance me all the money that should be necessary to enable me to take the whole business upon myself if that should be practicable; but they did not like my continuing the partnership with Meredith, who, as they said, was often seen drunk in the streets and playing at low games in alehouses, much to our discredit. These two friends were *William Coleman* and *Robert Grace*. I told them I could not propose a separation while any prospect remained of the Merediths fulfilling their part of our agreement, because I thought myself under great obligations to them for what they had done and would do if they could. But if they finally failed in their performance and our partnership must be dissolved, I should then think myself at liberty to accept the assistance of my friends.

Thus the matter rested for some time; when I said to my partner, "Perhaps your father is dissatisfied at the part you have undertaken in this affair of ours and is unwilling to advance for you and me what he would for you alone. If that is the case, tell me, and I will resign the whole to you and go about my business."

"No," says he, "my father has really been disappointed and is really unable; and I am unwilling to distress him further. I see this is a business I am not fit for. I was bred a farmer, and it was a folly in me to come to town and put myself at thirty years of age an apprentice to learn a new trade. Many of our Welsh people are going to settle in North Carolina, where land is cheap. I am inclined to go with them and follow my old employment.

You may find friends to assist you. If you will take the debts of the company upon you, return to my father the hundred pounds he has advanced, pay my little personal debts, and give me thirty pounds and a new saddle, I will relinquish the partnership and leave the whole in your hands."

I agreed to this proposal. It was drawn up in writing, signed and sealed immediately. I gave him what he demanded, and he went soon after to Carolina, from whence he sent me next year two long letters containing the best account that had been given of that country, the climate, soil, husbandry, etc., for in those matters he was very judicious. I printed them in the papers, and they gave great satisfaction to the public.

As soon as he was gone, I recurred to my two friends; and because I would not give an unkind preference to either, I took half what each had offered and I wanted of one, and half of the other, paid off the company's debts, and went on with the business in my own name, advertising that the partnership was dissolved. I think this was in or about the year 1729.

About this time there was a cry among the people for more paper money, only £15,000 being extant in the province and that soon to be sunk. The wealthy inhabitants opposed any addition, being against all paper currency, from the apprehension that it would depreciate as it had done in New England to the prejudice of all creditors. We had discussed this point in our Junto, where I was on the side of an addition, being persuaded that the first small sum struck in 1723 had done much good by increasing the trade, employment, and number of inhabitants in the province, since I now saw all the old houses inhabited and many new ones building where, as I remembered well that when I first walked about the streets of Philadelphia eating my roll, I saw most of the houses in Walnut Street between Second and Front Streets with bills on their doors, "To be Let," and many likewise in Chestnut Street and other streets — which made me then think the inhabitants of the city were one after another deserting it.

Our debates possessed me so fully of the subject that I wrote and printed an anonymous pamphlet on it entitled *The Nature and Necessity of a Paper Currency*. It was well received by the common people in general; but the rich men disliked it, for it increased and strengthened the clamour for more money; and they happening to have no writers among them that were able to answer it, their opposition slackened, and the point was carried by a majority in the House. My friends there, who considered I had been of some service, thought fit to reward me by employing me in printing the money — a very profitable job and a great help to me. This was another advantage gained by my being able to write.

The utility of this currency became by time and experience so evident, as never afterwards to be much disputed, so that it grew soon to £55,000 and in 1739 to £80,000 since which it arose during war to upwards of £350,000 — trade, building, and inhabitants all the while increasing — though I now think there are limits beyond which the quantity may be hurtful.

I soon afterwards obtained, thro' my friend Hamilton, the printing of the New Castle [1] paper money, another profitable job as I then thought it — small things appearing great to those in small circumstances — and these to me were really great advantages, as they were great encouragements. He procured me also the printing of the laws and votes of that government, which continued in my hands as long as I followed the business.

I now opened a small stationer's shop. I had in it blanks [2] of all sorts the correctest that ever appeared among us. I was assisted in that by my friend Breintnal. I had also paper, parchment, chapmen's books, etc. One Whitemash, a compositor I had known in London, an excellent workman, now came to me and worked with me constantly and diligently; and I took an apprentice, the son of Aquila Rose.

I began now gradually to pay off the debt I was under for the printing house. In order to secure my credit and character as a tradesman, I took care not only to be in *reality* industrious and frugal, but to avoid all *appearances* of the contrary. I dressed plain and was seen at no places of idle diversion. I never went out a fishing or shooting; a book, indeed, sometimes debauched me from my work, but that was seldom, snug, and gave no scandal; and to show that I was not above my business, I sometimes brought home the paper I purchased at the stores, thro' the streets on a wheelbarrow. Thus being esteemed an industrious, thriving, young man, and paying duly for what I

---

[1] Newcastle, Delaware.
[2] Legal forms, such as wills, deeds, etc.

bought, the merchants who imported stationery solicited my custom; others proposed supplying me with books, and I went on swimmingly. In the meantime Keimer's credit and business declining daily, he was at last forced to sell his printing house to satisfy his creditors. He went to Barbadoes and there lived some years in very poor circumstances.

His apprentice, David Harry, whom I had instructed while I worked with him, set up in his place at Philadelphia, having bought his materials. I was at first apprehensive of a powerful rival in Harry, as his friends were very able and had a good deal of interest. I therefore proposed a partnership to him, which he, fortunately for me, rejected with scorn. He was very proud, dressed like a gentleman, lived expensively, took much diversion and pleasure abroad, ran in debt, and neglected his business — upon which all business left him; and finding nothing to do, he followed Keimer to Barbadoes, taking the printing house with him. There this apprentice employed his former master as a journeyman. They quarrelled often, Harry went continually behind-hand and at length was forced to sell his types and return to his country work in Pennsylvania. The person who bought them employed Keimer to use them, but a few years after he died.

There remained now no other competitor with me at Philadelphia but the old one, Bradford, who was rich and easy, did a little printing now and then by straggling hands, but was not very anxious about the business. However, as he kept the Post Office, it was imagined he had better opportunities of obtaining news, his paper was thought a better distributor of advertisements than mine and therefore had many more — which was a profitable thing to him and a disadvantage to me. For tho' I did indeed receive and send papers by the post, yet the public opinion was otherwise; for what I did send was by bribing the riders, who took them privately — Bradford being unkind enough to forbid it, which occasioned some resentment on my part; and I thought so meanly of him for it that when I afterwards came into his situation, I took care never to imitate it.[1]

[1] Franklin paid the postal riders to deliver his papers. Bradford, who controlled the Post Office, refused to allow this, in order to stifle Franklin's competition. Franklin, when he became Deputy Postmaster of all the colonies in 1753, made the mails available to all publishers.

I had hitherto continued to board with Godfrey, who lived in part of my house with his wife and children, and had one side of the shop for his glazier's business, tho' he worked little, being always absorbed in his mathematics. Mrs. Godfrey projected a match for me with a relation's daughter, took opportunities of bringing us often together, till a serious courtship on my part ensued, the girl being in herself very deserving. The old folks encouraged me by continued invitations to supper and by leaving us together, till at length it was time to explain. Mrs. Godfrey managed our little treaty. I let her know that I expected as much money with their daughter as would pay off my remaining debt for the printing house, which I believe was not then above a hundred pounds. She brought me word they had no such sum to spare. I said they might mortgage their house in the Loan Office. The answer to this after some days was that they did not approve the match; that on enquiry of Bradford they had been informed the printing business was not a profitable one, the types would soon be worn out and more wanted; that S. Keimer and D. Harry had failed one after the other, and I should probably soon follow them; and therefore I was forbidden the house, and the daughter shut up. Whether this was a real change of sentiment or only artifice, on a supposition of our being too far engaged in affection to retract and therefore that we should steal a marriage, which would leave them at liberty to give or withhold what they pleased, I know not. But I suspected the motive, resented it, and went no more. Mrs. Godfrey brought me afterwards some more favourable accounts of their disposition and would have drawn me on again, but I declared absolutely my resolution to have nothing more to do with that family. This was resented by the Godfreys, we differed, and they removed, leaving me the whole house, and I resolved to take no more inmates. But this affair having turned my thoughts to marriage, I looked round me and made overtures of acquaintance in other places, but soon found that the business of a printer being generally thought a poor one, I was not to expect money with a wife, unless with such a one as I should not otherwise think agreeable. In the meantime that hard-to-be-governed passion of youth had hurried me frequently into intrigues with low women that fell in my way, which were attended with some expense and great inconvenience, besides a continual risk to my health by a distemper, which of all things I dreaded, tho' by great good luck I escaped it.

A friendly correspondence as neighbours and old acquaintances had continued between me and Miss Read's family, who all had a regard for me from the time of my first lodging in their house. I was often invited there and consulted in their affairs, wherein I sometimes was of service. I pitied poor Miss Read's unfortunate situation, who was generally dejected, seldom cheerful, and avoided company. I considered my giddiness and inconstancy when in London as in a great degree the cause of her unhappiness, tho' the mother was good enough to think the fault more her own than mine, as she had prevented our marrying before I went thither and persuaded the match in my absence. Our mutual affection was revived, but there were now great objections to our union. That match was indeed looked upon as invalid, a preceding wife being said to be living in England; but this could not easily be proved because of the distance. And tho' there was a report of his death, it was not certain. Then, tho' it should be true, he had left many debts which his successor might be called upon to pay. We ventured, however, over all these difficulties, and I took her to wife, Sept. 1, 1730. None of the inconveniencies happened that we had apprehended; she proved a good and faithful helpmate, assisted me much by attending the shop; we throve together and ever mutually endeavoured to make each other happy. Thus I corrected that great erratum as well as I could.

About this time our club meeting, not at a tavern, but in a little room of Mr. Grace's set apart for that purpose, a proposition was made by me that since our books were often referred to in our disquisitions upon the queries, it might be convenient to us to have them all together where we met, that upon occasion they might be consulted; and by thus clubbing our books to a common library, we should, while we liked to keep them together, have each of us the advantage of using the books of all the other members, which would be nearly as beneficial as if each owned the whole. It was liked and agreed to, and we filled one end of the room with such books as we could best spare. The number was not so great as we expected; and tho' they had been of great use, yet some inconveniencies occurring for want of due care of them, the collection after about a year was separated, and each took his books home again.

And now I set on foot my first project of a public nature, that for a subscription library. I drew up the proposals, got them put into form by our great scrivener, Brockden, and by the help of my friends in the Junto, procured fifty subscribers of forty shillings each to begin with, and ten shillings a year for fifty years — the term our company was to continue. We afterwards obtained a charter, the company being increased to one hundred. This was the mother of all the North American subscription libraries, now so numerous. It is become a great thing itself and continually increasing. These libraries have improved the general conversation of the Americans, made the common tradesmen and farmers as intelligent as most gentlemen from other countries, and perhaps have contributed in some degree to the stand so generally made throughout the Colonies in defence of their privileges.

Memo: Thus far was written with the intention expressed in the beginning and therefore contains several little family anecdotes of no importance to others. What follows was written many years after, in compliance with the advice contained in these letters, and accordingly intended for the public. The affairs of the Revolution occasioned the interruption.

Benjamin Franklin

*⌇ For ten years nothing was heard of Franklin's manu-
script. Franklin returned to America in 1775 and in 1776
sailed again for Europe as one of the commissioners as-
signed to negotiations for a French alliance. In late 1782
or early 1783, while he was living in Passy, a Paris suburb,
he received a letter from Abel James, a Philadelphia
printer and publisher, enclosing a copy of the unfinished
narrative and urging its completion. Franklin's papers
had apparently been left with Joseph Galloway near
Philadelphia during the war, and when Galloway, who
remained a Loyalist, left the country, they were retained
by his wife. Upon her death James, one of the executors
of her will, came into possession of the manuscript begun
at Twyford. Franklin sent the copy to Benjamin
Vaughan, a British diplomat who had already edited a
collection of Franklin's writings in 1779. On Vaughan's
advice, and that of his friend Guillaume le Veillard,
Mayor of Passy, Franklin resumed work on his narrative.*

My dear and honored friend:

I have often been desirous of writing to thee, but could not be
reconciled to the thoughts that the letter might fall into the hands
of the British, lest some printer or busybody should publish
some part of the contents and give our friends pain and myself
censure.

Sometimes since there fell into my hands to my great joy
about twenty-three sheets in thy own hand writing containing
an account of the parentage and life of thyself, directed to thy
son, ending in the year 1730, with which there were notes likewise in thy writing, a copy of which I enclose in hopes it may
be a means, if thou continuedst it up to a later period, that the
first and latter part may be put together; and if it is not yet continued, I hope thou wilt not delay it. Life is uncertain, as the
preacher tells us, and what will the world say if kind, humane,
and benevolent Ben Franklin should leave his friends and the
world deprived of so pleasing and profitable a work, a work
which would be useful and entertaining not only to a few but to
millions?

The influence writings under that class have on the minds of
youth is very great and has nowhere appeared so plain as in our

public friend's Journal. It almost insensibly leads the youth into the resolution of endeavouring to become as good and as eminent as the journalist. Should thine, for instance, when published — and I think it could not fail of it — lead the youth to equal the industry and temperance of thy early youth, what a blessing with that class would such a work be! I know of no character living, nor many of them put together, who has so much in his power as thyself to promote a greater spirit of industry and early attention to business, frugality, and temperance with the American youth. Not that I think the work would have no other merit and use in the world — far from it — but the first is of such vast importance, and I know nothing that can equal it. . . .

I trust I need make no apology to my good friend for mentioning to him these matters, believing he continues a relish for every exertion of the sort, in confidence of which I rest with great truth and perfect esteem his

Very affectionate friend,
(Signed) Abel James

The foregoing letter and the minutes accompanying it being shown to a friend, I received from him the following:

Paris, January 31, 1783.

My dearest sir:

When I had read over your sheets of minutes of the principal incidents of your life, recovered for you by your Quaker acquaintance, I told you I would send you a letter expressing my reasons why I thought it would be useful to complete and publish it as he desired. Various concerns have for sometime past prevented this letter being written, and I do not know whether it was worth any expectation; happening to be at leisure, however, at present, I shall by writing at least interest and instruct myself; but as the terms I am inclined to use may tend to offend a person of your manners, I shall only tell you how I would address any other person who was as good and as great as yourself but less diffident. I would say to him, sir, I solicit the history of your life from the following motives: Your history is so remarkable that if you do not give it, somebody else will certainly give it; and perhaps so as nearly to do as much harm, as your own management of the thing might do good. It will, moreover, present a table of the internal circumstances of your country which will very much tend to invite to it settlers of virtuous and manly minds. And considering the eagerness with which such information is sought by them, and the extent of your reputation, I do not know of a more efficacious advertisement than your biography would give. All that has happened to you is also connected with the detail of the manners and situation of a rising people; and in this respect I do not think that the writings of Caesar and Tacitus can be more interesting to a true judge of human nature and society. But these, sir, are small reasons, in my opinion, compared with the chance which your life will give for the forming of future great men; and in conjunction with your Art of Virtue (which you design to publish) of improving the features of private character, and consequently of aiding all happiness, both public and domestic. The two works I allude to, sir, will in particular give a noble rule and example of self-education. School and other education constantly proceed upon false principles and show a clumsy apparatus pointed at a false mark; but your apparatus is simple and the mark a true one; and while parents and young persons are left destitute of other just means of estimating and becoming prepared for a reasonable course in life, your discovery that the thing is in many a man's private power, will be invaluable! Influence upon the private character, late in life, is not only an influence late in life, but a weak influence. It is in youth that we plant our chief habits and prejudices; it is in youth that we take our party [1] as to profession, pursuits, and matrimony. In youth, therefore, the turn is given; in youth the education even of the next generation is given; in youth the private and public character is determined; and the term of life extending but from youth to age, life ought to begin well from youth, and more especially before we take our party as to our principal objects. But your biography will not merely teach self-education, but the education of a wise man; and the wisest man will receive lights and improve his progress, by seeing detailed the conduct of another wise man. And why are weaker men to be deprived of such helps, when we see our race has been blundering on in the dark, almost without a guide in this particular, from the farthest trace of time? Show then, sir, how much is to be done, both to sons and fathers; and invite all wise men to become like yourself, and other men to become wise. When we see how cruel statesmen and warriors can be to the

[1] Make our choice.

human race, and how absurd distinguished men can be to their acquaintance, it will be instructive to observe the instances multiply of pacific, acquiescing manners; and to find how compatible it is to be great and domestic, enviable and yet good-humored.

The little private incidents which you will also have to relate, will have considerable use, as we want, above all things, rules of prudence in ordinary affairs; and it will be curious to see how you have acted in these. It will be so far a sort of key to life, and explain many things that all men ought to have once explained to them, to give them a chance of becoming wise by foresight. The nearest thing to having experience of one's own, is to have other people's affairs brought before us in a shape that is interesting; this is sure to happen from your pen; our affairs and management will have an air of simplicity or importance that will not fail to strike; and I am convinced you have conducted them with as much originality as if you had been conducting discussions in politics or philosophy; and what more worthy of experiments and system (its importance and its errors considered) than human life?

Some men have been virtuous blindly, others have speculated fantastically, and others have been shrewd to bad purposes; but you, sir, I am sure, will give under your hand, nothing but what is at the same moment, wise, practical, and good. Your account of yourself (for I suppose the parallel I am drawing for Dr. Franklin, will hold not only in point of character but of private history) will show that you are ashamed of no origin — a thing the more important as you prove how little necessary all origin is to happiness, virtue, or greatness. As no end likewise happens without a means, so we shall find, sir, that even you yourself framed a plan by which you became considerable; but at the same time we may see that though the event is flattering, the means are as simple as wisdom could make them; that is, depending upon nature, virtue, thought, and habit. Another thing demonstrated will be the propriety of every man's waiting for his time for appearing upon the stage of the world. Our sensations being very much fixed to the moment, we are apt to forget that more moments are to follow the first, and consequently that man should arrange his conduct so as to suit the whole of a life. Your attribution appears to have been applied to your life, and the passing moments of it have been enlivened with content and enjoyment, instead of being tormented with foolish impatience or regrets. Such a conduct is easy for those who make virtue and themselves in countenance by examples of other truly great men, of whom patience is so often the characteristic. Your Quaker correspondent, sir (for here again I will suppose the subject of my letter resembling Dr. Franklin), praised your frugality, diligence, and temperance, which he considered as a pattern for all youth; but it is singular that he should have forgotten your modesty and your disinterestedness, without which you never could have waited for your advancement or found your situation in the meantime comfortable — which is a strong lesson to show the poverty of glory and the importance of regulating our minds. If this correspondent had known the nature of your reputation as well as I do, he would have said, Your former writings and measures would secure attention to your Biography, and Art of Virtue; and your Biography and Art of Virtue, in return, would secure attention to them. This is an advantage attendant upon a various character, and which brings all that belongs to it into greater play; and it is the more useful, as perhaps more persons are at a loss for the means of improving their minds and characters than they are for the time or the inclination to do it. But there is one concluding reflection, sir, that will shew the use of your life as a mere piece of biography. This style of writing seems a little gone out of vogue, and yet it is a very useful one; and your specimen of it may be particularly serviceable as it will make a subject of comparison with the lives of various public cut throats and intriguers, and with absurd monastic self-tormentors or vain literary triflers. If it encourages more writings of the same kind with your own and induces more men to spend lives fit to be written, it will be worth all Plutarch's *Lives* put together. But being tired of figuring to myself a character of which every feature suits only one man in the world, without giving him the praise of it, I shall end my letter, my dear Dr. Franklin, with a personal application to your proper self. I am earnestly desirous, then my dear sir, that you should let the world into the traits of your genuine character, as civil broils may otherwise tend to disguise or traduce it. Considering your great age, the caution of your character, and your peculiar style of thinking, it is not likely that any one besides yourself can be sufficiently master of the facts of your life or the intentions of your mind. Besides all this, the immense Revolution of the present period, will necessarily turn our attention towards the author of it, and when virtuous principles have been pretended in it, it will be highly important to shew that such have really influenced; and, as your own character will be the principal one to receive a scrutiny, it is proper (even for its effects upon your vast and rising country, as well as upon England and upon Europe) that it should stand respectable and eternal. For the furtherance of human happiness, I have always maintained that it is necessary to prove that man is not even at present a vicious and detestable animal, and still more to prove that good management may greatly amend him; and it is for much the same reason that I am anxious to see the opinion established that there are fair characters existing among the individuals of the race; for the moment that all men, without exception, shall be conceived abandoned, good people will cease efforts deemed to be hopeless, and perhaps think of taking their share in the scramble of life, or at least of making it comfortable principally for themselves. Take then, my dear sir, this work most speedily into hand: shew yourself good as you are good; temperate as you are temperate; and above all things, prove yourself as one who from your infancy have loved justice, liberty, and concord, in a way that has made it natural and consistent for you to have acted as we have seen you act in the last seventeen years of your life. Let Englishmen be made not only to respect, but even to love you. When they think well of individuals in your native country, they will go nearer to thinking well of your country; and when your countrymen see themselves well thought of by Englishmen, they will go nearer to thinking well of England. Extend your views even further; do not stop at those who speak the English tongue, but after having settled so many points in nature and politics, think of bettering the whole race of men. As I have not read any part of the life in question, but know only the character that lived it, I write somewhat at hazard. I am sure, however, that the life and the treatise I allude to (on the Art of Virtue) will necessarily fulfil the chief of my expectations, and still more so if you take up the measure of suiting these performances to the several views above stated. Should they even prove unsuccessful in all that a sanguine admirer of yours hopes from them, you will at least have framed pieces to interest the human mind; and whoever gives a feeling of pleasure that is innocent to man has added so much to the fair side of a life otherwise too much darkened by anxiety and too much injured by pain. In the hope, therefore, that you will listen to the prayer addressed to you in this letter, I beg to subscribe myself, my dearest sir, etc., etc.,

(Signed) Benj. Vaughan

Continuation of the Account of my Life.
Begun at Passy, 1784

It is some time since I received the above letters, but I have been too busy till now to think of complying with the request they contain. It might, too, be much better done if I were at home among my papers, which would aid my memory, and help to ascertain dates; but my return being uncertain, and having just now a little leisure, I will endeavour to recollect and write what I can. If I live to get home, it may there be corrected and improved.

Not having any copy here of what is already written, I know not whether an account is given of the means I used to establish the Philadelphia public library, which from a small beginning is now become so considerable, though I remember to have come down to near the time of that transaction, 1730. I will therefore begin here with an account of it, which may be struck out if found to have been already given.

At the time I established myself in Pennsylvania, there was not a good bookseller's shop in any of the Colonies to the southward of Boston. In New York and Philadelphia the printers were indeed stationers; they sold only paper, etc., almanacs, ballads, and a few common schoolbooks. Those who loved reading were obliged to send for their books from England. The members of the Junto had each a few. We had left the alehouse where we first met and hired a room to hold our club in. I proposed that we should all of us bring our books to that room, where they would not only be ready to consult in our conferences but become a common benefit, each of us being at liberty to borrow such as he wished to read at home. This was accordingly done and for some time contented us. Finding the advantage of this little collection, I proposed to render the benefit from books more common by commencing a public subscription library. I drew a sketch of the plan and rules that would be necessary, and got a skillful conveyancer, Mr. Charles Brockden, to put the whole in form of articles of agreement to be subscribed, by which each subscriber engaged to pay a certain sum down for the first purchase of books and an annual contribution for encreasing them. So few were the readers at that time in Philadelphia and the majority of us so poor that I was not able with great industry to find more than fifty persons, mostly young tradesmen, willing to pay down for this purpose forty shillings each and ten shillings per annum. With this little fund we began. The books were imported. The library was open one day in the week for lending them to the subscribers, on their promissory notes to pay double the value if not duly returned. The institution soon manifested its utility, was imitated by other towns and in other provinces; the libraries were augmented by donations; reading became fashionable; and our people, having no public amusements to divert their attention from study, became better acquainted with books, and in a few years were observed by strangers to be better instructed and more intelligent than people of the same rank generally are in other countries.

When we were about to sign the above-mentioned articles, which were to be binding on us, our heirs, etc., for fifty years, Mr. Brockden, the scrivener, said to us, "You are young men, but it is scarce probable that any of you will live to see the expiration of the term fixed in this instrument." A number of us, however, are yet living; but the instrument was after a few years rendered null by a charter that incorporated and gave perpetuity to the company.

The objections and reluctances I met with in soliciting the subscriptions made me soon feel the impropriety of presenting one's self as the proposer of any useful project that might be supposed to raise one's reputation in the smallest degree above that of one's neighbours when one has need of their assistance to accomplish that project. I therefore put myself as much as I could out of sight, and stated it as a scheme of a "number of friends" who had requested me to go about and propose it to such as they thought lovers of reading. In this way my affair went on more smoothly, and I ever after practised it on such occasions, and from my frequent successes can heartily recommend it. The present little sacrifice of your vanity will afterwards be amply repaid. If it remains a while uncertain to whom the merit belongs, someone more vain than yourself will be encouraged to claim it, and then even envy will be disposed to do you justice by plucking those assumed feathers and restoring them to their right owner.

This library afforded me the means of improvement by constant study, for which I set apart an hour or two each day, and thus repaired in some degree the loss of the learned education my father once intended for me. Reading was the only amusement I allowed myself. I spent no time in taverns, games, or frolics of any kind. And my industry in my business continued as indefatigable as it was necessary. I was in debt for my printing house, I had a young family coming on to be educated, and I had two competitors to contend with for business, who were established in the place before me. My circumstances, however, grew daily easier — my original habits of frugality continuing, and my father having among his instructions to me when a boy frequently repeated a proverb of Solomon, "Seeest thou a man diligent in his calling, he shall stand before kings, he shall not stand before mean men." I from thence considered industry as a means of obtaining wealth and distinction, which encouraged me, tho' I did not think that I should ever literally stand before kings, which, however, has since happened; for I have stood before five, and even had the honour of sitting down with one, the king of Denmark, to dinner.

We have an English proverb that says,

> He that would thrive
> Must ask his wife.

It was lucky for me that I had one as much disposed to industry and frugality as myself. She assisted me cheerfully in my business, folding and stitching pamphlets, tending shop, purchasing old linen rags for the papermakers, etc. We kept no idle servants, our table was plain and simple, our furniture of the cheapest. For instance, my breakfast was for a long time bread and milk, (no tea), and I ate it out of a twopenny earthen porringer with a pewter spoon. But mark how luxury will enter families and make a progress, in spite of principle. Being called one morning to breakfast, I found it in a china bowl, with a spoon of silver. They had been bought for me without my knowledge by my wife, and had cost her the enormous sum of three-and-twenty shillings, for which she had no other excuse or apology to make but that she thought *her* husband deserved a silver spoon and china bowl as well as any of his neighbours. This was the first appearance of plate and china in our house, which afterwards in a course of years as our wealth encreased, augmented gradually to several hundred pounds in value.

I had been religiously educated as a Presbyterian; and tho' some of the dogmas of that persuasion, such as the eternal decrees of God, election, reprobation, etc., appeared to me unintelligible, others doubtful, and I early absented myself from the public assemblies of the sect, Sunday being my studying-day, I never was without some religious principles. I never doubted, for instance, the existence of the Deity, that he made the world and governed it by his providence, that the most acceptable service of God was the doing good to man, that our souls are immortal, and that all crime will be punished and virtue rewarded either here or hereafter. These I esteemed the essentials of every religion, and being to be found in all the religions we had in our country, I respected them all, tho' with different degrees of respect as I found them more or less mixed with other articles which without any tendency to inspire, promote, or confirm morality, served principally to divide us and make us unfriendly to one another. This respect to all, with an opinion that the worst had some good effects, induced me to avoid all discourse that might tend to lessen the good opinion another might have of his own religion; and as our province increased in people and new places of worship were continually wanted and generally erected by voluntary contribution, my mite for such purpose, whatever might be the sect, was never refused.

Tho' I seldom attended any public worship, I had still an opinion of its propriety and of its utility when rightly conducted, and I regularly paid my annual subscription for the support of the only Presbyterian minister or meeting we had in Philadelphia. He used to visit me sometimes as a friend and admonish me to attend his administrations, and I was now and then prevailed on to do so, once for five Sundays successively. Had he been, *in my opinion*, a good preacher, perhaps I might have continued, notwithstanding the occasion I had for the Sunday's leisure in my course of study; but his discourses were chiefly either polemic arguments or explications of the peculiar doctrines of our sect, and were all to me very dry, uninteresting, and unedifying since not a single moral principle was inculcated or enforced, their aim seeming to be rather to make us Presbyterians than good citizens. At length he took for his text that verse of the fourth chapter of Philippians, "Finally, brethren, whatsoever things are true, honest, just, pure, lovely, or of good report, if there be any virtue, or any praise, think on these things"; and I imagined, in a sermon on such a text, we could not miss of having some morality. But he confined himself to five points only as meant by the apostle; viz., 1. Keeping holy the Sabbath day, 2. Being diligent in reading the Holy Scriptures, 3. Attending duly the public worship, 4. Partaking of the sacrament, 5. Paying a due respect to God's ministers. These might be all good things, but as they were not the kind of good things that I expected from that text, I despaired of ever meeting with them from any other, was disgusted, and attended his preaching no more. I had some years before composed a little liturgy or form of prayer for my own private use; viz., in 1728, entitled *Articles of Belief and Acts of Religion.* I returned to the use of this and went no more to the public assemblies. My conduct might be blamable, but I leave it without attempting further to excuse it, my present purpose being to relate facts and not to make apologies for them.

It was about this time I conceived the bold and arduous project of arriving at moral perfection. I wished to live without committing any fault at any time; I would conquer all that either natural inclination, custom, or company might lead me into. As I knew, or thought I knew, what was right and wrong, I did not see why I might not *always* do the one and avoid the other. But I soon found I had undertaken a task of more difficulty than I had imagined. While my attention was taken up and care employed in guarding against one fault, I was often surprized by another. Habit took the advantage of inattention. Inclination was sometimes too strong for reason. I concluded at length that the mere speculative conviction that it was our interest to be completely virtuous was not sufficient to prevent our slipping, and that the contrary habits must be broken and good ones acquired and established before we can have any dependence on a steady, uniform rectitude of conduct. For this purpose I therefore contrived the following method.

In the various enumerations of the moral virtues I had met with in my reading, I found the catalogue more or less numerous, as different writers included more or fewer ideas under the same name. Temperance, for example, was by some confined to eating and drinking, while by others it was extended to mean the moderating every other pleasure, appetite, inclination, or passion — bodily or mental, even to our avarice and ambition. I proposed to myself, for the sake of clearness, to use rather more names with fewer ideas annexed to each than a few names with more ideas; and I included under thirteen names of virtues all that at that time occurred to me as necessary or desirable, and annexed to each a short precept which fully expressed the extent I gave to its meaning.

These names of virtues with their precepts were

1. Temperance
Eat not to dulness. Drink not to elevation.

2. Silence
Speak not but what may benefit others or yourself. Avoid trifling conversation.

3. Order
Let all your things have their places. Let each part of your business have its time.

4. Resolution
Resolve to perform what you ought. Perform without fail what you resolve.

5. Frugality
Make no expence but to do good to others or yourself; i.e., waste nothing.

6. Industry
Lose no time. Be always employed in something useful. Cut off all unnecessary actions.

7. Sincerity
Use no hurtful deceit. Think innocently and justly; and, if you speak, speak accordingly.

8. Justice
Wrong none by doing injuries or omitting the benefits that are your duty.

9. Moderation
Avoid extremes. Forbear resenting injuries so much as you think they deserve.

10. Cleanliness

Tolerate no uncleanness in body, clothes or habitation.

11. Tranquillity

Be not disturbed at trifles or at accidents common or un-avoidable.

12. Chastity

Rarely use venery but for health or offspring — never to dul-ness, weakness, or the injury of your own or another's peace or reputation.

13. Humility

Imitate Jesus and Socrates.

My intention being to acquire the *habitude* of all these virtues, I judged it would be well not to distract my attention by at-tempting the whole at once but to fix it on one of them at a time, and when I should be master of that, then to proceed to another, and so on till I should have gone thro' the thirteen. And as the previous acquisition of some might facilitate the acquisition of certain others, I arranged them with that view as they stand above. *Temperance* first, as it tends to procure that coolness and clearness of head which is so necessary where constant vigilance was to be kept up, and guard maintained, against the unremitting attraction of ancient habits, and the force of perpetual tempta-tions. This being acquired and established, *Silence* would be more easy, and my desire being to gain knowledge at the same time that I improved in virtue, and considering that in conver-sation it was obtained rather by the use of the ear than of the tongue, and therefore wishing to break a habit I was getting into of prattling, punning, and joking, which only made me accepta-ble to trifling company, I gave *Silence* the second place. This and the next, *Order*, I expected would allow me more time for attending to my project and my studies. *Resolution*, once be-come habitual, would keep me firm in my endeavours to obtain all the subsequent virtues; *Frugality* and *Industry*, freeing me from my remaining debt and, producing affluence and inde-pendence, would make more easy the practice of *Sincerity* and *Justice*, etc., etc. Conceiving then that agreeable to the advice of Pythagoras in his golden verses, daily examination would be necessary, I contrived the following method for conducting that examination.

I made a little book in which I allotted a page for each of the virtues. I ruled each page with red ink so as to have seven columns, one for each day of the week, marking each column with a letter for the day. I crossed these columns with thirteen red lines, marking the beginning of each line with the first letter of one of the virtues, on which line and in its proper column I might mark by a little black spot every fault I found upon examination to have been committed respecting that virtue upon that day.

I determined to give a week's strict attention to each of the virtues successively. Thus in the first week my great guard was to avoid even the least offence against temperance, leaving the other virtues to their ordinary chance, only marking every evening the faults of the day. Thus if in the first week I could keep my first line marked "T." clear of spots, I supposed the habit of that virtue so much strengthened and its opposite weakened that I might venture extending my attention to include the next, and for the following week keep both lines clear of spots. Proceeding thus to the last, I could go thro' a course complete in thirteen weeks, and four courses in a year. And like him who, having a garden to weed, does not attempt to eradicate all the bad herbs at once, which would exceed his reach and his strength, but works on one of the beds at a time, and having accomplished the first, proceeds to a second; so I should have (I hoped) the encouraging pleasure of seeing on my pages the progress I made in virtue by clearing successively my lines of their spots, till in the end by a number of courses, I should be happy in viewing a clean book after a thirteen weeks' daily examination.

This my little book had for its motto these lines from Addison's *Cato;*

> Here will I hold: if there is a power above us,
> (And that there is, all Nature cries aloud
> Thro' all her works) he must delight in virtue,
> And that which he delights in must be happy.

Another from Cicero,

> *O vitae philosophia dux! O virtutum indagatrix, expultrixque vitiorum! Unus dies bene et ex preceptis tuis actus, peccanti immortalitati est anteponendus.*

FORM OF THE PAGES

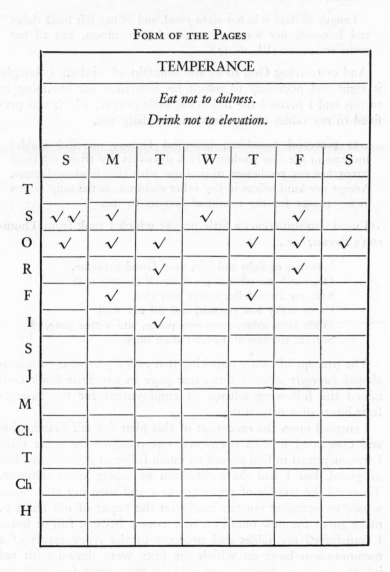

TEMPERANCE						
Eat not to dulness.						
Drink not to elevation.						
S	**M**	**T**	**W**	**T**	**F**	**S**
T						
S ✓✓	✓		✓		✓	
O ✓	✓	✓		✓	✓	✓
R			✓		✓	
F	✓			✓		
I		✓				
S						
J						
M						
Cl.						
T						
Ch						
H						

Another from the proverbs of Solomon speaking of wisdom or virtue;

> Length of days is in her right hand, and in her left hand riches and honours; her ways are ways of pleasantness, and all her paths are peace (III, 16, 17).

And conceiving God to be the fountain of wisdom, I thought it right and necessary to solicit his assistance for obtaining it; to this end I formed the following little prayer, which was prefixed to my tables of examination, for daily use.

> O powerful Goodness, bountiful Father, merciful Guide! Increase in me that wisdom which discovers my truest interests; strengthen my resolutions to perform what that wisdom dictates. Accept my kind offices to thy other children, as the only return in my power for thy continual favours to me.

I used also sometimes a little prayer which I took from Thomson's *Poems;* viz.,

> Father of light and life, thou Good supreme,
> Oh, teach me what is good, teach me thy self!
> Save me from folly, vanity and vice,
> From every low pursuit, and fill my soul
> With knowledge, conscious peace, and virtue pure,
> Sacred, substantial, never-fading bliss!

The precept of *Order* requiring that *every part of my business should have its allotted time,* one page in my little book contained the following scheme of employment for the twenty-four hours of a natural day.

I entered upon the execution of this plan for self-examination and continued it with occasional intermissions for some time. I was surprized to find myself so much fuller of faults than I had imagined, but I had the satisfaction of seeing them diminish. To avoid the trouble of renewing now and then my little book, which by scraping out the marks on the paper of old faults to make room for new ones in a new course became full of holes, I transferred my tables and precepts to the ivory leaves of a memorandum book on which the lines were drawn with red ink that made a durable stain, and on those lines I marked my faults with a black lead pencil, which marks I could easily wipe out with a wet sponge. After a while I went thro' one course

The morning question, What good shall I do this day?	5	Rise, wash, and address *Powerful Goodness;* contrive day's business and take the resolution of the day; prosecute the present study; and breakfast.
	6	
	7	
	8	
	9	Work.
	10	
	11	
	12	Read or overlook my accounts, and dine.
	1	
	2	Work.
	3	
	4	
	5	
	6	Put things in their places, supper, music, or diversion, or conversation; examination of the day.
	7	
	8	
	9	
Evening question, What good have I done today?	10	Sleep.
	11	
	12	
	1	
	2	
	3	
	4	

only in a year, and afterwards only one in several years, till at length I omitted them entirely, being employed in voyages and business abroad with a multiplicity of affairs that interfered; but I always carried my little book with me. My scheme of *Order* gave me the most trouble, and I found that tho' it might be practicable where a man's business was such as to leave him the disposition of his time, that of a journeyman printer for instance, it was not possible to be exactly observed by a master, who must mix with the world and often receive people of business at their own hours. Order, too, with regard to places for things, papers, etc., I found extremely difficult to acquire. I had not been early accustomed to *method*, and having an exceeding good memory, I was not so sensible of the inconvenience attending want of method. This article therefore cost me so much painful attention, and my faults in it vexed me so much, and I made so little progress in amendment and had such frequent relapses, that I was almost ready to give up the attempt and content myself with a faulty character in that respect. Like the man who in buying an ax of a smith my neighbour, desired to have the whole of its surface as bright as the edge; the smith consented to grind it bright for him if he would turn the wheel. He turned while the smith pressed the broad face of the ax hard and heavily on the stone, which made the turning of it very fatiguing. The man came every now and then from the wheel to see how the work went on; and at length would take his ax as it was, without further grinding. "No," says the smith, "turn on, turn on; we shall have it bright by and by; as yet 'tis only speckled." "Yes," says the man, "*but I think I like a speckled ax best.*" And I believe this may have been the case with many who having, for want of some such means as I employed, found the difficulty of obtaining good and breaking bad habits in other points of vice and virtue, have given up the struggle and concluded that "a speckled ax was best." For something that pretended to be reason was every now and then suggesting to me that such extreme nicety as I exacted of myself might be a kind of foppery in morals, which if it were known would make me ridiculous; that a perfect character might be attended with the inconvenience of being envied and hated; and that a benevolent man should allow a few faults in himself, to keep his friends in countenance. In truth, I found myself incorrigible with respect to *Order;* and now I am grown old and my memory bad, I feel very sensibly the want of it. But on the whole, tho' I never arrived at the perfection I had been so ambitious of obtaining but fell far short of it, yet I was by the endeavour a better and a happier man than I otherwise should have been if I had not attempted it; as those who aim at perfect writing by imitating the engraved copies, tho' they never reach the wished-for excellence of those copies, their hand is mended by the endeavour and is tolerable while it continues fair and legible.

It may be well my posterity should be informed that to this little artifice, with the blessing of God, their ancestor owed the constant felicity of his life down to his seventy-ninth year, in which this is written. What reverses may attend the remainder is in the hand of providence; but if they arrive, the reflection on past happiness enjoyed ought to help his bearing them with more resignation. To *Temperance* he ascribes his long-continued health and what is still left to him of a good constitution; to *Industry* and *Frugality*, the early easiness of his circumstances and acquisition of his fortune, with all that knowledge which enabled him to be an useful citizen and obtained for him some degree of reputation among the learned. To *Sincerity* and *Justice*, the confidence of his country and the honourable employs it conferred upon him; and to the joint influence of the whole mass of the virtues, even in the imperfect state he was able to acquire them, all that evenness of temper and that cheerfulness in conversation which makes his company still sought for and agreeable even to his younger acquaintance. I hope, therefore, that some of my descendants may follow the example and reap the benefit.

It will be remarked that, tho' my scheme was not wholly without religion, there was in it no mark of any of the distinguishing tenets of any particular sect. I had purposely avoided them; for being fully persuaded of the utility and excellency of my method, and that it might be serviceable to people in all religions, and intending sometime or other to publish it, I would not have anything in it that should prejudice anyone of any sect against it. I purposed writing a little comment on each virtue, in which I would have shown the advantages of possessing it and the mischiefs attending its opposite vice; I should have called my book *The Art of Virtue* because it would have shown the means and manner of obtaining virtue, which would have distinguished it from the mere exhortation to be good, that does not instruct and indicate the means, but is like the apostle's man of verbal charity, who only, without showing to the naked and hungry how or where they might get clothes or victuals, exhorted them to be fed and clothed (*James* II: 15, 16).

But it so happened that my intention of writing and publishing this comment was never fulfilled. I did, indeed, from time to time put down short hints of the sentiments, reasonings, etc., to be made use of in it, some of which I have still by me; but the necessary close attention to private business in the earlier part of life and public business since, have occasioned my postponing it. For it being connected in my mind with *a great and extensive project* that required the whole man to execute, and which an unforeseen succession of employs prevented my attending to, it has hitherto remained unfinished.

In this piece it was my design to explain and enforce this doctrine: That vicious actions are not hurtful because they are forbidden, but forbidden because they are hurtful, the nature of man alone considered; that it was therefore everyone's interest to be virtuous who wished to be happy even in this world. And I should from this circumstance, there being always in the world a number of rich merchants, nobility, states, and princes who have need of honest instruments for the management of their affairs, and such being so rare have endeavoured to convince young persons, that no qualities are so likely to make a poor man's fortune as those of probity and integrity.

My list of virtues contained at first but twelve. But a Quaker friend having kindly informed me that I was generally thought proud, that my pride showed itself frequently in conversation, that I was not content with being in the right when discussing any point, but was overbearing and rather insolent — of which he convinced me by mentioning several instances — I determined endeavouring to cure myself if I could of this vice or folly among the rest, and I added *Humility* to my list, giving an extensive meaning to the word. I cannot boast of much success in acquiring the *reality* of this virtue, but I had a good deal with regard to the *appearance* of it. I made it a rule to forbear all direct contradiction to the sentiments of others and all positive assertion

of my own. I even forbade myself agreeable to the old laws of
our Junto, the use of every word or expression in the language
that imported [1] a fixed opinion, such as "certainly," "undoubtedly," etc.; and I adopted instead of them, "I conceive,"
"I apprehend," or "I imagine" a thing to be so or so, or "It so
appears to me at present." When another asserted something that
I thought an error, I denied myself the pleasure of contradicting
him abruptly and of showing immediately some absurdity in his
proposition; and in answering I began by observing that in
certain cases or circumstances his opinion would be right, but
that in the present case there "appeared" or "seemed to me"
some difference, etc. I soon found the advantage of this change
in my manners: The conversations I engaged in went on more
pleasantly; the modest way in which I proposed my opinions
procured them a readier reception and less contradiction; I had
less mortification when I was found to be in the wrong, and I
more easily prevailed with others to give up their mistakes and
join with me when I happened to be in the right. And this mode,
which I at first put on with some violence to natural inclination,
became at length so easy and so habitual to me that perhaps for
these fifty years past no one has ever heard a dogmatical expression escape me. And to this habit (after my character of integrity) I think it principally owing that I had early so much weight
with my fellow citizens when I proposed new institutions or
alterations in the old, and so much influence in public councils
when I became a member. For I was but a bad speaker, never
eloquent, subject to much hesitation in my choice of words,
hardly correct in language, and yet I generally carried my point.

In reality there is perhaps no one of our natural passions so
hard to subdue as *pride;* disguise it, struggle with it, beat it down,
stifle it, mortify it as much as one pleases, it is still alive and will
every now and then peep out and show itself. You will see it
perhaps in this history. For even if I could conceive that I had
completely overcome it, I should probably be proud of my
humility.

[Thus far written at Passy, 1784] [2]
I am now about to write at home (Philadelphia), August 1788,

[1] Implied.
[2] Square brackets are Franklin's.

but cannot have the help expected from my papers, many of them being lost in the war. I have, however, found the following.

Having mentioned *a great and extensive project* which I had conceived, it seems proper that some account should be here given of that project and its object. Its first rise in my mind appears in the following little paper, accidentally preserved, viz.,

Observations on my Reading History in Library,
May 9, 1731.

"That the great affairs of the world, the wars, revolutions, etc., are carried on and effected by parties.

"That the view of these parties is their present general interest, or what they take to be such.

"That the different views of these different parties occasion all confusion.

"That while a party is carrying on a general design, each man has his particular private interest in view.

"That as soon as a party has gained its general point, each member becomes intent upon his particular interest, which thwarting others, breaks that party into divisions and occasions more confusion.

"That few in public affairs act from a mere view of the good of their country, whatever they may pretend; and tho' their actings bring real good to their country, yet men primarily considered that their own and their country's interest was united and did not act from a principle of benevolence.

"That fewer still in public affairs act with a view to the good of mankind.

"There seems to me at present to be great occasion for raising a united party for virtue, by forming the virtuous and good men of all nations into a regular body, to be governed by suitable good and wise rules, which good and wise men may probably be more unanimous in their obedience to than common people are to common laws.

"I at present think that whoever attempts this aright and is well qualified, cannot fail of pleasing God and of meeting with success.

B.F."

Revolving this project in my mind, as to be undertaken hereafter when my circumstances should afford me the necessary leisure, I put down from time to time on pieces of paper such thoughts as occurred to me respecting it. Most of these are lost, but I find one purporting to be the substance of an intended creed, containing, as I thought, the essentials of every known religion and being free of everything that might shock the professors of any religion. It is expressed in these words, viz.,

"That there is one God who made all things.

"That he governs the world by his providence.

"That he ought to be worshipped by adoration, prayer, and thanksgiving.

"But that the most acceptable service to God is doing good to man.

"That the soul is immortal.

"And that God will certainly reward virtue and punish vice, either here or hereafter."

My ideas at that time were that the sect should be begun and spread at first among young and single men only; that each person to be initiated should not only declare his assent to such creed but should have exercised himself with the thirteen weeks' examination and practice of the virtues, as in the before-mentioned model; that the existence of such a society should be kept a secret till it was become considerable, to prevent solicitations for the admission of improper persons; but that the members should each of them search among his acquaintance for ingenuous, well-disposed youths to whom, with prudent caution, the scheme should be gradually communicated; that the members should engage to afford their advice, assistance, and support to each other in promoting one another's interest, business, and advancement in life; that for distinction we should be called the Society of the Free and Easy: free, as being by the general practice and habit of the virtues; free from the dominion of vice, and particularly by the practice of industry and frugality; free from debt, which exposes a man to confinement and a species of slavery to his creditors. This is as much as I can now recollect of the project, except that I communicated it in part to two young men who adopted it with some enthusiasm. But my then narrow circumstances and the necessity I was under of sticking close to my business, occasioned my postponing the further prosecution of it at that time, and my multifarious occupations public and private induced me to continue postponing, so that it has been omitted till I have no longer strength or activity left sufficient for such an enterprize, tho' I am still of opinion that it was a practicable scheme and might have been very useful by forming a great number of good citizens. And I was not discouraged by the seeming magnitude of the undertaking, as I have always thought that one man of tolerable abilities may work great changes and accomplish great affairs among mankind if he first forms a good plan, and, cutting off all amusements or other employments that would divert his attention, makes the execution of that same plan his sole study and business.

In 1732 I first published my *Almanac*, under the name of Richard Saunders; it was continued by me about twenty-five years, commonly called *Poor Richard's Almanac*.[1] I endeavoured to make it both entertaining and useful, and it accordingly came to be in such demand that I reaped considerable profit from it, vending annually near ten thousand. And observing that it was generally read, scarce any neighbourhood in the province being without it, I considered it as a proper vehicle for conveying instruction among the common people, who bought scarce any other books. I therefore filled all the little spaces that occurred between the remarkable days in the calendar with proverbial sentences, chiefly such as inculcated industry and frugality as the means of procuring wealth and thereby securing virtue — it being more difficult for a man in want to act always honestly, as (to use here one of those proverbs) "it is hard for an empty sack to stand upright." These proverbs, which contained the wisdom of many ages and nations, I assembled and formed into a connected discourse prefixed to the *Almanac* of 1757, as the harangue of a wise old man to the people attending an auction. The bringing all these scattered counsels thus into a focus enabled them to make greater impression. The piece, being universally approved, was copied in all the newspapers of the Continent, reprinted in Britain on a broadside to be stuck up in houses,[2] two translations were made of it in French, and great numbers bought by the clergy and gentry to distribute gratis among their

---

[1] Franklin sold his *Almanac* in 1758, though it continued publication until 1796.

[2] A large page printed on one side, for posting in inns, taverns, and public places. The piece referred to is the famous *Way to Wealth*.

poor parishioners and tenants. In Pennsylvania, as it discouraged useless expence in foreign superfluities, some thought it had its share of influence in producing that growing plenty of money which was observable for several years after its publication.

I considered my newspaper also as another means of communicating instruction, and in that view frequently reprinted in it extracts from the *Spectator* and other moral writers, and sometimes published little pieces of my own which had been first composed for reading in our Junto. Of these are a Socratic dialogue tending to prove that whatever might be his parts and abilities, a vicious man could not properly be called a man of sense; and a discourse on self-denial showing that virtue was not secure till its practice became a habitude and was free from the opposition of contrary inclinations. These may be found in the papers about the beginning of 1735. In the conduct of my newspaper I carefully excluded all libelling and personal abuse, which is of late years become so disgraceful to our country. Whenever I was solicited to insert anything of that kind and the writers pleaded, as they generally did, the liberty of the press and that a newspaper was like a stagecoach in which any one who would pay had a right to a place, my answer was that I would print the piece separately if desired, and the author might have as many copies as he pleased to distribute himself, but that I would not take upon me to spread his detraction, and that having contracted with my subscribers to furnish them with what might be either useful or entertaining, I could not fill their papers with private altercation in which they had no concern without doing them manifest injustice. Now many of our printers make no scruple of gratifying the malice of individuals by false accusations of the fairest characters among ourselves, augmenting animosity even to the producing of duels, and are moreover so indiscreet as to print scurrilous reflections on the government of neighbouring states and even on the conduct of our best national allies, which may be attended with the most pernicious consequences. These things I mention as a caution to young printers, that they may be encouraged not to pollute their presses and disgrace their profession by such infamous practices but refuse steadily, as they may see by my example that such a course of conduct will not on the whole be injurious to their interests.

In 1733, I sent one of my journeymen to Charlestown, South

Carolina, where a printer was wanting. I furnished him with a press and letters on an agreement of partnership, by which I was to receive one-third of the profits of the business, paying one-third of the expence. He was a man of learning and honest, but ignorant in matters of account; and tho' he sometimes made me remittances, I could get no account from him nor any satisfactory state [1] of our partnership while he lived. On his decease, the business was continued by his widow, who being born and bred in Holland, where, as I have been informed, the knowledge of accompts makes a part of female education, she not only sent me as clear a state as she could find of the transactions past, but continued to account with the greatest regularity and exactitude every quarter afterwards, and managed the business with such success that she not only brought up reputably a family of children but at the expiration of the term was able to purchase of me the printing house and establish her son in it. I mention this affair chiefly for the sake of recommending that branch of education for our young females as likely to be of more use to them and their children in case of widowhood than either music or dancing, by preserving them from losses by imposition of crafty men, and enabling them to continue perhaps a profitable mercantile house with established correspondence till a son is grown up fit to undertake and go on with it, to the lasting advantage and enriching of the family.

About the year 1734 there arrived among us from Ireland a young Presbyterian preacher named Hemphill, who delivered with a good voice, and apparently extempore, most excellent discourses, which drew together considerable numbers of different persuasions, who joined in admiring them. Among the rest I became one of his constant hearers, his sermons pleasing me as they had little of the dogmatical kind but inculcated strongly the practice of virtue, or what in the religious style are called "good works." Those, however, of our congregation who considered themselves as orthodox Presbyterians disapproved his doctrine and were joined by most of the old clergy, who arraigned him of heterodoxy before the synod in order to have him silenced. I became his zealous partisan and contributed all I could to raise a party in his favour, and we combated for him awhile with some hopes of success. There was much scribbling pro and con

[1] Accounting or statement.

upon the occasion; and finding that tho' an elegant preacher he was but a poor writer, I lent him my pen and wrote for him two or three pamphlets, and one piece in the *Gazette* of April 1735. Those pamphlets, as is generally the case with controversial writings, tho' eagerly read at the time, were soon out of vogue, and I question whether a single copy of them now exists.

During the contest an unlucky occurrence hurt his cause exceedingly. One of our adversaries, having heard him preach a sermon that was much admired, thought he had somewhere read that sermon before, or at least a part of it. On search he found that part quoted at length in one of the British reviews, from a discourse of Dr. Foster's. This detection gave many of our party disgust, who accordingly abandoned his cause and occasioned our more speedy discomfiture in the synod. I stuck by him, however, as I rather approved his giving us good sermons composed by others than bad ones of his own manufacture, tho' the latter was the practice of our common teachers. He afterwards acknowledged to me that none of those he preached were his own; adding that his memory was such as enabled him to retain and repeat any sermon after one reading only. On our defeat he left us in search elsewhere of better fortune, and I quitted the congregation, never joining it after, tho' I continued many years my subscription for the support of its ministers.

I had begun in 1733 to study languages. I soon made myself so much a master of the French as to be able to read the books with ease. I then undertook the Italian. An acquaintance who was also learning it used often to tempt me to play chess with him. Finding this took up too much of the time I had to spare for study, I at length refused to play any more unless on this condition — that the victor in every game should have a right to impose a task, either in parts of the grammar to be got by heart, or in translation, etc., which tasks the vanquished was to perform upon honour before our next meeting. As we played pretty equally, we thus beat one another into that language. I afterwards with a little painstaking acquired as much of the Spanish as to read their books also. I have already mentioned that I had only one year's instruction in a Latin school, and that when very young, after which I neglected that language entirely. But when I had attained an acquaintance with the French, Italian, and Spanish, I was surprized to find, on looking over a Latin Testament, that I understood so much more of that language than I had imagined — which encouraged me to apply myself again to the study of it; and I met with the more success, as those preceding languages had greatly smoothed my way. From these circumstances I have thought that there is some inconsistency in our common mode of teaching languages. We are told that it is proper to begin first with the Latin, and having acquired that, it will be more easy to attain those modern languages which are derived from it; and yet we do not begin with the Greek in order more easily to acquire the Latin. It is true that if you can clamber and get to the top of a staircase without using the steps, you will more easily gain them in descending; but certainly if you begin with the lowest, you will with more ease ascend to the top. And I would therefore offer it to the consideration of those who superintend the educating of our youth, whether, since many of those who begin with the Latin quit the same after spending some years without having made any great proficiency, and what they have learned becomes almost useless so that their time has been lost, it would not have been better to have begun them with the French, proceeding to the Italian, etc., for tho' after spending the same time they should quit the study of languages and never arrive at the Latin, they would, however, have acquired another tongue or two that being in modern use might be serviceable to them in common life.

After ten years' absence from Boston and having become more easy in my circumstances, I made a journey thither to visit my relations, which I could not sooner well afford. In returning I called at Newport to see my brother then settled there with his printing house. Our former differences were forgotten, and our meeting was very cordial and affectionate. He was fast declining in his health and requested of me that in case of his death, which he apprehended not far distant, I would take home his son, then but ten years of age, and bring him up to the printing business. This I accordingly performed, sending him a few years to school before I took him into the office. His mother carried on the business till he was grown up, when I assisted him with an assortment of new types, those of his father being in a manner worn out. Thus it was that I made my brother ample amends for the service I had deprived him of by leaving him so early.

In 1736, I lost one of my sons, a fine boy of four years old, by the smallpox taken in the common way. I long regretted bitterly, and still regret, that I had not given it to him by inoculation. This I mention for the sake of parents who omit that operation on the supposition that they should never forgive themselves if a child died under it — my example showing that the regret may be the same either way, and that therefore the safer should be chosen.

Our club, the Junto, was found so useful and afforded such satisfaction to the members that several were desirous of introducing their friends, which could not well be done without exceeding what we had settled as a convenient number, viz., twelve. We had from the beginning made it a rule to keep our institution a secret, which was pretty well observed. The intention was to avoid applications of improper persons for admittance, some of whom perhaps we might find it difficult to refuse. I was one of those who were against any addition to our number, but instead of it made in writing a proposal that every member separately should endeavour to form a subordinate club with the same rules respecting queries, etc., and without informing them of the connection with the Junto. The advantages proposed were the improvement of so many more young citizens by the use of our institutions; our better acquaintance with the general sentiments of the inhabitants on any occasion, as the Junto member might propose what queries we should desire and was to report to the Junto what passed in his separate club; the promotion of our particular interests in business by more extensive recommendations; and the increase of our influence in public affairs and our power of doing good by spreading thro' the several clubs the sentiments of the Junto. The project was approved, and every member undertook to form his club, but they did not all succeed. Five or six only were completed, which were called by different names, as the Vine, the Union, the Band, etc. They were useful to themselves, and afforded us a good deal of amusement, information, and instruction, besides answering in some considerable degree our views of influencing the public opinion on particular occasions, of which I shall give some instances in course of time as they happened.

My first promotion was my being chosen in 1736 clerk of the General Assembly. The choice was made that year without opposition; but the year following when I was again proposed (the choice, like that of the members, being annual), a new member made a long speech against me in order to favour some other candidate. I was, however, chosen, which was the more agreeable to me, as besides the pay for immediate service as clerk, the place gave me a better opportunity of keeping up an interest among the members, which secured to me the business of printing the votes, laws, paper money, and other occasional jobs for the public, that, on the whole, were very profitable. I therefore did not like the opposition of this new member, who was a gentleman of fortune and education with talents that were likely to give him in time great influence in the House, which, indeed, afterwards happened. I did not, however, aim at gaining his favour by paying any servile respect to him, but after some time took this other method. Having heard that he had in his library a certain very scarce and curious book, I wrote a note to him expressing my desire of perusing that book and requesting he would do me the favour of lending it to me for a few days. He sent it immediately; and I returned it in about a week with another note expressing strongly my sense of the favour. When we next met in the House, he spoke to me (which he had never done before), and with great civility. And he ever afterwards manifested a readiness to serve me on all occasions, so that we became great friends, and our friendship continued to his death. This is another instance of the truth of an old maxim I had learned, which says, "He that has once done you a kindness will be more ready to do you another than he whom you yourself have obliged." And it shows how much more profitable it is prudently to remove, than to resent, return, and continue inimical proceedings.

In 1737, Col. Spotswood, late Governor of Virginia, and then Postmaster-General, being dissatisfied with the conduct of his deputy at Philadelphia respecting some negligence in rendering and want of exactness in framing his accounts, took from him the commission and offered it to me. I accepted it readily and found it of great advantage; for tho' the salary was small, it facilitated the correspondence that improved my newspaper, increased the number demanded as well as the advertisements to be inserted, so that it came to afford me a considerable income. My old competitor's newspaper declined proportionably, and I was satisfied without retaliating his refusal, while Postmaster, to permit my papers being carried by the riders. Thus he suffered greatly from his neglect in due accounting; and I mention it as a lesson to those young men who may be employed in managing affairs for others that they should always render accounts with great clearness and punctuality. The character of observing such a conduct is the most powerful of all recommendations to new employments and increase of business.

I began now to turn my thoughts a little to public affairs, beginning, however, with small matters. The city watch was one of the first things that I conceived to want regulation. It was managed by the constables of the respective wards in turn; the constable warned a number of housekeepers to attend him for the night.[1] Those who chose never to attend paid him six shillings a year to be excused, which was supposed to be for hiring substitutes, but was in reality much more than was necessary for that purpose and made the constableship a place of profit; and the constable for a little drink often got such raga-muffins about him as a watch that respectable housekeepers did not choose to mix with. Walking the rounds, too, was often neglected, and most of the nights spent in tippling. I thereupon wrote a paper to be read in Junto representing these irregularities but insisting more particularly on the inequality of this six-shilling tax of the constables, respecting the circumstances of those who paid it, since a poor widow housekeeper, all whose property to be guarded by the watch did not, perhaps, exceed the value of fifty pounds, paid as much as the wealthiest merchant who had thousands of pounds'-worth of goods in his stores. On the whole, I proposed as a more effectual watch the hiring of proper men to serve constantly in that business; and as a more equitable way of supporting the charge, the levying a tax that should be proportioned to the property. This idea, being approved by the Junto, was communicated to the other clubs, but as arising in each of them. And tho' the plan was not immediately carried into execution, yet by preparing the minds of people for the change, it paved the way for the law obtained a few years after, when the members of our clubs were grown into more influence.

[1] Cities were policed only at night, by constables and marshals who were assisted by houseowners serving in rotation.

About this time I wrote a paper (first to be read in Junto, but it was afterwards published) on the different accidents and carelessnesses by which houses were set on fire, with cautions against them and means proposed of avoiding them. This was much spoken of as a useful piece, and gave rise to a project which soon followed it of forming a company for the more ready extinguishing of fires, and mutual assistance in removing and securing of goods when in danger. Associates in this scheme were presently found amounting to thirty. Our articles of agreement obliged every member to keep always in good order and fit for use a certain number of leather buckets with strong bags and baskets (for packing and transporting of goods) which were to be brought to every fire; and we agreed to meet once a month and spend a social evening together in discoursing and communicating such ideas as occurred to us upon the subject of fires as might be useful in our conduct on such occasions. The utility of this institution soon appeared, and many more desiring to be admitted than we thought convenient for one company, they were advised to form another, which was accordingly done. And this went on, one new company being formed after another till they became so numerous as to include most of the inhabitants who were men of property; and now at the time of my writing this, tho' upwards of fifty years since its establishment, that which I first formed, called the Union Fire Company,[1] still subsists and flourishes, tho' the first members are all deceased but myself and one, who is older by a year than I am. The small fines that have been paid by members for absence at the monthly meetings have been applied to the purchase of fire engines, ladders, firehooks, and other useful implements for each company, so that I question whether there is a city in the world better provided with the means of putting a stop to beginning conflagrations; and in fact since those institutions, the city has never lost by fire more than one or two houses at a time, and the flames have often been extinguished before the house in which they began has been half consumed.

In 1739 arrived among us from England the Rev. Mr. Whitefield, who had made himself remarkable there as an itinerant preacher.[2] He was at first permitted to preach in some of our

---

[1] Organized December 7, 1736.
[2] George Whitefield (1714–1770), an English Methodist evangelist whose

churches; but the clergy, taking a dislike to him, soon refused him their pulpits, and he was obliged to preach in the fields. The multitudes of all sects and denominations that attended his sermons were enormous, and it was matter of speculation to me, who was one of the number, to observe the extraordinary influence of his oratory on his hearers and how much they admired and respected him, notwithstanding his common abuse of them, by assuring them they were naturally "half beasts and half devils." It was wonderful to see the change soon made in the manners of our inhabitants; from being thoughtless or indifferent about religion, it seemed as if all the world were growing religious, so that one could not walk thro' the town in an evening without hearing psalms sung in different families of every street. And it being found inconvenient to assemble in the open air subject to its inclemencies, the building of a house to meet in was no sooner proposed and persons appointed to receive contributions, but sufficient sums were soon received to procure the ground and erect the building which was one hundred feet long and seventy broad, about the size of Westminster Hall; and the work was carried on with such spirit as to be finished in a much shorter time than could have been expected. Both house and ground were vested in trustees expressly for the use of any preacher of any religious persuasion who might desire to say something to the people of Philadelphia, the design in building not being to accommodate any particular sect but the inhabitants in general, so that even if the Mufti of Constantinople were to send a missionary to preach Mahometanism to us, he would find a pulpit at his service.

Mr. Whitfield, in leaving us, went preaching all the way thro' the Colonies to Georgia. The settlement of that province had lately been begun; but instead of being made with hardy, industrious husbandmen accustomed to labour, the only people fit for such an enterprise, it was with families of broken shopkeepers and other insolvent debtors, many of indolent and idle habits, taken out of the gaols — who, being set down in the woods, unqualified for clearing land and unable to endure the hardships of a new settlement, perished in numbers, leaving many

---

tour provided the initial impetus for the American Methodist movement and played an important part in generating the evangelistic "Great Awakening" of the 1740's. Franklin here spells his name as it was pronounced.

helpless children unprovided for. The sight of their miserable situation inspired the benevolent heart of Mr. Whitfield with the idea of building an orphan house there in which they might be supported and educated. Returning northward he preached up this charity and made large collections; for his eloquence had a wonderful power over the hearts and purses of his hearers, of which I myself was an instance. I did not disapprove of the design, but as Georgia was then destitute of materials and workmen and it was proposed to send them from Philadelphia at a great expence, I thought it would have been better to have built the house here and brought the children to it. This I advised, but he was resolute in his first project and rejected my counsel, and I thereupon refused to contribute. I happened soon after to attend one of his sermons, in the course of which I perceived he intended to finish with a collection, and I silently resolved he should get nothing from me. I had in my pocket a handful of copper money, three or four silver dollars, and five pistoles in gold. As he proceeded, I began to soften and concluded to give the coppers. Another stroke of his oratory made me ashamed of that and determined me to give the silver; and he finished so admirably that I emptied my pocket wholly into the collector's dish, gold and all. At this sermon there was also one of our club, who being of my sentiments respecting the building in Georgia and suspecting a collection might be intended, had by precaution emptied his pockets before he came from home; towards the conclusion of the discourse, however, he felt a strong desire to give and applied to a neighbour who stood near him to borrow some money for the purpose. The application was unfortunately made to perhaps the only man in the company who had the firmness not to be affected by the preacher. His answer was, "At any other time, Friend Hopkinson, I would lend to thee freely, but not now; for thee seems to be out of thy right senses."

Some of Mr. Whitfield's enemies affected to suppose that he would apply these collections to his own private emolument, but I who was intimately acquainted with him (being employed in printing his sermons and journals, etc.) never had the least suspicion of his integrity, but am to this day decidedly of opinion that he was in all his conduct a perfectly *honest man*. And methinks my testimony in his favour ought to have the more weight as we had no religious connection. He used, indeed, sometimes to pray for my conversion but never had the satisfaction of believing that his prayers were heard. Ours was a mere civil friendship, sincere on both sides, and lasted to his death.

The following instance will show something of the terms on which we stood. Upon one of his arrivals from England at Boston, he wrote to me that he should come soon to Philadelphia but knew not where he could lodge when there, as he understood his old, kind host, Mr. Benezet, was removed to Germantown.[1] My answer was, "You know my house; if you can make shift its scanty accommodations, you will be most heartily welcome." He replied that if I made that kind offer for Christ's sake, I should not miss of a reward. And I returned, "Don't let me be mistaken; it was not for Christ's sake but for your sake." One of our common acquaintance jocosely remarked that knowing it to be the custom of the saints when they received any favour to shift the burthen of the obligation from off their own shoulders and place it in Heaven, I had contrived to fix it on earth.

The last time I saw Mr. Whitfield was in London, when he consulted me about his orphan house concern and his purpose of appropriating it to the establishment of a college.

He had a loud and clear voice, and articulated his words and sentences so perfectly that he might be heard and understood at a great distance, especially as his auditories, however numerous, observed the most exact silence. He preached one evening from the top of the courthouse steps, which are in the middle of Market Street and on the west side of Second Street, which crosses it at right angles. Both streets were filled with his hearers to a considerable distance. Being among the hindmost in Market Street, I had the curiosity to learn how far he could be heard by retiring backwards down the street towards the river, and I found his voice distinct till I came near Front Street, when some noise in that street obscured it. Imagining then a semicircle, of which my distance should be the radius, and that it were filled with auditors, to each of whom I allowed two square feet,

[1] Anthony Benezet (1713–1784), French-born Quaker who settled in Philadelphia and became a leader in the early temperance and anti-slavery movements.

I computed that he might well be heard by more than thirty thousand. This reconciled me to the newspaper accounts of his having preached to twenty-five thousand people in the fie'ds, and to the antient histories of generals haranguing whole armies, of which I had sometimes doubted.

By hearing him often I came to distinguish easily between sermons newly composed and those which he had often preached in the course of his travels. His delivery of the latter was so improved by frequent repetitions that every accent, every emphasis, every modulation of voice was so perfectly well turned and well placed that, without being interested in the subject, one could not help being pleased with the discourse, a pleasure of much the same kind with that received from an excellent piece of music. This is an advantage itinerant preachers have over those who are stationary, as the latter cannot well improve their delivery of a sermon by so many rehearsals.

His writing and printing from time to time gave great advantage to his enemies. Unguarded expressions and even erroneous opinions delivered in preaching might have been afterwards explained or qualified by supposing others that might have accompanied them, or they might have been denied, but *litera scripta manet*.[1] Critics attacked his writings violently and with so much appearance of reason as to diminish the number of his votaries and prevent their encrease; so that I am of opinion if he had never written anything, he would have left behind him a much more numerous and important sect. And his reputation might in that case have been still growing, even after his death; as there being nothing of his writing on which to found a censure and give him a lower character, his proselytes would be left at liberty to feign for him as great a variety of excellencies as their enthusiastic admiration might wish him to have possessed.

My business was now continually augmenting and my circumstances growing daily easier, my newspaper having become very profitable, as being for a time almost the only one in this and the neighbouring provinces. I experienced, too, the truth of the observation that "after getting the first hundred pound, it is more easy to get the second:" — money itself being of a prolific nature.

The partnership at Carolina having succeeded, I was en-

1 The written letter remains.

couraged to engage in others and to promote several of my workmen who had behaved well, by establishing them with printing houses in different colonies on the same terms with that in Carolina. Most of them did well, being enabled at the end of our term, six years, to purchase the types of me and go on working for themselves, by which means several families were raised. Partnerships often finish in quarrels, but I was happy in this, that mine were all carried on and ended amicably, owing, I think, a good deal to the precaution of having very explicitly settled in our articles everything to be done by or expected from each partner, so that there was nothing to dispute — which precaution I would therefore recommend to all who enter into partnerships, for whatever esteem partners may have for and confidence in each other at the time of the contract, little jealousies and disgusts may arise, with ideas of inequality in the care and burthen of the business, etc., which are attended often with breach of friendship and of the connection, perhaps with lawsuits and other disagreeable consequences.

I had on the whole abundant reason to be satisfied with my being established in Pennsylvania. There were, however, two things that I regretted: there being no provision for defence nor for a complete education of youth, no militia nor any college. I therefore in 1743 drew up a proposal for establishing an academy; and at that time thinking the Reverend Mr. Peters, who was out of employ, a fit person to superintend such an institution, I communicated the project to him. But he, having more profitable views in the service of the Proprietors, which succeeded, declining the undertaking.[1] And not knowing another at that time suitable for such a trust, I let the scheme lie awhile dormant. I succeeded better the next year, 1744, in proposing and establishing a philosophical society.[2] The paper I wrote for that purpose will be found among my writings when collected.

With respect to defence, Spain having been several years at war against Britain and being at length joined by France,[3] which brought us into greater danger, and the laboured and long-continued endeavours of our Governor Thomas to prevail with

[1] The Reverend Richard Peters of Christ Church, Philadelphia, who hoped instead to obtain a post in the colonial government from the Penns, the proprietors of Pennsylvania.

[2] The American Philosophical Society.

[3] England and Spain went to war in 1739, England and France in 1744.

our Quaker Assembly to pass a militia law and make other provisions for the security of the province having proved abortive,
I determined to try what might be done by a voluntary association of the people. To promote this, I first wrote and published
a pamphlet, intitled *Plain Truth*,[1] in which I stated our defence-
less situation in strong lights, with the necessity of union and
discipline for our defence, and promised to propose in a few days
an association to be generally signed for that purpose. The
pamphlet had a sudden and surprizing effect. I was called upon
for the instrument of association; and having settled the draft of
it with a few friends, I appointed a meeting of the citizens in the
large building before-mentioned. The house was pretty full. I
had prepared a number of printed copies, and provided pens and
ink dispersed all over the room. I harangued them a little on the
subject, read the paper, and explained it, and then distributed
the copies, which were eagerly signed, not the least objection
being made. When the company separated and the papers were
collected, we found about twelve hundred hands; and other
copies being dispersed in the country, the subscribers amounted
at length to upwards of ten thousand. These all furnished themselves as soon as they could with arms, formed themselves into
companies and regiments, chose their own officers, and met every
week to be instructed in the manual exercise and other parts of
military discipline. The women, by subscriptions among themselves, provided silk colours, which they presented to the companies, painted with different devices and mottos which I supplied. The officers of the companies composing the Philadelphia
regiment being met, chose me for their colonel; but conceiving
myself unfit, I declined that station and recommended Mr.
Lawrence, a fine person and man of influence, who was accordingly appointed. I then proposed a lottery to defray the expence
of building a battery below the town and furnishing it with
cannon. It filled expeditiously, and the battery was soon erected,
the merlons [2] being framed of logs and filled with earth. We
bought some old cannon from Boston, but these not being
sufficient, we wrote to England for more, soliciting at the same
time our Proprietaries for some assistance, tho' without much
expectation of obtaining it. Meanwhile Colonel Lawrence,

[1] Published in 1747.
[2] Battlements.

William Allen, Abraham Taylor, Esquires, and myself were sent to New York by the associators, commissioned to borrow some cannon of Governor Clinton. He at first refused us peremptorily; but at a dinner with his council where there was great drinking of Madeira wine, as the custom at that place then was, he softened by degrees and said he would lend us six. After a few more bumpers he advanced to ten. And at length he very good-naturedly conceded eighteen. They were fine cannon, eighteen-pounders, with their carriages, which we soon transported and mounted on our battery, where the associators kept a nightly guard while the war lasted. And among the rest I regularly took my turn of duty there as a common soldier.

My activity in these operations was agreeable to the Governor and Council; they took me into confidence, and I was consulted by them in every measure wherein their concurrence was thought useful to the association. Calling in the aid of religion, I proposed to them the proclaiming a fast to promote reformation and implore the blessing of Heaven on our undertaking. They embraced the motion, but as it was the first fast ever thought of in the province, the Secretary had no precedent from which to draw the proclamation. My education in New England, where a fast is proclaimed every year, was here of some advantage. I drew it in the accustomed style; it was translated into German, printed in both languages, and circulated thro' the province. This gave the clergy of the different sects an opportunity of influencing their congregations to join in the association; and it would probably have been general among all but Quakers if the peace had not soon intervened.

It was thought by some of my friends that by my activity in these affairs, I should offend that sect and thereby lose my interest in the Assembly, where they were a great majority. A young gentleman who had likewise some friends in the House and wished to succeed me as their clerk, acquainted me that it was decided to displace me at the next election, and he therefore in good will advised me to resign, as more consistent with my honour than being turned out. My answer to him was that I had read or heard of some public man who made it a rule never to ask for an office and never to refuse one when offered to him. "I approve," says I, "of his rule and will practise it with a small addition; I shall never *ask*, never *refuse*, nor ever *resign* an

office. If they will have my office of clerk to dispose of to
another, they shall take it from me. I will not, by giving it up,
lose my right of sometime or other making reprisals on my
adversaries." I heard, however, no more of this. I was chosen
again, unanimously as usual, at the next election. Possibly as
they disliked my late intimacy with the members of Council
who had joined the governors in all the disputes about military
preparations with which the House had long been harassed, they
might have been pleased if I would voluntarily have left them;
but they did not care to displace me on account merely of my
zeal for the association, and they could not well give another
reason. Indeed, I had some cause to believe that the defence of
the country was not disagreeable to any of them, provided they
were not required to assist in it. And I found that a much
greater number of them than I could have imagined, tho' against
offensive war, were clearly for the defensive. Many pamphlets
pro and con were published on the subject, and some by good
Quakers in favour of defence, which I believe convinced most
of their younger people. A transaction in our fire company gave
me some insight into their prevailing sentiments. It had been proposed that we should encourage the scheme for building a
battery by laying out the present stock, then about sixty pounds,
in tickets of the lottery. By our rules no money could be disposed of till the next meeting after the proposal. The company
consisted of thirty members, of which twenty-two were Quakers,
and eight only of other persuasions. We eight punctually attended the meeting; but tho' we thought that some of the
Quakers would join us, we were by no means sure of a majority.
Only one Quaker, Mr. James Morris, appeared to oppose the
measure. He expressed much sorrow that it had ever been proposed, as he said "Friends" [1] were all against it, and it would
create such discord as might break up the company. We told
him that we saw no reason for that; we were the minority, and
if "Friends" were against the measure and outvoted us, we must
and should, agreeable to the usage of all societies, submit. When
the hour for business arrived, it was moved to put the vote. He
allowed we might then do it by the rules, but as he could assure
us that a number of members intended to be present for the
purpose of opposing it, it would be but candid to allow a little

[1] Quakers, i.e., the Society of Friends.

time for their appearing. While we were disputing this, a waiter came to tell me two gentlemen below desired to speak with me. I went down and found they were two of our Quaker members. They told me there were eight of them assembled at a tavern just by; that they were determined to come and vote with us if there should be occasion, which they hoped would not be the case; and desired we would not call for their assistance if we could do without it, as their voting for such a measure might embroil them with their elders and friends. Being thus secure of a majority, I went up, and after a little seeming hesitation, agreed to a delay of another hour. This Mr. Morris allowed to be extremely fair. Not one of his opposing friends appeared, at which he expressed great surprize; and at the expiration of the hour, we carried the resolution eight to one; and as of the twenty-two Quakers, eight were ready to vote with us and thirteen by their absence manifested that they were not inclined to oppose the measure, I afterwards estimated the proportion of Quakers sincerely against defence as one to twenty-two only. For these were all regular members of that society, and in good reputation among them, and had due notice of what was proposed at that meeting.

The honourable and learned Mr. Logan,[1] who had always been of that sect, was one who wrote an address to them declaring his approbation of defensive war and supporting his opinion by many strong arguments. He put into my hands sixty pounds to be laid out in lottery tickets for the battery, with directions to apply what prizes might be drawn wholly to that service. He told me the following anecdote of his old master William Penn, respecting defence. He came over from England when a young man with that Proprietary, and as his secretary. It was war time, and their ship was chased by an armed vessel supposed to be an enemy. Their captain prepared for defence, but told William Penn and his company of Quakers that he did not expect their assistance and they might retire into the cabin, which they did, except James Logan, who chose to stay upon deck and was quartered to a gun. The supposed enemy proved a friend, so there was no fighting. But when the secretary went down to communicate the intelligence, William Penn rebuked him severely

---

[1] James Logan, Irish-born Philadelphian who was business secretary to the Penn family.

for staying upon deck and undertaking to assist in defending the vessel contrary to the principles of Friends, especially as it had not been required by the captain. This reproof being before all the company, piqued the secretary, who answered: "I being thy servant, why did thee not order me to come down? But thee was willing enough that I should stay and help to fight the ship when thee thought there was danger."

My being many years in the Assembly, the majority of which were constantly Quakers, gave me frequent opportunities of seeing the embarrassment given them by their principle against war whenever application was made to them by order of the Crown to grant aids for military purposes. They were unwilling to offend government, on the one hand, by a direct refusal and their Friends, the body of Quakers, on the other, by a compliance contrary to their principles — hence a variety of evasions to avoid complying and modes of disguising the compliance when it became unavoidable. The common mode at last was to grant money under the phrase of its being "for the King's use," and never to enquire how it was applied. But if the demand was not directly from the Crown, that phrase was found not so proper, and some other was to be invented. As when powder was wanting (I think it was for the garrison at Louisburg) and the government of New England solicited a grant of some from Pennsylvania (which was much urged on the House by Governor Thomas), they could not grant money to buy powder because that was an ingredient of war, but they voted an aid to New England of three thousand pounds, to be put into the hands of the Governor, and appropriated it for the purchasing of bread, flour, wheat, "or other grain." Some of the Council, desirous of giving the House still further embarrassment, advised the Governor not to accept provision as not being the thing he had demanded. But he replied, "I shall take the money, for I understand very well their meaning; 'other grain' is gunpowder" — which he accordingly bought, and they never objected to it. It was in allusion to this fact that when in our fire company we feared the success of our proposal in favour of the lottery and I had said to my friend Mr. Syng, one of our members, "If we fail, let us move the purchase of a fire engine with the money; the Quakers can have no objection to that. And then if you nominate me, and I you, as a committee for that purpose, we will

buy a great gun, which is certainly a 'fire engine.' " "I see," says
he, "you have improved by being so long in the Assembly; your
equivocal project would be just a match for their wheat 'or other
grain.' "

These embarrassments that the Quakers suffered from having
established and published it as one of their principles that no kind
of war was lawful, and which being once published, they could
not afterwards, however they might change their minds, easily
get rid of, reminds me of what I think a more prudent conduct
in another sect among us, that of the Dunkers.[1] I was acquainted
with one of its founders, Michael Welfare, soon after it appeared.
He complained to me that they were grievously calumniated by
the zealots of other persuasions, and charged with abominable
principles and practices to which they were utter strangers. I
told him this had always been the case with new sects and that
to put a stop to such abuse, I imagined it might be well to
publish the articles of their belief and the rules of their discipline.
He said that it had been proposed among them, but not agreed to
for this reason: "When we were first drawn together as a
society," says he, "it had pleased God to enlighten our minds so
far as to see that some doctrines which we once esteemed truths
were errors, and that others which we had esteemed errors were
real truths. From time to time he has been pleased to afford us
further light, and our principles have been improving and our
errors diminishing. Now we are not sure that we are arrived at
the end of this progression, and at the perfection of spiritual
or theological knowledge; and we fear that if we should once
print our confession of faith, we should feel ourselves as if
bound and confined by it, and perhaps be unwilling to receive
further improvement, and our successors still more so, as conceiving what their elders and founders had done to be something
sacred, never to be departed from." This modesty in a sect
is perhaps a singular instance in the history of mankind, every
other sect supposing itself in possession of all truth, and that
those who differ are so far in the wrong — like a man travelling
in foggy weather: Those at some distance before him on the
road he sees wrapped up in the fog, as well as those behind
him, and also the people in the fields on each side; but near him

---

[1] Members of a German Baptist sect, also known as Dunkards, many of
whom emigrated to Pennsylvania in the early eighteenth century.

all appears clear, tho' in truth he is as much in the fog as any of them. To avoid this kind of embarrassment, the Quakers have of late years been gradually declining the public service in the Assembly and in the magistracy, choosing rather to quit their power than their principle.

In order of time, I should have mentioned before that, having in 1742 invented an open stove for the better warming of rooms and at the same time saving fuel, as the fresh air admitted was warmed in entering, I made a present of the model to Mr. Robert Grace, one of my early friends, who having an iron furnace, found the casting of the plates for these stoves a profitable thing, as they were growing in demand. To promote that demand, I wrote and published a pamphlet entitled, *An Account of the New-Invented Pennsylvania Fireplaces: Wherein Their Construction and Manner of Operation is Particularly Explained, Their Advantages above Every Other Method of Warming Rooms Demonstrated; and All Objections That Have Been Raised against the Use of Them Answered and Obviated, etc.* This pamphlet had a good effect. Governor Thomas was so pleased with the construction of this stove as described in it that he offered to give me a patent for the sole vending of them for a term of years; but I declined it from a principle which has ever weighed with me on such occasions; viz., *that as we enjoy great advantages from the inventions of others, we should be glad of an opportunity to serve others by any invention of ours, and this we should do freely and generously.* An ironmonger in London, however, after assuming[1] a good deal of my pamphlet, and working up into his own, and making some small changes in the machine, which rather hurt its operation, got a patent for it there, and made, as I was told, a little fortune by it. And this is not the only instance of patents taken out for my inventions by others, tho' not always with the same success, which I never contested, as having no desire of profiting by patents myself and hating disputes. The use of these fireplaces in very many houses both of this and the neighbouring colonies, has been and is a great saving of wood to the inhabitants.

Peace being concluded and the association business therefore at an end, I turned my thoughts again to the affair of establishing an academy. The first step I took was to associate in the design

[1] Appropriating.

a number of active friends, of whom the Junto furnished a good part, the next was to write and publish a pamphlet entitled *Proposals Relating to the Education of Youth in Pennsylvania.* This I distributed among the principal inhabitants gratis; and as soon as I could suppose their minds a little prepared by the perusal of it, I set on foot a subscription for opening and supporting an academy; it was to be paid in quotas yearly for five years; by so dividing it I judged the subscription might be larger, and I believe it was so, amounting to no less, if I remember right, than five thousand pounds.

In the introduction to these proposals, I stated their publication not as an act of mine, but of some "public-spirited gentlemen"; avoiding as much as I could, according to my usual rule, the presenting myself to the public as the author of any scheme for their benefit.

The subscribers, to carry the project into immedate execution, chose out of their number twenty-four trustees and appointed Mr. Francis, then Attorney-General, and myself to draw up constitutions for the government of the academy, which being done and signed, a house was hired, masters engaged, and the schools opened, I think, in the same year, 1749.

The scholars encreasing fast, the house was soon found too small, and we were looking out for a piece of ground properly situated, with intention to build, when Providence threw into our way a large house ready built, which with a few alterations might well serve our purpose. This was the building beforementioned, erected by the hearers of Mr. Whitfield, and was obtained for us in the following manner.

It is to be noted that the contributions to this building being made by people of different sects, care was taken in the nomination of trustees, in whom the building and ground were to be vested, that a predominancy should not be given to any sect, lest in time that predominancy might be a means of appropriating the whole to the use of such sect contrary to the original intention; it was for this reason that one of each sect was appointed, viz., one Church of England man, one Presbyterian, one Baptist, one Moravian,[1] etc.; those in case of vacancy by death were to

---

[1] An evangelical sect which arose in Austria and Germany among followers of John Huss, also known as Bohemian Brethren and United Brethren. Large numbers settled in southern and western Pennsylvania.

fill it by election from among the contributors. The Moravian happened not to please his colleagues, and on his death they resolved to have no other of that sect. The difficulty then was, how to avoid having two of some other sect by means of the new choice. Several persons were named and for that reason not agreed to. At length one mentioned me, with the observation that I was merely an honest man, and of *no sect* at all — which prevailed with them to choose me. The enthusiasm which existed when the house was built had long since abated, and its trustees had not been able to procure fresh contributions for paying the ground rent and discharging some other debts the building had occasioned, which embarrassed them greatly. Being now a member of both boards of trustees, that for the building and that for the academy, I had a good opportunity of negotiating with both, and brought them finally to an agreement by which the trustees for the building were to cede it to those of the academy, the latter undertaking to discharge the debt, to keep forever open in the building a large hall for occasional preachers according to the original intention, and maintain a free school for the instruction of poor children. Writings were accordingly drawn, and on paying the debts the trustees of the academy were put in possession of the premises, and by dividing the great and lofty hall into stories, and different rooms above and below for the several schools, and purchasing some additional ground, the whole was soon made fit for our purpose, and the scholars removed into the building. The care and trouble of agreeing with the workmen, purchasing materials, and superintending the work fell upon me, and I went thro' it the more cheerfully, as it did not then interfere with my private business, having the year before taken a very able, industrious, and honest partner, Mr. David Hall, with whose character I was well acquainted as he had worked for me four years. He took off my hands all care of the printing office, paying me punctually my share of the profits. This partnership continued eighteen years, successfully for us both.

The trustees of the academy after a while were incorporated by a charter from the Governor; their funds were increased by contributions in Britain and grants of land from the Proprietaries, to which the Assembly has since made considerable addition, and thus was established the present University of Philadelphia.[1] I have been continued one of its trustees from the beginning, now near forty years, and have had the very great pleasure of seeing a number of the youth who have received their education in it distinguished by their improved abilities, serviceable in public stations, and ornaments to their country.

When I disengaged myself, as above mentioned, from private business, I flattered myself that, by the sufficient tho' moderate fortune I had acquired, I had secured leisure during the rest of my life for philosophical studies and amusements; I purchased all Dr. Spence's apparatus, who had come from England to lecture here; and I proceeded in my electrical experiments with great alacrity; but the public now considering me as a man of leisure, laid hold of me for their purposes — every part of our civil government, and almost at the same time, imposing some duty upon me. The Governor put me into the commission of the peace; the corporation of the city chose me of the common council and soon after an alderman; and the citizens at large elected me a burgess to represent them in Assembly. This latter station was the more agreeable to me, as I was at length tired with sitting there to hear debates in which as clerk I could take no part, and which were often so uninteresting that I was induced to amuse myself with making magic squares or circles or anything to avoid weariness. And I conceived my becoming a member would enlarge my power of doing good. I would not, however, insinuate that my ambition was not flattered by all these promotions. It certainly was. For considering my low beginning they were great things to me. And they were still more pleasing as being so many spontaneous testimonies of the public's good opinion, and by me entirely unsolicited.

The office of justice of the peace I tried a little, by attending a few courts and sitting on the bench to hear causes. But finding that more knowledge of the common law than I possessed was necessary to act in that station with credit, I gradually withdrew from it, excusing myself by my being obliged to attend the higher duties of a legislator in the Assembly. My election to this trust was repeated every year for ten years without my ever asking any elector for his vote or signifying either directly or in-

[1] The present University of Pennsylvania.

directly any desire of being chosen. On taking my seat in the House, my son was appointed their clerk.

The year following, a treaty being to be held with the Indians at Carlisle, the Governor sent a message to the House proposing that they should nominate some of their members to be joined with some members of Council as commissioners for that purpose. The House named the Speaker (Mr. Norris) and myself; and being commissioned, we went to Carlisle and met the Indians accordingly. As those people are extremely apt to get drunk and when so are very quarrelsome and disorderly, we strictly forbade the selling any liquor to them; and when they complained of this restriction, we told them that if they would continue sober during the treaty, we would give them plenty of rum when business was over. They promised this, and they kept their promise because they could get no liquor, and the treaty was conducted very orderly and concluded to mutual satisfaction. They then claimed and received the rum. This was in the afternoon. They were near one hundred men, women, and children, and were lodged in temporary cabins built in the form of a square, just without the town. In the evening, hearing a great noise among them, the commssioners walked out to see what was the matter. We found they had made a great bonfire in the middle of the square. They were all drunk, men and women, quarrelling and fighting. Their dark-coloured bodies, half naked, seen only by the gloomy light of the bonfire, running after and beating one another with firebrands, accompanied by their horrid yellings, formed a scene the most resembling our ideas of hell that could well be imagined. There was no appeasing the tumult, and we retired to our lodging. At midnight a number of them came thundering at our door demanding more rum — of which we took no notice. The next day, sensible they had misbehaved in giving us that disturbance, they sent three of their old counsellors to make their apology. The orator acknowledged the fault, but laid it upon the rum, and then endeavoured to excuse the rum by saying, "The Great Spirit who made all things made everything for some use, and whatever use he designed anything for, that use it should always be put to. Now, when he made rum, he said, 'LET THIS BE FOR INDIANS TO GET DRUNK WITH.' And it must be so." And indeed if it be the design of Providence to extirpate these savages in order to make room for cultivators of the earth, it seems not improbable that rum may be the appointed means. It has already annihiliated all the tribes who formerly inhabited the seacoast.

In 1751 Dr. Thomas Bond, a particular friend of mine, conceived the idea of establishing a hospital in Philadelphia for the reception and cure of poor, sick persons, whether inhabitants of the province or strangers — a very beneficent design, which has been ascribed to me but was originally his. He was zealous and active in endeavouring to procure subscriptions for it; but the proposal being a novelty in America and at first not well understood, he met with small success. At length he came to me with the compliment that he found there was no such thing as carrying a public-spirited project through without my being concerned in it. "For," say he, "I am often asked by those to whom I propose subscribing, 'Have you consulted Franklin upon this business, and what does he think of it?' And when I tell them that I have not (supposing it rather out of your line), they do not subscribe but say they will consider it." I enquired into the nature and probable utility of his scheme, and receiving from him a very satisfactory explanation, I not only subscribed to it myself but engaged heartily in the design of procuring subscriptions from others. Previous, however, to the solicitation, I endeavoured to prepare the minds of the people by writing on the subject in the newspapers, which was my usual custom in such cases, but which he had omitted. The subscriptions afterwards were more free and generous, but beginning to flag, I saw they would be insufficient without some assistance from the Assembly and therefore proposed to petition for it, which was done. The country members did not at first relish the project. They objected that it could only be serviceable to the city, and therefore the citizens should alone be at the expence of it; and they doubted whether the citizens themselves generally approved of it. My allegation on the contrary that it met with such approbation as to leave no doubt of our being able to raise £2000 by voluntary donations, they considered as a most extravagant supposition and utterly impossible. On this I formed my plan; and asking leave to bring in a bill for incorporating the contributors according to the prayer of their petition and granting them a blank sum of money, which leave was obtained chiefly on the consideration that the House could throw the bill out if they did not like it, I drew it so as to make the important clause a conditional one; viz., "And be it enacted by the authority aforesaid that when the said contributors shall have met and chosen their managers and treasurer, *and shall have raised by their contributions a capital stock of £2000 value* (the yearly interest of which is to be applied to the accommodating of the sick poor in the said hospital, free of charge for diet, attendance, advice, and medicines) and *shall make the same appear to the satisfaction of the Speaker of the Assembly* for the time being, that *then* it shall and may be lawful for the said Speaker; and he is hereby required to sign an order on the provincial treasurer for the payment of £2000 in two yearly payments, to the treasurer of the said hospital, to be applied to the founding, building, and finishing of the same." This condition carried the bill through; for the members who had opposed the grant and now conceived they might have the credit of being charitable without the expence, agreed to its passage; and then in soliciting subscriptions among the people, we urged the conditional promise of the law as an additional motive to give, since every man's donation would be doubled. Thus the clause worked both ways. The subscriptions accordingly soon exceeded the requisite sum, and we claimed and received the public gift, which enabled us to carry the design into execution. A convenient and handsome building was soon erected, the institution has by constant experience been found useful and flourishes to this day. And I do not remember any of my political manoeuvres, the success of which gave me at the time more pleasure; or that in after-thinking of it, I more easily excused myself for having made use of cunning.

It was about this time that another projector, the Rev. Gilbert Tennent,[1] came to me with a request that I would assist him in procuring a subscription for erecting a new meetinghouse. It was to be for the use of a congregation he had gathered among the Presbyterians who were originally disciples of Mr. Whitfield. Unwilling to make myself disagreeable to my fellow citizens by too frequently soliciting their contributions, I absolutely refused. He then desired I would furnish him with a list of the names of persons I knew by experience to be generous and public-

---

[1] Tennent, who accompanied Whitefield on part of his American tour, became one of the most influential American preachers during the decade of the "Great Awakening."

spirited. I thought it would be unbecoming in me, after their kind compliance with my solicitations, to mark them out to be worried by other beggars, and therefore refused also to give such a list. He then desired I would at least give him my advice. "That I will readily do," said I, "and, in the first place, I advise you to apply to all those who you know will give something; next, to those who you are uncertain whether they will give anything or not, and show them the list of those who have given; and lastly, do not neglect those who you are sure will give nothing, for in some of them you may be mistaken." He laughed and thanked me, and said he would take my advice. He did so, for he asked of *everybody;* and he obtained a much larger sum than he expected, with which he erected the capacious and very elegant meetinghouse that stands in Arch Street.

Our city, tho' laid out with a beautiful regularity, the streets large, straight, and crossing each other at right angles, had the disgrace of suffering those streets to remain long unpaved; and in wet weather the wheels of heavy carriages ploughed them into a quagmire so that it was difficult to cross them. And in dry weather the dust was offensive. I had lived near what was called the Jersey Market and saw with pain the inhabitants wading in mud while purchasing their provisions. A strip of ground down the middle of that market was at length paved with brick so that being once in the market they had firm footing, but were often over shoes in dirt to get there. By talking and writing on the subject, I was at length instrumental in getting the street paved with stone between the market and the bricked foot pavement that was on each side next the houses. This for some time gave an easy access to the market, dry-shod. But the rest of the street not being paved, whenever a carriage came out of the mud upon this pavement, it shook off and left its dirt upon it, and it was soon covered with mire, which was not removed, the city as yet having no scavengers.[1] After some enquiry I found a poor, industrious man who was willing to undertake keeping the pavement clean by sweeping it twice a week and carrying off the dirt from before all the neighbours' doors, for the sum of sixpence per month, to be paid by each house. I then wrote and printed a paper, setting forth the advantages to the neighborhood that might be obtained by this small expence: the greater ease in keep-

---

[1] Street cleaners.

ing our houses clean, so much dirt not being brought in by people's feet; the benefit to the shops by more custom, as buyers could more easily get at them; and by not having in windy weather the dust blown in upon their goods, etc., etc. I sent one of these papers to each house and in a day or two went round to see who would subscribe an agreement to pay these sixpences. It was unanimously signed and for a time well executed. All the inhabitants of the city were delighted with the cleanliness of the pavement that surrounded the market, it being a convenience to all; and this raised a general desire to have all the streets paved, and made the people more willing to submit to a tax for that purpose. After some time I drew a bill for paving the city and brought it into the Assembly. It was just before I went to England in 1757 and did not pass till I was gone, and then with an alteration in the mode of assessment, which I thought not for the better, but with an additional provision for lighting as well as paving the streets, which was a great improvement. It was by a private person, the late Mr. John Clifton, giving a sample of the utility of lamps by placing one at his door that the people were first impressed with the idea of lighting all the city. The honour of this public benefit has also been ascribed to me, but it belongs truly to that gentleman. I did but follow his example and have only some merit to claim respecting the form of our lamps as differing from the globe lamps we at first were supplied with from London. Those we found inconvenient in these respects: They admitted no air below; the smoke therefore did not readily go out above, but circulated in the globe, lodged on its inside, and soon obstructed the light they were intended to afford, giving, besides, the daily trouble of wiping them clean; and an accidental stroke on one of them would demolish it and render it totally useless. I therefore suggested the composing them of four flat panes, with a long funnel above, to draw up the smoke, and crevices admitting air below, to facilitate the ascent of the smoke. By this means they were kept clean, and did not grow dark in a few hours as the London lamps do, but continued bright till morning; and an accidental stroke would generally break but a single pane, easily repaired. I have sometimes wondered that the Londoners did not, from the effect holes in the bottom of the globe lamps used at Vauxhall [1] have in keeping them clean, learn

---

[1] Vauxhall Gardens, an amusement park on the outskirts of London.

to have such holes in their street lamps. But those holes being made for another purpose, viz., to communicate flame more suddenly to the wick by a little flax hanging down thro' them, the other use of letting in airs seems not to have been thought of. And therefore, after the lamps have been lit a few hours, the streets of London are very poorly illuminated.

The mention of these improvements puts me in mind of one I proposed when in London to Dr. Fothergill,[1] who was among the best men I have known and a great promoter of useful projects. I had observed that the streets when dry were never swept and the light dust carried away, but it was suffered to accumulate till wet weather reduced it to mud; and then after lying some days so deep on the pavement that there was no crossing but in paths kept clean by poor people with brooms, it was with great labour raked together and thrown up into carts open above, the sides of which suffered some of the slush at every jolt on the pavement to shake out and fall, sometimes to the annoyance of foot passengers. The reason given for not sweeping the dusty streets was that the dust would fly into the windows of shops and houses. An accidental occurrence had instructed me how much sweeping might be done in a little time. I found at my door in Craven Street one morning a poor woman sweeping my pavement with a birch broom. She appeared very pale and feeble as just come out of a fit of sickness. I asked who employed her to sweep there. She said, "Nobody. But I am very poor and in distress, and I sweeps before gentlefolkses doors and hopes they will give me something." I bid her sweep the whole street clean and I would give her a shilling. This was at nine o'clock. At twelve she came for the shilling. From the slowness I saw at first in her working, I could scarce believe that the work was done so soon and sent my servant to examine it, who reported that the whole street was swept perfectly clean and all the dust placed in the gutter which was in the middle; and the next rain washed it quite away so that the pavement and even the kennel [2] were perfectly clean. I then judged that if that feeble woman could sweep such a street in three hours, a strong, active man might have done it in half the time. And here let me remark the convenience of having but one gutter in such a narrow street

[1] Dr. John Fothergill (1712–1780), noted British physician.
[2] Gutter.

running down its middle instead of two, one on each side near the footway. For where all the rain that falls on a street runs from the sides and meets in the middle, it forms there a current strong enough to wash away all the mud it meets with. But when divided into two channels, it is often too weak to cleanse either and only makes the mud it finds more fluid so that the wheels of carriages and feet of horses throw and dash it up on the foot pavement, which is thereby rendered foul and slippery, and sometimes splash it upon those who are walking. My proposal communicated to the good doctor was as follows:

"For the more effectual cleaning and keeping clean the streets of London and Westminster, it is proposed that the several watchmen be contracted with to have the dust swept up in dry seasons and the mud raked up at other times, each in the several streets and lanes of his round; that they be furnished with brooms and other proper instruments for these purposes, to be kept at their respective stands, ready to furnish the poor people they may employ in the service.

"That in the dry, summer months the dust be all swept up into heaps at proper distances before the shops and windows of houses are usually opened, when the scavengers with close-covered carts shall also carry it all away.

"That the mud when raked up be not left in heaps to be spread abroad again by the wheels of carriages and trampling of horses; but that the scavengers be provided with bodies of carts, not placed high upon wheels, but low upon sliders, with lattice bottoms, which being covered with straw, will retain the mud thrown into them and permit the water to drain from it, whereby it will become much lighter, water making the greatest part of its weight — these bodies of carts to be placed at convenient distances and the mud brought to them in wheelbarrows, they remaining where placed till the mud is drained, and then horses brought to draw them away."

I have since had doubts of the practicability of the latter part of this proposal, on account of the narrowness of some streets and the difficulty of placing the draining sleds so as not to encumber too much the passage. But I am still of opinion that the former, requiring the dust to be swept up and carried away before the shops are open, is very practicable in the summer when the days are long; for in walking thro' the Strand and Fleet

Street one morning at seven o'clock, I observed there was not one shop open tho' it had been daylight and the sun up above three hours — the inhabitants of London choosing voluntarily to live much by candlelight and sleep by sunshine, and yet often complaining a little absurdly of the duty on candles and the high prices of tallow.

Some may think these trifling matters not worth minding or relating. But when they consider that tho' dust blown into the eyes of a single person or into a single shop on a windy day is but of small importance, yet the great number of the instances in a populous city and its frequent repetitions give it weight and consequence; perhaps they will not censure very severely those who bestow some attention to affairs of this seemingly low nature. Human felicity is produced not so much by great pieces of good fortune that seldom happen as by little advantages that occur every day. Thus, if you teach a poor young man to shave himself and keep his razor in order, you may contribute more to the happiness of his life than in giving him a thousand guineas. The money may be soon spent, the regret only remaining of having foolishly consumed it. But in the other case he escapes the frequent vexation of waiting for barbers and of their sometimes dirty fingers, offensive breaths, and dull razors. He shaves when most convenient to him and enjoys daily the pleasure of its being done with a good instrument. With these sentiments I have hazarded the few preceding pages, hoping they may afford hints which sometime or other may be useful to a city I love, having lived many years in it very happily — and perhaps to some of our towns in America.

Having been for some time employed by the Postmaster-General of America as his comptroller, in regulating the several offices and bringing the officers to account, I was upon his death in 1753 appointed jointly with Mr. William Hunter to succeed him by a commission from the Postmaster-General in England. The American office had never hitherto paid anything to that of Britain. We were to have £600 a year between us if we could make that sum out of the profits of the office. To do this, a variety of improvements were necessary; some of these were inevitably at first expensive, so that in the first four years the office became above £900 in debt to us. But it soon after began to repay us, and before I was displaced by a freak of the ministers, of which I shall speak hereafter, we had brought it to yield *three times* as much clear revenue to the Crown as the Post Office of Ireland. Since that imprudent transaction, they have received from it — not one farthing.

The business of the Post Office occasioned my taking a journey this year to New England, where the College of Cambridge, of their own motion, presented me with the degree of Master of Arts. Yale College in Connecticut had before made me a similar compliment. Thus without studying in any college I came to partake of their honours. They were conferred in consideration of my improvements and discoveries in the electric branch of natural philosophy.

In 1754 war with France being again apprehended, a congress of commissioners from the different Colonies was by an order of the Lords of Trade to be assembled at Albany, there to confer with the chiefs of the six nations concerning the means of defending both their country and ours. Governor Hamilton having received this order, acquainted the House with it, requesting they would furnish proper presents for the Indians to be given on this occasion, and naming the Speaker (Mr. Norris) and myself to join Mr. Thomas Penn and Mr. Secretary Peters as commissioners to act for Pennsylvania. The House approved the nomination and provided the goods for the presents, tho' they did not much like treating out of the province, and we met the other commissioners at Albany about the middle of June. In our way thither, I projected and drew up a plan for the union of all the Colonies under one government, so far as might be necessary for defence and other important general purposes. As we passed thro' New York, I had there shown my project to Mr. James Alexander and Mr. Kennedy, two gentlemen of great knowledge in public affairs; and being fortified by their approbation, I ventured to lay it before the Congress. It then appeared that several of the commissioners had formed plans of the same kind. A previous question was first taken whether a union should be established, which passed in the affirmative unanimously. A committee was then appointed, one member from each colony, to consider the several plans and report. Mine happened to be preferred, and with a few amendments was accordingly reported. By this plan the general government was to be administered by a president-general appointed and supported by the Crown and a grand council to be chosen by the representatives of the people of the several Colonies met in their respective Assemblies. The debates upon it in Congress went on daily hand in hand with the Indian business. Many objections and difficulties were started, but in length they were all overcome, and the plan was unanimously agreed to, and copies ordered to be transmitted to the Board of Trade and to the Assemblies of the several provinces. Its fate was singular. The Assemblies did not adopt it, as they all thought there was too much *prerogative* in it;[1] and in England it was judged to have too much of the *democratic*. The Board of Trade therefore did not approve of it; nor recommend it for the approbation of His Majesty; but another scheme was formed, supposed better to answer the same purpose, whereby the Governors of the provinces with some members of their respective Councils were to meet and order the raising of troops, building of forts, etc., and to draw on the Treasury of Great Britain for the expence, which was afterwards to be refunded by an act of Parliament laying a tax on America. My plan, with my reasons in support of it, is to be found among my political papers that are printed. Being the winter following in Boston, I had much conversation with Governor Shirley upon both the plans. Part of what passed between us on the occasion may also be seen among those papers. The different and contrary reasons of dislike to my plan make me suspect that it was really the true medium; and I am still of opinion it would have been happy for both sides the water if it had been adopted. The Colonies so united would have been sufficiently strong to have defended themselves; there would then have been no need of troops from England; of course the subsequent pretence for taxing America and the bloody contest it occasioned would have been avoided. But such mistakes are not new; history is full of the errors of states and princes.

> Look round the habitable world, how few
> Know their own good, or knowing it pursue.

Those who govern, having much business on their hands, do not generally like to take the trouble of considering and carrying

[1] I.e., *royal* prerogative.

into execution new projects. The best public measures are therefore seldom *adopted from previous wisdom, but forced by the
occasion.*

The Governor of Pennsylvania in sending it down to the
Assembly, expressed his approbation of the plan "as appearing
to him to be drawn up with great clearness and strength of judgment, and therefore recommended it as well worthy their closest
and most serious attention." The House, however, by the management of a certain member, took it up when I happened to be
absent, which I thought not very fair, and reprobated it without
paying any attention to it at all, to my no small mortification.

In my journey to Boston this year, I met at New York with
our new Governor, Mr. Morris, just arrived there from England,
with whom I had been before intimately acquainted. He brought
a commission to supersede Mr. Hamilton, who, tired with the
disputes his proprietary instructions subjected him to, had re-
signed. Mr. Morris asked me if I thought he must expect as
uncomfortable an administration.

I said, "No, you may on the contrary have a very comfortable
one, if you will only take care not to enter into any dispute with
the Assembly."

"My dear friend," says he pleasantly, "how can you advise my
avoiding disputes? You know I love disputing; it is one of my
greatest pleasures. However, to show the regard I have for
your counsel, I promise you I will, if possible, avoid them." He
had some reason for loving to dispute, being eloquent, an acute
sophister, and therefore generally successful in argumentative
conversation. He had been brought up to it from a boy, his
father, as I have heard, accustoming his children to dispute with
one another for his diversion while sitting at table after dinner.
But I think the practice was not wise, for in the course of my
observation, these disputing, contradicting, and confuting people
are generally unfortunate in their affairs. They get victory
sometimes, but they never get good will, which would be of
more use to them. We parted, he going to Philadelphia, and I
to Boston. In returning I met at New York with the votes of
the Assembly, by which it appeared that notwithstanding his
promise to me, he and the House were already in high contention, and it was a continual battle between them as long as he
retained the government. I had my share of it, for as soon as I got

back to my seat in the Assembly, I was put on every committee for answering his speeches and messages, and by the committees always desired to make the drafts. Our answers as well as his messages were often tart, and sometimes indecently abusive. And as he knew I wrote for the Assembly, one might have imagined that when we met we could hardly avoid cutting throats. But he was so good-natured a man that no personal difference between him and me was occasioned by the contest, and we often dined together. One afternoon, in the height of this public quarrel, we met in the street. "Franklin," says he, "you must go home with me and spend the evening. I am to have some company that you will like"; and taking me by the arm, he led me to his house. In gay conversation over our wine after supper he told us jokingly that he much admired the idea of Sancho Panza, who, when it was proposed to give him a government, requested it might be a government of *blacks*, as then, if he could not agree with his people, he might sell them. One of his friends who sat next to me says, "Franklin, why do you continue to side with these damned Quakers? Had not you better sell them? The Proprietor would give you a good price." "The Governor," says I, "has not yet *blacked* them enough." He had indeed laboured hard to blacken the Assembly in all his messages, but they wiped off his colouring as fast as he laid it on, and placed it in return thick upon his own face; so that finding he was likely to be negrofied himself, he, as well as Mr. Hamilton, grew tired of the contest and quitted the government.

These public quarrels were all at bottom owing to the Proprietaries, our hereditary governors, who when any expence was to be incurred for the defence of their province, with incredible meanness instructed their deputies to pass no act for levying the necessary taxes unless their vast estates were in the same act expressly excused; and they had even taken bonds of those deputies to observe such instructions. The Assemblies for three years held out against this injustice, tho' constrained to bend at last. At length Captain Denny, who was Governor Morris's successor, ventured to disobey those instructions; how that was brought about I shall show hereafter.

But I am got forward too fast with my story; there are still some transactions to be mentioned that happened during the administration of Governor Morris.

War being in a manner commenced with France,[1] the government of Massachusetts Bay projected an attack upon Crown Point, and sent Mr. Quincy to Pennsylvania and Mr. Pownall, afterwards Governor Pownall, to New York to solicit assistance. As I was in the Assembly, knew its temper, and was Mr. Quincy's countryman, he applied to me for my influence and assistance. I dictated his address to them, which was well received. They voted an aid of £ 10,000, to be laid out in provisions. But the Governor refusing his assent to their bill (which included this with other sums granted for the use of the Crown) unless a clause were inserted exempting the proprietary estate from bearing any part of the tax that would be necessary, the Assembly, tho' very desirous of making their grant to New England effectual, were at a loss how to accomplish it. Mr. Quincy laboured hard with the Governor to obtain his assent, but he was obstinate. I then suggested a method of doing the business without the Governor, by orders on the Trustees of the Loan Office, which by law the Assembly had the right of drawing. There was indeed little or no money at that time in the office, and therefore I proposed that the orders should be payable in a year and to bear an interest of 5 per cent. With these orders I supposed the provisions might easily be purchased. The Assembly with very little hesitation adopted the proposal. The orders were immediately printed, and I was one of the committee directed to sign and dispose of them. The fund for paying them was the interest of all the paper currency then extant in the province upon loan, together with the revenue arising from the excise,[2] which being known to be more than sufficient, they obtained instant credit, and were not only received in payment for the provisions, but many monied people who had cash lying by them vested it in those orders, which they found advantageous as they bore interest while upon hand and might on any occasion be used as money, so that they were eagerly all bought up, and in a few weeks none of them were to be seen. Thus this important affair was by my means completed. Mr. Quincy returned thanks to the Assembly in a handsome memorial, went home highly pleased with the success of his

[1] The opening of the French and Indian Wars, 1754–1763.
[2] The tax on whiskey, tobacco, and other items collected within the colonies.

embassy, and ever after bore for me the most cordial and affectionate friendship.

The British government not choosing to permit the union of the Colonies as proposed at Albany and to trust that union with their defence, lest they should thereby grow too military and feel their own strength, suspicions, and jealousies at this time being entertained of them, sent over General Braddock with two regiments of regular English troops for that purpose. He landed at Alexandria in Virginia and thence marched to Frederick [1] in Maryland, where he halted for carriages. Our Assembly apprehending, from some information, that he had conceived violent prejudices against them, as averse to the service, wished me to wait upon him, not as from them, but as Postmaster-General, under the guise of proposing to settle with him the mode of conducting with most celerity and certainty the dispatches between him and the Governors of the several provinces, with whom he must necessarily have continual correspondence, and of which they proposed to pay the expence. My son accompanied me on this journey. We found the General at Frederick, waiting impatiently for the return of those he had sent thro' the back parts of Maryland and Virginia to collect waggons. I stayed with him several days, dined with him daily, and had full opportunity of removing all his prejudices by the information of what the Assembly had before his arrival actually done and were still willing to do to facilitate his operations. When I was about to depart, the returns of waggons to be obtained were brought in, by which it appeared that they amounted only to twenty-five, and not all of those were in serviceable condition. The General and all the officers were surprized, declared the expedition was then at an end, being impossible, and exclaimed against the ministers for ignorantly landing them in a country destitute of the means of conveying their stores, baggage, etc., not less than 150 waggons being necessary. I happened to say I thought it was pity they had not been landed rather in Pennsylvania, as in that country almost every farmer had his waggon. The General eagerly laid hold of my words and said, "Then you, sir, who are a man of interest there, can probably procure them for us; and I beg you will undertake it." I asked what terms were to be

[1] Franklin originally wrote: "Frederic Town." [*Farrand's note*]

offered the owners of the waggons, and I was desired to put on paper the terms that appeared to me necessary. This I did, and they were agreed to, and a commission and instructions accordingly prepared immediately. What those terms were will appear in the advertisement I published as soon as I arrived at Lancaster; which being, from the great and sudden effect it produced, a piece of some curiosity, I shall insert it at length, as follows.

ADVERTISEMENT
Lancaster, April 26, 1753

Whereas, 150 waggons, with 4 horses to each waggon, and 1,500 saddle or pack horses are wanted for the service of His Majesty's forces, now about to rendezvous at Wills's Creek, and His Excellency, General Braddock, having been pleased to empower me to contract for the hire of the same; I hereby give notice that I shall attend for that purpose at Lancaster from this day to next Wednesday evening, and at York from next Thursday morning till Friday evening, where I shall be ready to agree for waggons and teams, or single horses, on the following terms; viz., 1. That there shall be paid for each waggon with 4 good horses and a driver, fifteen shillings per diem. And for each able horse with a pack-saddle or other saddle and furniture, two shillings per diem. And for each able horse without a saddle, eighteen pence per diem. 2. That the pay commence from the time of their joining the forces at Wills's Creek (which must be on or before the 20th May ensuing) and that a reasonable allowance be paid over and above for the time necessary for their travelling to Wills's Creek and home again after their discharge. 3. Each waggon and team, and every saddle or pack-horse is to be valued by indifferent [1] persons chosen between me and the owner; and in case of the loss of any waggon, team, or other horse in the service, the price according to such valuation is to be allowed and paid. 4. Seven days' pay is to be advanced and paid in hand by me to the owner of each waggon and team, or horse, at the time of contracting, if required; and the remainder to be paid by General Braddock or by the paymaster of the army at the time of their discharge, or from time to time as it shall be demanded. 5. No drivers of waggons or persons taking care of the hired horses are on any account to be called upon to do the duty of

[1] Neutral.

soldiers, or be otherwise employed than in conducting or taking care of their carriages or horses. 6. All oats, Indian corn, or other forage that waggons or horses bring to the camp, more than is necessary for the subsistence of the horses, are to be taken for the use of the army, and a reasonable price paid for the same.

Note — My son, William Franklin, is empowered to enter into like contracts with any person in Cumberland County.

B. Franklin.

To the Inhabitants of the Counties of Lancaster, York, and Cumberland

FRIENDS AND COUNTRYMEN,

Being occasionally at the camp at Frederick, a few days since, I found the General and officers extremely exasperated on account of their not being supplied with horses and carriages, which had been expected from this province, as most able to furnish them; but through the dissensions between our Governor and Assembly, money had not been provided, nor any steps taken for that purpose.

It was proposed to send an armed force immediately into these counties to seize as many of the best carriages and horses as should be wanted and compel as many persons into the service as would be necessary to drive and take care of them.

I apprehended that the progress of British soldiers through these counties on such an occasion (especially considering the temper they are in and their resentment against us) would be attended with many and great inconveniences to the inhabitants, and therefore more willingly took the trouble of trying first what might be done by fair and equitable means. The people of these back counties have lately complained to the Assembly that a sufficient currency was wanting; you have an opportunity of receiving and dividing among you a very considerable sum; for if the service of this expedition should continue (as it is more than probable it will) for 120 days, the hire of these wagons and horses will amount to upwards of £30,000, which will be paid you in silver and gold of the King's money.

The service will be light and easy, for the army will scarce march above twelve miles per day, and the waggons and baggage horses, as they carry those things that are absolutely necessary to the welfare of the army, must march with the army and no faster, and are, for the army's sake, always placed where they can be most secure, whether in a march or in a camp.

If you are really, as I believe you are, good and loyal subjects to His Majesty, you may now do a most acceptable service and make it easy to yourselves; for three or four of such as cannot separately spare from the business of their plantations a waggon and four horses and a driver, may do it together — one furnishing the waggon, another one or two horses, and another the driver — and divide the pay proportionally between you. But if you do not this service to your King and country voluntarily when such good pay and reasonable terms are offered to you, your loyalty will be strongly suspected. The King's business must be done; so many brave troops, come so far for your defence, must not stand idle through your backwardness to do what may be reasonably expected from you; waggons and horses must be had, violent measures will probably be used; and you will be to seek for a recompence where you can find it, and your case perhaps be little pitied or regarded.

I have no particular interest in this affair, as (except the satisfaction of endeavouring to do good) I shall have only my labour for my pains. If this method of obtaining the waggons and horses is not likely to succeed, I am obliged to send word to the General in fourteen days; and I suppose Sir John St. Clair, the hussar, with a body of soldiers, will immediately enter the province for the purpose — which I shall be sorry to hear because I am very sincerely and truly

Your friend and well-wisher,
B. Franklin

I received of the General about £800 to be disbursed in advance money to the waggon owners, etc.; but that sum being insufficient, I advanced upwards of £200 more, and in two weeks the 150 waggons with 259 carrying horses were on their march for the camp. The advertisement promised payment according to the valuation in case any waggon or horse should be lost. The owners, however, alleging they did not know General Braddock, or what dependence might be had on his promise, insisted on my bond for the performance, which I accordingly gave them.

While I was at the camp supping one evening with the officers of Col. Dunbar's regiment, he represented to me his concern for the subalterns, who he said were generally not in affluence, and could ill afford in this dear [1] country to lay in the stores that might be necessary in so long a march thro' a wilderness where nothing was to be purchased. I commiserated their case and resolved to endeavour procuring them some relief. I said nothing, however, to him of my intention, but wrote the next morning to the Committee of Assembly, who had the disposition of some public money, warmly recommending the case of these officers to their consideration and proposing that a present should be sent them of necessaries and refreshments. My son, who had had some experience of a camp life and of its wants, drew up a list for me, which I enclosed in my letter. The Committee approved and used such diligence that, conducted by my son, the stores arrived at the camp as soon as the waggons. They consisted of twenty parcels, each containing

6 lb. loaf sugar
6 lb. good muscovado do
1 lb. good green tea
1 lb. good bohea do
6 lb. good ground coffee
6 lb. chocolate
½ cwt. best white biscuit
½ lb. pepper
1 quart best white wine vinegar
1 Gloucester cheese
1 keg containing 20 lb. good butter
2 doz. old Madeira wine
2 gallons Jamaica spirits
1 bottle flour of mustard
2 well-cured hams
½ doz. dried tongues
6 lb. rice
6 lb. raisins

These twenty parcels, well-packed, were placed on as many horses, each parcel with the horse being intended as a present for one officer. They were very thankfully received and the kindness acknowledged by letters to me from the colonels of both regiments in the most grateful terms. The General, too, was

[1] Expensive.

highly satisfied with my conduct in procuring him the waggons, etc., etc., and readily paid my account of disbursements, thanking me repeatedly and requesting my further assistance in sending provisions after him. I undertook this also and was busily employed in it till we heard of his defeat, advancing, for the service, of my own money upwards of £1,000 sterling, of which I sent him an account. It came to his hands, luckily for me, a few days before the battle, and he returned me immediately an order on the paymaster for the round sum of £1,000, leaving the remainder to the next account. I consider this payment as good luck, having never been able to obtain that remainder — of which more hereafter.

This General was, I think, a brave man, and might probably have made a figure as a good officer in some European war. But he had too much self-confidence, too high an opinion of the validity of regular troops, and too mean a one of both Americans and Indians. George Croghan, our Indian interpreter, joined him on his march with one hundred of those people, who might have been of great use to his army as guides, scouts, etc., if he had treated them kindly; but he slighted and neglected them, and they gradually left him. In conversation with him one day, he was giving me some account of his intended progress. "After taking Fort Duquesne," says he, "I am to proceed to Niagara, and having taken that, to Frontenac,[1] if the season will allow time, and I suppose it will; for Duquesne can hardly detain me above three or four days; and then I see nothing that can obstruct my march to Niagara." Having before revolved in my mind the long line his army must make in their march by a very narrow road to be cut for them thro' the woods and bushes, and also what I had read of a former defeat of 1,500 French who invaded the Iroquois country, I had conceived some doubts and some fears for the event of the campaign. But I ventured only to say, "To be sure, sir, if you arrive well before Duquesne with these fine troops so well provided with artillery, that place, not yet completely fortified and, as we hear, with no very strong garrison, can probably make but a short resistance. The only danger I apprehend of obstruction to your march, is from the ambuscades of Indians, who

---

[1] Braddock's plan was to capture the fort at what is now Pittsburgh, cross into Canada at Niagara, and proceed to the French fort at what is now Kingston, Ontario.

by constant practice are dextrous in laying and executing them. And the slender line, near four miles long, which your army must make, may expose it to be attacked by surprize in its flanks, and to be cut like a thread into several pieces, which from their distance cannot come up in time to support each other." He smiled at my ignorance and replied, "These savages may indeed be a formidable enemy to your raw American militia; but upon the King's regular and disciplined troops, sir, it is impossible they should make any impression." I was conscious of an impropriety in my disputing with a military man in matters of his profession and said no more. The enemy, however, did not take the advantage of his army which I apprehended its long line of march exposed it to, but let it advance without interruption till within nine miles of the place; and then when more in a body (for it had just passed a river, where the front had halted till all were come over) and in a more open part of the woods than any it had passed, attacked its advance guard by a heavy fire from behind trees and bushes — which was the first intelligence the General had of an enemy's being near him. This guard being disordered, the General hurried the troops up to their assistance, which was done in great confusion thro' waggons, baggage, and cattle. And presently the fire came upon their flank; the officers, being on horseback, were more easily distinguished, picked out as marks, and fell very fast; and the soldiers were crowded together in a huddle, having or hearing no orders, and standing to be shot at till two-thirds of them were killed, and then being seized with a panic the whole fled with precipitation. The waggoners took each a horse out of his team and scampered; their example was immediately followed by others so that all the waggons, provisions, artillery, and stores were left to the enemy. The General, being wounded, was brought off with difficulty; his secretary, Mr. Shirley, was killed by his side; and out of 86 officers, 63 were killed or wounded, and 714 men killed out of 1,100. These 1,100 had been picked men from the whole army, the rest had been left behind with Col. Dunbar, who was to follow with the heavier part of the stores, provisions, and baggage. The flyers, not being pursued, arrived at Dunbar's camp, and the panic they brought with them instantly seized him and all his people. And tho' he had now above 1,000 men and the enemy who had beaten Braddock did not at most exceed 400 Indians and French together, instead of proceeding and endeavouring to recover some of the lost honour, he ordered all the stores, ammunition, etc., to be destroyed that he might have more horses to assist his flight towards the settlements and less lumber to remove. He was there met with requests from the governors of Virginia, Maryland, and Pennsylvania that he would post his troops on the frontiers so as to afford some protection to the inhabitants; but he continued his hasty march thro' all the country, not thinking himself safe till he arrived at Philadelphia, where the inhabitants could protect him. This whole transaction gave us Americans the first suspicion that our exalted ideas of the prowess of British regulars had not been well founded.

In their first march, too, from their landing till they got beyond the settlements, they had plundered and stripped the inhabitants, totally ruining some poor families, besides insulting, abusing, and confining the people if they remonstrated. This was enough to put us out of conceit [1] of such defenders if we had really wanted any. How different was the conduct of our French friends in 1781, who during a march thro' the most inhabited part of our country from Rhode Island to Virginia, near seven hundred miles, occasioned not the smallest complaint for the loss of a pig, a chicken, or even an apple!

Captain Orme, who was one of the General's aides-de-camp and, being grievously wounded, was brought off with him and continued with him to his death, which happened in a few days, told me that he was totally silent all the first day and at night only said, "Who would have thought it?"; that he was silent again the following day, only saying at last, "We shall better know how to deal with them another time," and died a few minutes after.

The secretary's papers with all the General's orders, instructions, and correspondence falling into the enemy's hands, they selected and translated into French a number of the articles, which they printed to prove the hostile intentions of the British court before the declaration of war. Among these I saw some letters of the General to the ministry speaking highly of the great service I had rendered the army and recommending me to their notice. David Hume, too, who was some years after secretary to Lord Hertford when Minister in France and after-

[1] Out of patience.

wards to General Conway when Secretary of State, told me he had seen among the papers in that office letters from Braddock highly recommending me. But the expedition having been unfortunate, my service, it seems, was not thought of much value, for those recommendations were never of any use to me. As to rewards from himself, I asked only one, which was that he would give orders to his officers not to enlist any more of our bought servants [1] and that he would discharge such as had been already enlisted. This he readily granted, and several were accordingly returned to their masters on my application. Dunbar, when the command devolved on him, was not so generous. He being at Philadelphia on his retreat, or rather flight, I applied to him for the discharge of the servants of three poor farmers of Lancaster County that he had enlisted, reminding him of the late General's orders on that head. He promised me that if the masters would come to him at Trenton, where he should be in a few days on his march to New York, he would there deliver their men to them. They accordingly were at the expence and trouble of going to Trenton, and there he refused to perform his promise, to their great loss and disappointment.

As soon as the loss of the waggons and horses was generally known, all the owners came upon me for the valuation which I had given bond to pay. Their demands gave me a great deal of trouble. I acquainted them that the money was ready in the paymaster's hands, but that orders for paying it must first be obtained from General Shirley, and that I had applied for it; but he being at a distance, an answer could not soon be received, and they must have patience. All this was not sufficient to satisfy, and some began to sue me. General Shirley at length relieved me from this terrible situation by appointing commissioners to examine the claims and ordering payment. They amounted to near £20,000, which to pay would have ruined me.

Before we had the news of this defeat, the two Doctors Bond came to me with a subscription paper for raising money to defray the expence of a grand firework, which it was intended to exhibit at a rejoicing on receipt of the news of our taking Fort Duquesne. I looked grave and said it would, I thought, be time enough to prepare for the rejoicing when we knew we should have occasion to rejoice. They seemed surprized that I did not im-

[1] Indentured servants.

mediately comply with their proposal. "Why, the d——l," says one of them, "you surely don't suppose that the fort will not be taken?" "I don't know that it will not be taken; but I know that the events of war are subject to great uncertainty." I gave them the reasons of my doubting. The subscription was dropped and the projectors thereby missed the mortification they would have undergone if the firework had been prepared. Dr. Bond on some other occasions afterwards said that he did not like Franklin's forebodings.

Governor Morris, who had continually worried the Assembly with message after message before the defeat of Braddock to beat them into the making of acts to raise money for the defence of the province without taxing, among others, the proprietary estates, and had rejected all their bills for not having such an exempting clause, now redoubled his attacks, with more hope of success, the danger and necessity being greater. The Assembly, however, continued firm, believing they had justice on their side and that it would be giving up an essential right if they suffered the Governor to amend their money bills. In one of the last, indeed, which was for granting £50,000, his proposed amendment was only of a single word: the bill expressed that all estates real and personal were to be taxed, those of the Proprietaries *not* excepted. His amendment was, for "not" read "only"—a small but very material alteration! However, when the news of this disaster reached England, our friends there whom we had taken care to furnish with all the Assembly's answers to the Governor's messages, raised a clamour against the Proprietaries for their meanness and injustice in giving their Governor such instructions, some going so far as to say that by obstructing the defence of their province, they forfeited their right to it. They were intimidated by this, and sent orders to their receiver-general to add £5,000 of their money to whatever sum might be given by the Assembly for such purpose. This, being notified to the House, was accepted in lieu of their share of a general tax, and a new bill was formed with an exempting clause which passed accordingly. By this act I was appointed one of the commissioners for disposing of the money, £60,000. I had been active in modelling it and procuring its passage, and had at the same time drawn a bill for establishing and disciplining a voluntary militia, which I carried thro' the House without much difficulty, as care was taken in it to leave the Quakers at their liberty. To promote the association necessary to form the militia, I wrote a dialogue [1] stating and answering all the objections I could think of to such a militia, which was printed and had, as I thought, great effect. While the several companies in the city and country were forming and learning their exercise, the Governor prevailed with me to take charge of our northwestern frontier, which was infested by the enemy, and provide for the defence of the inhabitants by raising troops, and building a line of forts. I undertook this military business, tho' I did not conceive myself well-qualified for it. He gave me a commission with full powers and a parcel of blank commissions for officers, to be given to whom I thought fit. I had but little difficulty in raising men, having some 560 under my command. My son, who had in the preceding war been an officer in the army raised against Canada, was my aide-de-camp, and of great use to me. The Indians had burned Gnadenhut,[2] a village settled by the Moravians, and massacred the inhabitants, but the place was thought a good situation for one of the forts. In order to march thither, I assembled the companies at Bethlehem,[3] the chief establishment of those people. I was surprized to find it in so good a posture of defence. The destruction of Gnadenhut had made them apprehend danger. The principal buildings were defended by a stockade. They had purchased a quantity of arms and ammunition from New York, and had even placed quantities of small paving stones between the windows of their high stone houses, for their women to throw down upon the heads of any Indians that should attempt to force into them. The armed brethren, too, kept watch, and relieved [4] as methodically as in any garrison town. In conversation with Bishop Spangenberg, I mentioned my surprize; for knowing they had obtained an act of Parliament exempting them from military duties in the Colonies, I had supposed they were conscientiously scrupulous of bearing arms. He answered me that it was not one of their established principles, but that at the time of their obtaining that

[1] This dialogue and the Militia Act are in the *Gentleman's Magazine* for February and March, 1756. [*Farrand's note*]
[2] Gnadenhütten, a village of Christianized Indians in eastern Ohio, founded by Moravian missionaries.
[3] Bethlehem, Pennsylvania.
[4] Kept and relieved the guard.

act it was thought to be a principle with many of their people. On this occasion, however, they to their surprize found it adopted by but a few. It seems they were either deceived in themselves or deceived the Parliament. But common sense, aided by present danger, will sometimes be too strong for whimsical opinions.

It was the beginning of January when we set out upon this business of building forts. I sent one detachment towards the Minisinks,[1] with instructions to erect one for the security of that upper part of the country; and another to the lower part, with similar instructions. And I concluded to go myself with the rest of my force to Gnadenhut, where a fort was thought more immediately necessary. The Moravians procured me five waggons for our tools, stores, baggage, etc. Just before we left Bethlehem, eleven farmers who had been driven from their plantations by the Indians, came to me requesting a supply of firearms, that they might go back and fetch off their cattle. I gave them each a gun with suitable ammunition. We had not marched many miles before it began to rain, and it continued raining all day. There were no habitations on the road to shelter us till we arrived near night at the house of a German, where, and in his barn, we were all huddled together as wet as water could make us. It was well we were not attacked in our march, for our arms were of the most ordinary sort and our men could not keep their gunlocks dry. The Indians are dextrous in contrivances for that purpose, which we had not. They met that day the eleven poor farmers above-mentioned and killed ten of them. The one who escaped informed us that his and his companions' guns would not go off, the priming being wet with the rain. The next day being fair, we continued our march and arrived at the desolated Gnadenhut. There was a sawmill near, round which were left several piles of boards, with which we soon hutted ourselves — an operation the more necessary at that inclement season as we had no tents. Our first work was to bury more effectually the dead we found there, who had been half interred by the country people. The next morning our fort was planned and marked out, the circumference measuring 455 feet, which would require as many palisades to be made of trees, one with another of a foot diameter each. Our axes, of which we

[1] Falls on Stony Creek in Pennsylvania.

had seventy, were immediately set to work to cut down trees; and our men being dextrous in the use of them, great dispatch was made. Seeing the trees fall so fast, I had the curiosity to look at my watch when two men began to cut at a pine. In six minutes they had it upon the ground, and I found it of fourteen inches diameter. Each pine made three palisades of eighteen feet long, pointed at one end. While these were preparing, our other men dug a trench all round of three feet deep in which the palisades were to be planted, and the bodies being taken off our waggons and the fore and hind wheels separated by taking out the pin which united the two parts of the perch,[1] we had ten carriages with two horses each, to bring the palisades from the woods to the spot. When they were set up, our carpenters built a stage of boards all round within, about six feet high, for the men to stand on when to fire thro' the loopholes. We had one swivel gun which we mounted on one of the angles and fired it as soon as fixed, to let the Indians know, if any were within hearing, that we had such pieces; and thus our fort (if such a magnificent name may be given to so miserable a stockade) was finished in a week, tho' it rained so hard every other day that the men could not work.

This gave me occasion to observe that when men are employed they are best contented. For on the days they worked they were good-natured and cheerful, and with the consciousness of having done a good day's work they spent the evenings jollily; but on the idle days they were mutinous and quarrelsome, finding fault with their pork, the bread, etc., and in continual ill-humour — which put me in mind of a sea captain whose rule it was to keep his men constantly at work; and when his mate once told him that they had done everything and there was nothing further to employ them about, "Oh," says he, "make them scour the anchor."

This kind of fort, however contemptible, is a sufficient defence against Indians who have no cannon. Finding ourselves now posted securely and having a place to retreat to on occasion, we ventured out in parties to scour the adjacent country. We met with no Indians, but we found the places on the neighbouring hills where they had lain to watch our proceedings. There was an art in their contrivance of those places that seems worth

[1] The pole connecting the front and rear axles.

mention. It being winter, a fire was necessary for them. But a common fire on the surface of the ground would by its light have discovered their position at a distance. They had therefore dug holes in the ground about three feet diameter and somewhat deeper. We saw where they had with their hatchets cut off the charcoal from the sides of burnt logs lying in the woods. With these coals they had made small fires in the bottom of the holes, and we observed among the weeds and grass the prints of their bodies made by their laying all round with their legs hanging down in the holes to keep their feet warm, which with them is an essential point. This kind of fire, so managed, could not discover them either by its light, flame, sparks, or even smoke. It appeared that their number was not great, and it seems they saw we were too many to be attacked by them with prospect of advantage.

We had for our chaplain a zealous Presbyterian minister, Mr. Beatty, who complained to me that the men did not generally attend his prayers and exhortations. When they enlisted, they were promised, besides pay and provisions, a gill of rum a day, which was punctually served out to them half in the morning and the other half in the evening, and I observed they were as punctual in attending to receive it. Upon which I said to Mr. Beatty, "It is perhaps below the dignity of your profession to act as steward of the rum. But if you were to deal it out, and only just after prayers, you would have them all about you." He liked the thought, undertook the office, and with the help of a few hands to measure out the liquor executed it to satisfaction; and never were prayers more generally and more punctually attended — so that I thought this method preferable to the punishments inflicted by some military laws for non-attendance on divine service.

I had hardly finished this business and got my fort well stored with provisions when I received a letter from the Governor, acquainting me that he had called the Assembly and wished my attendance there, if the posture of affairs on the frontiers was such that my remaining there was no longer necessary. My friends, too, of the Assembly pressing me by their letters to be, if possible, at the meeting, and my three intended forts being now completed, and the inhabitants contented to remain on their farms under that protection, I resolved to return — the more willingly as a New England officer, Col. Clapham, experienced in Indian war, being on a visit to our establishment, consented to accept the command. I gave him a commission, and, parading the garrison, had it read before them, and introduced him to them as an officer who from his skill in military affairs was much more fit to command them than myself, and giving them a little exhortation, took my leave. I was escorted as far as Bethlehem, where I rested a few days to recover from the fatigue I had undergone. The first night being in a good bed, I could hardly sleep, it was so different from my hard lodging on the floor of our hut at Gnaden, wrapped only in a blanket or two.

While at Bethlehem, I enquired a little into the practices of the Moravians. Some of them had accompanied me, and all were very kind to me. I found they worked for a common stock, eat at common tables, and slept in common dormitories, great numbers together. In the dormitories I observed loopholes at certain distances all along just under the ceiling, which I thought judiciously placed for change of air. I was at their church, where I was entertained with good music, the organ being accompanied with violins, hautboys, flutes, clarinets, etc. I understood that their sermons were not usually preached to mixed congregations of men, women, and children, as is our common practice; but that they assembled sometimes the married men, at other times their wives, then the young men, the young women, and the little children, each division by itself. The sermon I heard was to the latter, who came in and were placed in rows on benches, the boys under the conduct of a young man their tutor, and the girls conducted by a young woman. The discourse seemed well adapted to their capacities and was delivered in a pleasing, familiar manner, coaxing them, as it were, to be good. They behaved very orderly, but looked pale and unhealthy, which made me suspect they were kept too much within-doors or not allowed sufficient exercise. I enquired concerning the Moravian marriages, whether the report was true that they were by lot. I was told that lots were used only in particular cases; that generally when a young man found himself disposed to marry, he informed the elders of his class, who consulted the elder ladies that governed the young women. As these elders of the different sexes were well acquainted with the tempers and dispositions of their respective pupils, they could best judge what matches were suitable, and their judgments were generally acquiesced in. But if, for example, it should happen that two or three young women were found to be equally proper for the young man, the lot was then recurred to. I objected, "If the matches are not made by the mutual choice of the parties, some of them may chance to be very unhappy." "And so they may," answered by informer, "if you let the parties choose for themselves" — which, indeed, I could not deny.

Being returned to Philadelphia, I found the association went on swimmingly, the inhabitants that were not Quakers having pretty generally come into it, formed themselves into companies, and [had] chosen their captains, lieutenants, and ensigns according to the new law. Dr. Bond visited me, and gave me an account of the pains he had taken to spread a general good liking to the law, and ascribed much to those endeavours. I had had the vanity to ascribe all to my dialogue; however, not knowing but that he might be in the right, I let him enjoy his opinion, which I take to be generally the best way in such cases. The officers' meeting chose me to be colonel of the regiment, which I this time accepted. I forget how many companies we had, but we paraded about 1,200 well-looking men, with a company of artillery who had been furnished with six brass field pieces, which they had become so expert in the use of as to fire twelve times in a minute. The first time I reviewed my regiment, they accompanied me to my house and would salute me with some rounds fired before my door, which shook down and broke several glasses of my electrical apparatus. And my new honour proved not much less brittle, for all our commissions were soon after broke by a repeal of the law in England.

During the short time of my colonelship, being about to set out on a journey to Virginia, the officers of my regiment took it into their heads that it would be proper for them to escort me out of town as far as the lower ferry. Just as I was getting on horseback, they came to my door, between thirty and forty, mounted, and all in their uniforms. I had not been previously acquainted with the project or I should have prevented it, being naturally averse to the assuming of state on any occasion, and I was a good deal chagrined at their appearance as I could not avoid their accompanying me. What made it worse was that as soon as we began to move, they drew their swords and rode with them naked all the way. Somebody wrote an account of this to the Proprietor, and it gave him great offence. No such honour had been paid him when in the province, nor to any of his governors; and he said it was only proper to princes of the blood royal — which may be true for aught I know, who was, and still am, ignorant of the etiquette in such cases. This silly affair, however, greatly increased his rancour against me which was before not a little on account of my conduct in the Assembly respecting the exemption of his estate from taxation, which I had always opposed very warmly, and not without severe reflections on his meanness and injustice in contending for it. He accused me to the ministry as being the great obstacle to the King's service, preventing by my influence in the House the proper form of the bills for raising money; and he instanced this parade with my officers as a proof of my having an intention to take the government of the province out of his hands by force. He also applied to Sir Everard Fauckener, the Postmaster-General. to deprive me of my office. But it had no other effect than to procure from Sir Everard a gentle admonition.

Notwithstanding the continual wrangle between the Governor and the House, in which I as a member had so large a share, there still subsisted a civil intercourse between that gentleman and myself, and we never had any personal difference. I have sometimes since thought that his little or no resentment against me for the answers it was known I drew up to his messages, might be the effect of professional habit, and that, being bred a lawyer, he might consider us both as merely advocates for contending clients in a suit, he for the Proprietaries and I for the Assembly. He would therefore sometimes call in a friendly way to advise with me on difficult points and sometimes, tho' not often, take my advice. We acted in concert to supply Braddock's army with provisions, and when the shocking news arrived of his defeat, the Governor sent in haste for me to consult with him on measures for preventing the desertion of the back countries. I forget now the advice I gave, but I think it was that Dunbar should be written to and prevailed with, if possible, to post his troops on the frontiers for their protection, till by reinforcements from the Colonies he might be able to proceed on the expedition. And after my return from the frontier, he would have had me undertake the conduct of such an expedition with provincial troops for the reduction of Fort Duquesne, Dunbar and his men being otherwise employed; and he proposed to commission me as general. I had not so good an opinion of my military abilities as he professed to have, and I believe his professions must have exceeded his real sentiments. But probably he might think that my popularity would facilitate the raising of the men and my influence in Assembly the grant of money to pay them, and that, perhaps, without taxing the proprietary estate. Finding me not so forward to engage as he expected, the project was dropped; and he soon after left the government, being superseded by Capt. Denny.

Before I proceed in relating the part I had in public affairs under this new Governor's administration, it may not be amiss here to give some account of the rise and progress of my philosophical reputation.

In 1746 being at Boston, I met there with a Dr. Spence, who was lately arrived from Scotland, and showed me some electric experiments. They were imperfectly performed, as he was not very expert; but being on a subject quite new to me, they equally surprized and pleased me. Soon after my return to Philadelphia, our library company received from Mr. Peter Colinson,[1] F.R.S., of London, a present of a glass tube, with some account of the use of it in making such experiments. I eagerly seized the opportunity of repeating what I had seen at Boston, and by much practice acquired great readiness in performing those also which we had an account of from England, adding a number of new ones. I say much practice, for my house was continually full for some time with people who came to see these new wonders. To divide a little this incumbrance among my friends, I caused a number of similar tubes to be blown at our glass house, with which they furnished themselves, so that we had at length several performers. Among these the principal was Mr. Kinnersley, an ingenious neighbour, who, being out of business, I encouraged to undertake showing the experiment for money, and drew up for him two lectures in which the experiments were ranged in such order and accompanied with explanations, in such method as that the foregoing should assist in comprehending the following. He procured an

---

[1] Peter Collinson (1694–1768), brilliant English botanist, who helped to publish the results of Franklin's electrical researches in 1751.

elegant apparatus for the purpose, in which all the little machines that I had roughly made for myself were nicely formed by instrument makers. His lectures were well attended and gave great satisfaction, and after some time he went thro' the Colonies exhibiting them in every capital town and picked up some money.[1] In the West India Islands, indeed, it was with difficulty the experiments could be made, from the general moisture of the air.

Obliged as we were to Mr. Colinson for his present of the tube, etc., I thought it right he should be informed of our success in using it and wrote him several letters containing accounts of our experiments. He got them read in the Royal Society, where they were not at first thought worth so much notice as to be printed in their transactions. One paper which I wrote for Mr. Kinnersley, on the sameness of lightning with electricity, I sent to Dr. Mitchel, an acquaintance of mine and one of the members also of that Society, who wrote me word that it had been read but was laughed at by the connoisseurs. The papers, however, being shown to Dr. Fothergill, he thought them of too much value to be stifled and advised the printing of them. Mr. Colinson then gave them to Cave for publication in his *Gentleman's Magazine;* but he chose to print them separately in a pamphlet, and Dr. Fothergill wrote the preface. Cave, it seems, judged rightly for his profit; for by the additions that arrived afterwards, they swelled to a quarto volume, which has had five editions and cost him nothing for copy-money.[2]

It was, however, some time before those papers were much taken notice of in England. A copy of them happening to fall into the hands of the Count de Buffon, a philosopher deservedly of great reputation in France and indeed all over Europe, he prevailed with M. Dalibard to translate them into French, and they were printed at Paris.[3] The publication offended the Abbé Nollet, preceptor in natural philosophy to the royal family, and

[1] Ebenezer Kinnersley, a Baptist minister, gave these lectures in 1751–52, and taught at the Academy of Philadelphia from 1753 to 1773.

[2] Dr. John Mitchell of London assisted Franklin in getting his researches before the Royal Society, while Edward Cave's magazine (1731–54) was among the most respected of British periodicals. Franklin points out, however, that Cave paid him no "copy-money," or royalties.

[3] Count de Buffon (1707–1788) was perhaps the ranking French scientist. D'Alibard set up a lightning rod near Paris in 1752, working from Franklin's pamphlet, and tested it successfully. See Franklin's reference below.

an able experimenter who had formed and published a theory of electricity which then had the general vogue. He could not at first believe that such a work came from America and said it must have been fabricated by his enemies at Paris to decry his system. Afterwards having been assured that there really existed such a person as Franklin of Philadelphia, which he had doubted, he wrote and published a volume of letters, chiefly addressed to me, defending his theory and denying the verity of my experiments and of the positions deduced from them. I once purposed answering the Abbé and actually began the answer. But on consideration that my writings contained only a description of experiments which anyone might repeat and verify, and, if not to be verified, could not be defended; or of observations offered as conjectures and not delivered dogmatically, therefore not laying me under any obligation to defend them; and reflecting that a dispute between two persons writing in different languages might be lengthened greatly by mistranslations, and thence misconceptions, of one another's meaning — much of one of the Abbé's letters being founded on an error in the translation; I concluded to let my papers shift for themselves, believing it was better to spend what time I could spare from public business in making new experiments than in disputing about those already made. I therefore never answered M. Nollet, and the event gave me no cause to repent my silence, for my friend M. le Roy of the Royal Academy of Sciences took up my cause and refuted him; my book was translated into the Italian, German, and Latin languages; and the doctrine it contained was by degrees universally adopted by the philosophers of Europe in preference to that of the Abbé, so that he lived to see himself the last of his sect — except Mr. B——, his *élève* and immediate disciple.

What gave my book the more sudden and general celebrity was the success of one of its proposed experiments, made by Messrs. Dalibard and Delor at Marly for drawing lightning from the clouds. This engaged the public attention everywhere. M. Delor, who had an apparatus for experimental philosophy and lectured in that branch of science, undertook to repeat what he called the "Philadelphia Experiments," and after they were performed before the King and court, all the curious of Paris flocked to see them. I will not swell this narrative with an account of that capital experiment, nor of the infinite pleasure

I received in the success of a similar one I made soon after with a kite at Philadelphia, as both are to be found in the histories of electricity. Dr. Wright, an English physician then at Paris, wrote to a friend who was of the Royal Society an account of the high esteem my experiments were in among the learned abroad, and of their wonder that my writings had been so little noticed in England. The Society on this resumed the consideration of the letters that had been read to them, and the celebrated Dr. Watson drew up a summary account of them and of all I had afterwards sent to England on the subject, which he accompanied with some praise of the writer. This summary was then printed in their transactions. And some members of the Society in London, particularly the very ingenious Mr. Canton, having verified the experiment of procuring lightning from the clouds by a pointed rod and acquainting them with the success, they soon made me more than amends for the slight with which they had before treated me. Without my having made any application for that honour, they chose me a member and voted that I should be excused the customary payments, which would have amounted to twenty-five guineas, and ever since have given me their transactions gratis. They also presented me with the gold medal of Sir Godfrey Copley for the year 1753, the delivery of which was accompanied by a very handsome speech of the president, Lord Macclesfield, wherein I was highly honoured.[1]

Our new Governor, Capt. Denny, brought over for me the before-mentioned medal from the Royal Society, which he presented to me at an entertainment given him by the city. He accompanied it with very polite expressions of his esteem for me, having, as he said, been long acquainted with my character. After dinner, when the company, as was customary at that time, were engaged in drinking, he took me aside into another room and acquainted me that he had been advised by his friends in England to cultivate a friendship with me, as one who was capable of giving him the best advice and of contributing most effectually to the making his administration easy, that he there-

---

[1] Doctor (later Sir William) Watson (1715–1787) was interested in electrical research, while Joseph Canton was the first English physicist to validate Franklin's identification of lightning and electricity. The Copley Medal is one of the Royal Society's highest awards.

fore desired of all things to have a good understanding with me; and he begged me to be assured of his readiness on all occasions to render me every service that might be in his power. He said much to me also of the Proprietor's good dispositions towards the province and of the advantage it might be to us all, and to me in particular, if the opposition that had been so long continued to his measures were dropped and harmony restored between him and the people, in effecting which it was thought no one could be more serviceable than myself, and I might depend on adequate acknowledgments and recompenses, etc., etc. The drinkers, finding we did not return immediately to the table, sent us a decanter of Madeira, which the Governor made liberal use of, and in proportion became more profuse of his solicitations and promises. My answers were to this purpose: that my circumstances, thanks to God, were such as to make proprietary favours unnecessary to me; and that being a member of the Assembly, I could not possibly accept of any; that, however, I had no personal enmity to the Proprietary; and that whenever the public measures he proposed should appear to be for the good of the people, no one should espouse and forward them more zealously than myself, my past opposition having been founded on this — that the measures which had been urged were evidently intended to serve the proprietary interest with great prejudice to that of the people; that I was much obliged to him (the Governor) for his professions of regard to me, and that he might rely on everything in my power to make his administration as easy to him as possible, hoping at the same time that he had not brought with him the same unfortunate instructions his predecessor had been hampered with. On this he did not then explain himself. But when he afterwards came to do business with the Assembly, they appeared again; the disputes were renewed; and I was as active as ever in the opposition, being the penman first of the request to have a communication of the instructions and then of the remarks upon them, which may be found in the votes of the time and in the historical review I afterwards published. But between us personally no enmity arose; we were often together; he was a man of letters, had seen much of the world, and was very entertaining and pleasing in conversation. He gave me the first information that my old friend Jas. Ralph was still alive, that he was esteemed one of the best political writers in England, had been employed in the dispute between Prince Frederick and the King, and had obtained a pension of three hundred a year; that his reputation was indeed small as a poet, Pope having damned his poetry in the *Dunciad*, but his prose was thought as good as any man's.

The Assembly finally, finding the Proprietaries obstinately persisted in manacling their deputies with instructions inconsistent not only with the privileges of the people but with the service of the Crown, resolved to petition the King against them, and appointed me their agent to go over to England to present and support the petition.[1] The House had sent up a bill to the Governor granting a sum of £60,000 for the King's use (£10,000 of which was subjected to the orders of the then General, Lord Loudon), which the Governor absolutely refused to pass in compliance with his instructions. I had agreed with Captain Morris of the packet at New York for my passage, and my stores were put on board, when Lord Loudon arrived at Philadelphia, expressly, as he told me, to endeavour an accommodation between the Governor and Assembly, that His Majesty's service might not be obstructed by their dissensions. Accordingly, he desired the Governor and myself to meet him, that he might hear what was to be said on both sides. We met and discussed the business. In behalf of the Assembly I urged all the arguments that may be found in the public papers of that time, which were of my writing and are printed with the minutes of the Assembly; and the Governor pleaded his instructions, the bond he had given to observe them, and his ruin if he disobeyed, yet seemed not unwilling to hazard himself if Lord Loudon would advise it. This His Lordship did not choose to do, tho' I once thought I had nearly prevailed with him to do it; but finally he rather chose to urge the compliance of the Assembly; and he entreated me to use my endeavours with them for that purpose, declaring he could spare none of the King's troops for the defence of our frontiers, and that if we did not continue to provide for that defence ourselves, they must remain exposed to the enemy. I acquainted the House with what had passed; and

[1] Franklin arrived in London as Pennsylvania's agent in July, 1757. He returned to America in 1762, and again served as Pennsylvania's London agent from 1764 to 1775. In 1768 he was appointed agent for Georgia, in 1769 for New Jersey, and in 1770 for Massachusetts.

presenting them with a set of resolutions I had drawn up, declaring our rights and that we did not relinquish our claim to those rights but only suspended the exercise of them on this occasion thro' *force*, against which we protested; they at length agreed to drop that bill and frame another conformable to the proprietary instructions. This of course the Governor passed, and I was then at liberty to proceed on my voyage. But in the meantime the packet had sailed with my sea stores, which was some loss to me, and my only recompense was His Lordship's thanks for my service, all the credit of obtaining the accommodation falling to his share.

He set out for New York before me; and as the time for dispatching the packet boats was in his disposition and there were two then remaining there, one of which he said was to sail very soon, I requested to know the precise time that I might not miss her by any delay of mine. His answer was, "I have given out that she is to sail on Saturday next, but I may let you know, *entre nous*, that if you are there by Monday morning you will be in time, but do not delay longer." By some accidental hindrance at a ferry, it was Monday noon before I arrived, and I was much afraid she might have sailed as the wind was fair, but I was soon made easy by the information that she was still in the harbour and would not move till the next day.

One would imagine that I was now on the very point of departing for Europe. I thought so; but I was not then so well acquainted with His Lordship's character, of which *indecision* was one of the strongest features. I shall give some instances. It was about the beginning of April that I came to New York, and I think it was near the end of June before we sailed. There were then two of the packet boats which had been long in port but were detained for the General's letters, which were always to be ready tomorrow. Another packet arrived, and she too was detained, and before we sailed a fourth was expected. Ours was the first to be dispatched, as having been there longest. Passengers were engaged in all, and some extremely impatient to be gone, and the merchants uneasy about their letters, and the orders they had given for insurance (it being wartime), and for fall goods. But their anxiety availed nothing; His Lordship's letters were not ready. And yet whoever waited on him found him always at his desk, pen in hand, and concluded he must needs write abundantly. Going myself one morning to pay my respects, I found in his anti-chamber one Innis, a messenger of Philadelphia, who had come from thence express with a packet from Governor Denny for the General. He delivered to me some letters from my friends there, which occasioned my enquiring when he was to return and where he lodged, that I might send some letters by him. He told me he was ordered to call tomorrow at nine for the General's answer to the Governor and should set off immediately. I put my letters into his hands the same day. A fortnight after I met him again in the same place.

"So you are soon returned, Innis!"

"Returned! No, I am not gone yet."

"How so?"

"I have called here by order every morning these two weeks past for His Lordship's letter, and it is not yet ready."

"Is it possible, when he is so great a writer, for I see him constantly at his scritoire." [1]

"Yes," says Innis, "but he is like St. George on the signs, *always on horseback, and never rides on.*"

This observation of the messenger was, it seems, well founded; for when in England, I understood that Mr. Pit gave it as one reason for removing this General and sending Amherst and Wolf, that "the ministers never heard from him, and could not know what he was doing."

This daily expectation of sailing, and all the three packets going down to Sandy Hook to join the fleet there, the passengers thought it best to be on board, lest by a sudden order the ships should sail and they be left behind. There, if I remember right, we were about six weeks, consuming our sea stores and obliged to procure more. At length the fleet sailed, the General and all his army on board, bound to Louisburg with intent to besiege and take that fortress;[2] all the packet boats in company, ordered to attend the General's ship, ready to receive his dispatches when they should be ready. We were out five days before we got a letter with leave to part, and then our ship quitted the fleet and steered for England. The other two packets he still detained, carried them with him to Halifax, where he stayed some time to exercise the men in sham attacks upon sham forts, then altered his mind as to besieging Louisburg and returned to New York with all his troops, together with the two packets above-

---

[1] Escritoire, or writing desk.
[2] Louisburg, Nova Scotia, fell to the British in 1758.

mentioned and all their passengers. During his absence the French and savages had taken Fort George on the frontier of that province, and the savages had massacred many of the garrison after capitulation. I saw afterwards in London Capt. Bonnell, who commanded one of those packets. He told me that when he had been detained a month, he acquainted His Lordship that his ship was grown foul to a degree that must necessarily hinder her fast sailing — a point of consequence for a packet boat — and requested an allowance of time to heave her down and clean her bottom. He was asked how long time that would require. He answered three days. The General replied, "If you can do it in one day, I give leave; otherwise not, for you must certainly sail the day after tomorrow." So he never obtained leave, tho' detained afterwards from day to day during full three months. I saw also in London one of Bonnell's passengers who was so enraged against His Lordship for deceiving and detaining him so long at New York and then carrying him to Halifax and back again, that he swore he would sue him for damages. Whether he did or not, I never heard; but as he represented the injury to his affairs, it was very considerable. On the whole I then wondered much how such a man came to be entrusted with so important a business as the conduct of a great army; but having since seen more of the great world, and the means of obtaining and motives for giving places, my wonder is diminished. General Shirley, on whom the command of the army devolved upon the death of Braddock, would in my opinion, if continued in place, have made a much better campaign than that of Loudon in 1757, which was frivolous, expensive, and disgraceful to our nation beyond conception. For tho' Shirley was not a bred soldier, he was sensible and sagacious in himself, and attentive to good advice from others, capable of forming judicious plans, and quick and active in carrying them into execution. Loudon, instead of defending the Colonies with his great army, left them totally exposed while he paraded it idly at Halifax, by which means Fort George was lost; besides he deranged all our mercantile operations and distressed our trade by a long embargo on the exportation of provisions, on pretence of keeping supplies from being obtained by the enemy, but in reality for beating down their price in favour of the contractors, in whose profits, it was said — perhaps from suspicion only — he had a share.

And when at length the embargo was taken off, by neglecting to send notice of it to Charlestown, the Carolina fleet was detained near three months longer, whereby their bottoms were so much damaged by the worm that a great part of them foundered in the passage home. Shirley was, I believe, sincerely glad of being relieved from so burthensome a charge as the conduct of an army must be to a man unacquainted with military business. I was at the entertainment given by the City of New York, to Lord Loudon on his taking upon him the command. Shirley, tho' thereby superseded, was present also. There was a great company of officers, citizens, and strangers, and some chairs having been borrowed in the neighbourhood, there was one among them very low which fell to the lot of Mr. Shirley. Perceiving it as I sat by him, I said, "They have given you, sir, too low a seat." "No matter," says he, "Mr. Franklin, I find *a low seat the easiest!*"

While I was, as aforementioned, detained at New York, I received all the accounts of the provisions, etc., that I had furnished to Braddock, some of which accounts could not sooner be obtained from the different persons I had employed to assist in the business. I presented them to Lord Loudon, desiring to be paid the balance. He caused them to be regularly examined by the proper officer, who, after comparing every article with its voucher, certified them to be right and the balance due, for which His Lordship promised to give me an order on the paymaster. This, however, was put off from time to time, and tho' I called often for it by appointment, I did not get it. At length, just before my departure, he told me he had on better consideration concluded not to mix his accounts with those of his predecessors. "And you," says he, "when in England, have only to exhibit your accounts at the Treasury, and you will be paid immediately." I mentioned, but without effect, the great and unexpected expence I had been put to by being detained so long at New York, as a reason for my desiring to be presently paid; and on my observing that it was not right I should be put to any further trouble or delay in obtaining the money I had advanced, as I charged no commissions for my service, "O, sir," says he, "you must not think of persuading us that you are no gainer. We understand better those affairs and know that everyone concerned in supplying the army finds means in the doing it to fill his own pockets." I assured him that was not my case and that I had not pocketed a farthing. But he appeared clearly not to believe me, and indeed I have since learned that immense fortunes are often made in such employments. As to my balance, I am not paid it to this day, of which more hereafter.

Our captain of the packet had boasted much before we sailed of the swiftness of his ship. Unfortunately, when we came to sea, she proved the dullest of ninety-six sail, to his no small mortification. After many conjectures respecting the cause, when we were near another ship almost as dull as ours (which, however, gained upon us), the captain ordered all hands to come aft and stand as near the ensign staff as possible. We were, passengers included, about forty persons. While we stood there, the ship mended her pace and soon left her neighbour far behind, which proved clearly what our captain suspected, that she was loaded too much by the head. The casks of water, it seems, had been all placed forward. These he therefore ordered to be removed farther aft, on which the ship recovered her character and proved the best sailer in the fleet. The captain said she had once gone at the rate of thirteen knots, which is accounted thirteen miles per hour. We had on board as a passenger Captain Kennedy of the Royal Navy, who contended that it was impossible, that no ship ever sailed so fast, and that there must have been some error in the division of the log line or some mistake in heaving the log. A wager ensued between the two captains, to be decided when there should be sufficient wind. Kennedy thereupon examined rigorously the log line, and being satisfied with that, he determined to throw the log himself. Accordingly, some days after when the wind blew very fair and fresh and the captain of the packet *(Lutwidge)* said he believed she then went at the rate of thirteen knots, Kennedy made the experiment and owned his wager lost. The above fact I give for the sake of the following observation. It has been remarked as an imperfection in the art of shipbuilding that it can never be known 'till she is tried whether a new ship will or will not be a good sailer, for that the model of a good sailing ship has been exactly followed in a new one, which has proved, on the contrary, remarkably dull. I apprehend this may be partly occasioned by the different opinions of seamen respecting the modes of lading, rigging, and sailing of a ship. Each has his system. And the same vessel laden by the judgment and orders of one captain shall sail better or worse than when by the orders of another. Besides, it scarce ever happens that a ship is formed, fitted for the sea, and sailed by the same person. One man builds the hull, another rigs her, a third lades and sails her. No one of these has the advantage of knowing all the ideas and experience of the others, and therefore cannot draw just conclusions from a combination of the whole. Even in the simple operation of sailing when at sea, I have often observed different judgments in the officers who commanded the successive watches, the wind being the same. One would have the sails trimmed sharper or flatter than another, so that they seemed to have no certain rule to govern by. Yet I think a set of experiments might be instituted: first, to determine the most proper form of the hull for swift sailing; next, the best dimensions and properest place for the masts; then, the form and quantity of sails, and their position as the winds may be; and lastly, the disposition of the lading. This is the age of experiments, and such a set accurately made and combined would be of great use. I am therefore persuaded that ere long some ingenious philosopher will undertake it — to whom I wish success.

We were several times chased in our passage, but outsailed everything and in thirty days had soundings. We had a good observation, and the captain judged himself so near our port (Falmouth) that if we made a good run in the night, we might be off the mouth of the harbour in the morning, and by running in the night might escape the notice of the enemy's privateers, who often cruised near the entrance of the Channel. Accordingly, all the sail was set that we could possibly make, and the wind being very fresh and fair, we went right before it and made great way. The captain after his observation, shaped his course — as he thought — so as to pass wide of the Scilly Isles; but it seems there is sometimes a strong indraught setting up St. George's Channel which deceives seamen and caused the loss of Sir Cloudsley Shovel's squadron.[1] This indraught was probably the cause of what happened to us. We had a watchman placed in the bow to whom they often called, "Look well out before, there"; and he as often answered, "Aye, aye!" But perhaps had his eyes shut and was half asleep at the time, they sometimes

---

[1] British naval disaster in 1707.

answering, as is said, mechanically. For he did not see a light just before us which had been hid by the studding sails from the man at helm and from the rest of the watch, but by an accidental yaw of the ship was discovered and occasioned a great alarm — we being very near it, the light appearing to me as big as a cart wheel. It was midnight, and our captain fast asleep. But Capt. Kennedy jumping upon deck and seeing the danger, ordered the ship to wear round, all sails standing — an operation dangerous to the masts, but it carried us clear, and we escaped shipwreck, for we were running right upon the rocks on which the lighthouse was erected. This deliverance impressed me strongly with the utility of lighthouses and made me resolve to encourage the building more of them in America, if I should live to return there.

In the morning it was found by the soundings, etc., that we were near our port, but a thick fog hid the land from our sight. About nine o'clock the fog began to rise and seemed to be lifted up from the water like the curtain at a playhouse, discovering underneath the town of Falmouth, the vessels in its harbour, and the fields that surrounded it. A most pleasing spectacle to those who had been so long without any other prospects than the uniform view of a vacant ocean! And it gave us the more pleasure, as we were now freed from the anxieties which the state of war occasioned.

I set out immediately with my son [1] for London, and we only stopped a little by the way to view Stonehenge on Salisbury Plain, and Lord Pembroke's house and gardens, with his very curious antiquities, at Wilton.

We arrived in London the 27th of July, 1757.[2] As soon as I was settled in a lodging Mr. Charles had provided for me, I went to visit Dr. Fothergill, to whom I was strongly recommended and whose counsel respecting my proceedings I was advised to obtain. He was against an immediate complaint to government and thought the Proprietaries should first be personally applied to, who might possibly be induced by the interposition and persuasion of some private friends to accommodate matters amicably. I then waited on my old friend and correspondent, Mr. Peter

[1] William Franklin.
[2] The second portion of Franklin's manuscript ends at this point. The remainder was written shortly before his death in April, 1790.

Collinson, who told me that John Hanbury, the great Virginia merchant, had requested to be informed when I should arrive that he might carry me to Lord Granville's, who was then President of the Council, and wished to see me as soon as possible. I agreed to go with him the next morning. Accordingly, Mr. Hanbury called for me and took me in his carriage to that nobleman's, who received me with great civility; and after some questions respecting the present state of affairs in America, and discourse thereupon, he said to me, "You Americans have wrong ideas of the nature of your constitution; you contend that the King's instructions to his governors are not laws and think yourselves at liberty to regard or disregard them at your own discretion. But those instructions are not like the pocket instructions given to a minister going abroad for regulating his conduct in some trifling point of ceremony. They are first drawn up by judges learned in the laws; they are then considered, debated, and perhaps amended in Council, after which they are signed by the King. They are then so far as relates to you, the *law of the land;* for THE KING IS THE LEGISLATOR OF THE COLONIES." I told His Lordship this was new doctrine to me. I had always understood from our charters that our laws were to be made by our Assemblies, to be presented, indeed, to the King for his royal assent, but that being once given, the King could not repeal or alter them. And as the Assemblies could not make permanent laws without his assent, so neither could he make a law for them without theirs. He assured me I was totally mistaken. I did not think so, however. And His Lordship's conversation having a little alarmed me as to what might be the sentiments of the court concerning us, I wrote it down as soon as I returned to my lodgings. I recollected that about twenty years before a clause in a bill brought into Parliament by the ministry had proposed to make the King's instructions laws in the Colonies; but the clause was thrown out by the Commons, for which we adored them as our friends and friends of liberty, till by their conduct towards us in 1765, it seemed that they had refused that point of sovereignty to the King only that they might reserve it for themselves.

After some days, Dr. Fothergill having spoken to the Proprietaries, they agreed to a meeting with me at Mr. T. Penn's house in Spring Garden. The conversation at first consisted of mutual declarations of disposition to reasonable accommodation, but I suppose each party had its own ideas of what should be meant by *reasonable*. We then went into consideration of our several points of complaint which I enumerated. The Proprietaries justified their conduct as well as they could, and I the Assembly's. We now appeared very wide, and so far from each other in our opinions as to discourage all hope of agreement. However, it was concluded that I should give them the heads of our complaints in writing, and they promised then to consider them. I did so soon after; but they put the paper into the hands of their solicitor, Ferdinando John Paris, who managed for them all their law business in their great suit with the neighbouring Proprietary of Maryland, Lord Baltimore, which had subsisted seventy years, and wrote for them all their papers and messages in their dispute with the Assembly. He was a proud, angry man; and as I had occasionally in the answers of the Assembly treated his papers with some severity, they being really weak in point of argument, and haughty in expression, he had conceived a mortal enmity to me, which discovering itself whenever we met, I declined the Proprietary's proposal that he and I should discuss the heads of complaint between our two selves and refused treating with any one but them. They then by his advice put the paper into the hands of the Attorney- and Solicitor-General for their opinion and counsel upon it, where it lay unanswered a year wanting eight days, during which time I made frequent demands of an answer from the Proprietaries but without obtaining any other than that they had not yet received the opinion of the Attorney- and Solicitor-General. What it was when they did receive it, I never learned, for they did not communicate it to me, but sent a long message to the Assembly drawn and signed by Paris reciting my paper, complaining of its want of formality as a rudeness on my part, and giving a flimsy justification of their conduct, adding that they should be willing to accommodate matters if the Assembly would send over "some person of candour" to treat with them for that purpose, intimating thereby that I was not such.

The want of formality or rudeness was probably my not having addressed the paper to them with their assumed titles of true and absolute Proprietaries of the Province of Pennsylvania, which I omitted as not thinking it necessary in a paper, the intention of which was only to reduce to a certainty by writing what in conversation I had delivered *viva voce*. But during this delay, the Assembly having prevailed with Governor Denny to pass an act taxing the proprietary estate in common with the estates of the people, which was the grand point in dispute, they omitted answering the message.

When this act, however, came over, the Proprietaries counselled by Paris determined to oppose its receiving the royal assent. Accordingly, they petitioned the King in Council, and a hearing was appointed, in which two lawyers were employed by them against the act and two by me in support of it. They alleged that the act was intended to load the proprietary estate in order to spare those of the people, and that if it were suffered to continue in force and the Proprietaries, who were in odium with the people, left to their mercy in proportioning the taxes, they would inevitably be ruined. We replied that the act had no such intention and would have no such effect, that the assessors were honest and discreet men, under an oath to assess fairly and equitably, and that any advantage each of them might expect in lessening his own tax by augmenting that of the Proprietaries was too trifling to induce them to perjure themselves. This is the purport of what I remember as urged by both sides, except that we insisted strongly on the mischievous consequences that must attend a repeal; for that the money (£100,000) being printed and given to the King's use, expended in his service, and now spread among the people, the repeal would strike it dead in their hands to the ruin of many and the total discouragement of future grants; and the selfishness of the Proprietors in soliciting such a general catastrophe, merely from a groundless fear of their estate being taxed too highly, was insisted on in the strongest terms. On this Lord Mansfield, one of the Council, rose, and beckoning to me, took me into the clerks' chamber, while the lawyers were pleading, and asked me if I was really of opinion that no injury would be done the proprietary estate in the execution of the act. I said, "Certainly." "Then," says he, "you can have little objection to enter into an engagement to assure that point." I answered, "None at all." He then called in Paris, and after some discourse His Lordship's proposition was accepted on both sides; a paper to the purpose was drawn up by the clerk of the Council, which I signed with Mr. Charles, who was also an agent of the province for their ordinary affairs, when Lord Mansfield returned to the council chamber, where finally the law was allowed to pass. Some changes were, however, recommended, and we also engaged they should be made by a subsequent law; but the Assembly did not think them necessary. For one year's tax having been levied by the act before the order of Council arrived, they appointed a committee to examine the proceedings of the assessors, and on this committee they put several particular friends of the Proprietaries. After a full enquiry they unanimously signed a report that they found the tax had been assessed with perfect equity. The Assembly looked on my entering into the first part of the engagement as an essential service to the province, since it secured the credit of the paper money then spread over all the country; and they gave me their thanks in form when I returned. But the Proprietaries were enraged at Governor Denny for having passed the act and turned him out, with threats of suing him for breach of instructions which he had given bond to observe. He, however, having done it at the instance of the General and for His Majesty's service, and having some powerful interest at court, despised the threats, and they were never put in execution.

The Silence Dogood Papers

⮑ *Published anonymously in 1722 under the circumstances described in the* Autobiography. *"Silence Dogood" was presumably the widow of a country parson,
with strong opinions on various aspects of American life.
The influence of Addison and Steele on the youthful
essayist is quite evident.*

(From Monday May 21. to Monday May 28. 1722.)

Mulier Muliere magis congruet. TER.[1]

To the *Author* of the New-England Courant.

SIR,

I shall here present your Readers with a Letter from one, who
informs me that I have begun at the wrong End of my Business,
and that I ought to begin at Home, and censure the Vices and
Follies of my own Sex, before I venture to meddle with your's:
Nevertheless, I am resolved to dedicate this Speculation to the
Fair Tribe, and endeavour to show, that Mr. *Ephraim* charges
Women with being particularly guilty of Pride, Idleness, &c.
wrongfully, inasmuch as the Men have not only as great a Share
in those Vices as the Women, but are likewise in a great Measure
the Cause of that which the Women are guilty of. I think it
will be best to produce my Antagonist, before I encounter him.

To *Mrs.* Dogood.

Madam,

My Design in troubling you with this Letter is, to desire you
would begin with your own Sex first: Let the first Volley of your
Resentments be directed against *Female* Vice; let Female Idleness,
Ignorance and Folly, (which are Vices more peculiar to your
Sex than to our's,) be the Subject of your Satyrs, but more
especially Female Pride, which I think is intolerable. Here is a
large Field that wants Cultivation, and which I believe you are
able (if willing) to improve with Advantage; and when you have
once reformed the Women, you will find it a much easier Task

[1] "A woman deals much better with a woman." — Terence, *Phormio*,
V, i, 1.

159

to reform the Men, because Women are the prime Causes of a great many Male Enormities. This is all at present from

Your Friendly Wellwisher,

Ephraim Censorious.

After Thanks to my Correspondent for his Kindness in cutting out Work for me, I must assure him, that I find it a very difficult Matter to reprove Women separate from the Men; for what Vice is there in which the Men have not as great a Share as the Women? and in some have they not a far greater, as in Drunkenness, Swearing, &c.? And if they have, then it follows, that when a Vice is to be reproved, Men, who are most culpable, deserve the most Reprehension, and certainly therefore, ought to have it. But will wave this point at present, and proceed to a particular Consideration of what my Correspondent calls *Female Vice.*

As for Idleness, if I should *Quære,*[1] Where are the greatest Number of its Votaries to be found, with us or the Men? it might I believe be easily and truly answer'd, *With the latter.* For, notwithstanding the Men are commonly complaining how hard they are forc'd to labour, only to maintain their Wives in Pomp and Idleness, yet if you go among the Women, you will learn, that *they have always more Work upon their Hands than they are able to do,* and that *a Woman's Work is never done,* &c. But however, Suppose we should grant for once, that we are generally more idle than the Men, (without making any Allowance for the *Weakness of the Sex,*) I desire to know whose Fault it is? Are not the Men to blame for their Folly in maintaining us in Idleness? Who is there that can be handsomely supported in Affluence, Ease and Pleasure by another, that will chuse rather to earn his Bread by the Sweat of his own Brows? And if a Man will be so fond and so foolish, as to labour hard himself for a Livelihood, and suffer his Wife in the mean Time to sit in Ease and Idleness, let him not blame her if she does so, for it is in a great Measure his own Fault.

And now for the Ignorance and Folly which he reproaches us with, let us see (if we are Fools and Ignoramus's) whose is the Fault, the Men's or our's. An ingenious Writer, having this

[1] Ask.

Subject in Hand, has the following Words, wherein he lays the Fault wholly on the Men, for not allowing Women the Advantages of Education.

"I have (says he) often thought of it as one of the most barbarous Customs in the World, considering us as a civiliz'd and Christian Country, that we deny the Advantages of Learning to Women. We reproach the Sex every Day with Folly and Impertinence, while I am confident, had they the Advantages of Education equal to us, they would be guilty of less than our selves. One would wonder indeed how it should happen that Women are conversible at all, since they are only beholding to natural Parts for all their Knowledge. Their Youth is spent to teach them to stitch and sow, or make Baubles. They are taught to read indeed, and perhaps to write their Names, or so; and that is the Heigth of a Womans Education. And I would but ask any who slight the Sex for their Understanding, What is a Man (a Gentleman, I mean) good for that is taught no more? If Knowledge and Understanding had been useless Additions to the Sex, God Almighty would never have given them Capacities, for he made nothing Needless. What has the Woman done to forfeit the Priviledge of being taught? Does she plague us with her Pride and Impertinence? Why did we not let her learn, that she might have had more Wit? Shall we upbraid Women with Folly, when 'tis only the Error of this inhumane Custom that hindered them being made wiser."

So much for Female Ignorance and Folly; and now let us a little consider the Pride which my Correspondent thinks is *intolerable*. By this Expression of his, one would think he is some dejected Swain, tyranniz'd over by some cruel haughty Nymph, who (perhaps he thinks) has no more Reason to be proud than himself. *Alas-a-day!* What shall we say in this Case! Why truly, if Women are proud, it is certainly owing to the Men still; for if they will be such *Simpletons* as to humble themselves at their Feet, and fill their credulous Ears with extravagant Praises of their Wit, Beauty, and other Accomplishments (perhaps where there are none too,) and when Women are by this Means perswaded that they are Something more than humane, what Wonder is it, if they carry themselves haughtily, and live extravagantly. Notwithstanding, I believe there are more Instances of extravagant Pride to be found among Men than among Women, and this Fault is certainly more hainous in the former than in the latter.

Upon the whole, I conclude, that it will be impossible to lash any Vice, of which the Men, are not equally guilty with the Women, and consequently deserve an equal (if not a greater) Share in the Censure. However, I exhort both to amend, where both are culpable, otherwise they may expect to be severely handled by   Sir,

Your Humble Servant,

SILENCE DOGOOD.

N. B. *Mrs.* Dogood *has lately left her Seat in the Country, and come to Boston, where she intends to tarry for the Summer Season, in order to compleat her Observations of the present reigning Vices of the Town.*

Articles of Belief and Acts of Religion

IN TWO PARTS [1]

~§ Written in 1728, a year after the founding of the Junto, and perhaps the most complete statement of his religious creed.

> *Here will I hold. If there is a Pow'r above us,*
> *(And that there is, all Nature cries aloud,*
> *Thro' all her Works) He must delight in Virtue;*
> *And that which he delights in must be Happy.*
>   CATO.

PART I

Philadᵃ, Nov. 20: 1728

First Principles

I believe there is one supreme, most perfect Being, Author and Father of the Gods themselves. For I believe that Man is not the most perfect Being but one, rather than as there are many Degrees of Beings his Inferiors, so there are many Degrees of Beings superior to him.

Also when I stretch my Imagination thro' and beyond our System of Planets, beyond the visible fix'd Stars themselves, into that Space that is every Way infinite, and conceive it fill'd with Suns like ours, each with a Chorus of Worlds forever moving round him, then this little Ball on which we move, seems, even in my narrow Imagination, to be almost Nothing, and myself less than nothing, and of no sort of Consequence.

When I think thus, I imagine it great Vanity in me to suppose, that the *Supremely Perfect* does in the least regard such an inconsiderable Nothing as Man. More especially, since it is impossible for me to have any positive clear idea of that which is infinite and incomprehensible, I cannot conceive otherwise than that he *the Infinite Father* expects or requires no Worship or Praise from us, but that he is even infinitely above it.

But, since there is in all Men something like a natural principle,

---

[1] No second part has been found.

163

which inclines them to DEVOTION, or the Worship of some unseen Power;

And since Men are endued with Reason superior to all other Animals, that we are in our World acquainted with;

Therefore I think it seems required of me, and my Duty as a Man, to pay Divine Regards to SOMETHING.

I conceive then, that the INFINITE has created many beings or Gods, vastly superior to Man, who can better conceive his Perfections than we, and return him a more rational and glorious Praise.

As, among Men, the Praise of the Ignorant or of Children is not regarded by the ingenious Painter or Architect, who is rather honour'd and pleas'd with the approbation of Wise Men & Artists.

It may be that these created Gods are immortal; or it may be that after many Ages, they are changed, and others Supply their Places.

Howbeit, I conceive that each of these is exceeding wise and good, and very powerful; and that Each has made for himself one glorious Sun, attended with a beautiful and admirable System of Planets.

It is that particular Wise and good God, who is the author and owner of our System, that I propose for the object of my praise and adoration.

For I conceive that he has in himself some of those Passions he has planted in us, and that, since he has given us Reason whereby we are capable of observing his Wisdom in the Creation, he is not above caring for us, being pleas'd with our Praise, and offended when we slight Him, or neglect his Glory.

I conceive for many Reasons, that he is a *good Being,* and as I should be happy to have so wise, good, and powerful a Being my Friend, let me consider in what manner I shall make myself most acceptable to him.

Next to the Praise resulting from and due to his Wisdom, I believe he is pleas'd and delights in the Happiness of those he has created; and since without Virtue Man can have no Happiness in this World, I firmly believe he delights to see me Virtuous, because he is pleased when he sees me Happy.

And since he has created many Things, which seem purely designed for the Delight of Man, I believe he is not offended, when he sees his Children solace themselves in any manner of pleasant exercises and Innocent Delights; and I think no Pleasure innocent, that is to Man hurtful.

I *love* him therefore for his Goodness, and I *adore* him for his Wisdom.

Let me then not fail to praise my God continually, for it is his Due, and it is all I can return for his many Favours and great Goodness to me; and let me resolve to be virtuous, that I may be happy, that I may please Him, who is delighted to see me happy. Amen!

Advice to a Young Tradesman

*❧ Written in 1748, as Franklin was retiring from active
business life to devote himself to science and public service.*

To My Friend, A.B.:

As you have desired it of me, I write the following hints, which
have been of service to me, and may, if observed, be so to you.

Remember, that *time* is money. He that can earn ten shillings
a day by his labour, and goes abroad, or sits idle, one half of that
day, though he spends but sixpence during his diversion or idleness, ought not to reckon *that* the only expense; he has really
spent, or rather thrown away, five shillings besides.

Remember, that *credit* is money. If a man lets his money lie
in my hands after it is due, he gives me the interest, or so much
as I can make of it during that time. This amounts to a considerable sum where a man has good and large credit, and makes
good use of it.

Remember, that money is of the prolific, generating nature.
Money can beget money, and its offspring can beget more, and
so on. Five shillings turned is six, turned again it is seven and
three-pence, and so on till it becomes an hundred pounds. The
more there is of it, the more it produces every turning, so that
the profits rise quicker and quicker. He that kills a breeding sow,
destroys all her offspring to the thousandth generation. He that
murders a crown, destroys all that it might have produced, even
scores of pounds.

Remember, that six pounds a year is but a groat a day. For
this little sum (which may be daily wasted either in time or
expense unperceived) a man of credit may, on his own security,
have the constant possession and use of an hundred pounds. So
much in stock, briskly turned by an industrious man, produces
great advantage.

Remember this saying, *The good paymaster is lord of another
man's purse*. He that is known to pay punctually and exactly to
the time he promises, may at any time, and on any occasion,
raise all the money his friends can spare. This is sometimes of
great use. After industry and frugality, nothing contributes more

to the raising of a young man in the world than punctuality and justice in all his dealings; therefore never keep borrowed money an hour beyond the time you promised, lest a disappointment shut up your friend's purse for ever.

The most trifling actions that affect a man's credit are to be regarded. The sound of your hammer at five in the morning, or nine at night, heard by a creditor, makes him easy six months longer; but, if he see you at a billiard table, or hears your voice at a tavern, when you should be at work, he sends for his money the next day; demands it, before he can receive it, in a lump.

It shows, besides, that you are mindful of what you owe; it makes you appear a careful as well as an honest man, and that still increases your credit.

Beware of thinking all your own that you possess, and of living accordingly. It is a mistake that many people who have credit fall into. To prevent this, keep an exact account for some time, both of your expenses and your income. If you take the pains at first to mention particulars, it will have this good effect: you will discover how wonderfully small, trifling expenses mount up to large sums, and will discern what might have been, and may for the future be saved, without occasioning any great inconvenience.

In short, the way to wealth, if you desire it, is as plain as the way to market. It depends chiefly on two words, *industry* and *frugality;* that is, waste neither *time* nor *money*, but make the best use of both. Without industry and frugality nothing will do, and with them every thing. He that gets all he can honestly, and saves all he gets (necessary expenses excepted), will certainly become *rich*, if that Being who governs the world, to whom all should look for a blessing on their honest endeavors, doth not, in his wise providence, otherwise determine.

AN OLD TRADESMAN.

The Way to Wealth

◄§ Printed first as a preface to Poor Richard's Almanac
for 1758. Reprinted later as "Father Abraham's Speech"
and finally in 1774 as The Way to Wealth. *Since that time*
it has been reprinted innumerable times in fourteen
languages.

COURTEOUS READER:

I have heard that nothing gives an Author so great Pleasure,
as to find his Works respectfully quoted by other learned
Authors. This Pleasure I have seldom enjoyed; for tho' I have
been, if I may say it without Vanity, an *eminent Author* of
Almanacks annually now a full Quarter of a Century, my
Brother Authors in the same Way, for what Reason I know not,
have ever been very sparing in their Applauses, and no other
Author has taken the least Notice of me, so that did not my
Writings produce me some solid *Pudding,* the great Deficiency
of *Praise* would have quite discouraged me.

I concluded at length, that the People were the best Judges of
my merit; for they buy my Works; and besides, in my Rambles,
where I am not personally known, I have frequently heard one or
other of my Adages repeated, with, *as Poor Richard says,* at the
End on 't; this gave me some Satisfaction, as it showed not only
that my Instructions were regarded, but discovered likewise some
Respect for my Authority; and I own, that to encourage the
Practice of remembering and repeating those wise Sentences, I
have sometimes *quoted myself* with great Gravity.

Judge, then how much I must have been gratified by an
Incident I am going to relate to you. I stopt my Horse lately
where a great Number of People were collected at a Vendue of
Merchant Goods. The Hour of Sale not being come, they were
conversing on the Badness of the Times and one of the Company
call'd to a plain clean old Man, with white Locks, "Pray, Father
Abraham, what think you of the Times? Won't these heavy
Taxes quite ruin the Country? How shall we be ever able to pay
them? What would you advise us to?" Father *Abraham* stood
up, and reply'd, "If you'd have my Advice, I'll give it you in

short, for *A Word to the Wise is enough,* and *many Words won't fill a Bushel,* as *Poor Richard* says." They join'd in desiring him to speak his Mind, and gathering round him, he proceeded as follows;

"Friends," says he, "and Neighbours, the Taxes are indeed very heavy, and if those laid on by the Government were the only Ones we had to pay, we might more easily discharge them; but we have many others, and much more grievous to some of us. We are taxed twice as much by our *Idleness,* three times as much by our *Pride,* and four times as much by our *Folly;* and from these Taxes the Commissioners cannot ease or deliver us by allowing an Abatement. However let us hearken to good Advice, and something may be done for us; *God helps them that help themselves,* as *Poor Richard* says, in his Almanack of 1733.

It would be thought a hard Government that should tax its People one-tenth Part of their *Time,* to be employed in its Service. But *Idleness* taxes many of us much more, if we reckon all that is spent in absolute *Sloth,* or doing of nothing, with that which is spent in idle Employments or Amusements, that amount to nothing. *Sloth,* by bringing on Diseases, absolutely shortens Life. *Sloth, like Rust, consumes faster than Labour wears; while the used Key is always bright,* as *Poor Richard* says. *But dost thou love Life, then do not squander Time; for that's the stuff Life is made of,* as *Poor Richard* says. How much more than is necessary do we spend in sleep, forgetting that *The Sleeping Fox catches no Poultry,* and that *There will be sleeping enough in the Grave,* as *Poor Richard* says.

If Time be of all Things the most precious, wasting Time must be, as *Poor Richard* says, *the greatest Prodigality;* since, as he elsewhere tells us, *Lost Time is never found again; and what we call Time enough, always proves little enough:* Let us then up and be doing, and doing to the Purpose; so by Diligence shall we do more with less Perplexity. *Sloth makes all Things difficult, but Industry all easy,* as *Poor Richard* says; and *He that riseth late must trot all Day, and shall scarce overtake his Business at Night;* while *Laziness travels so slowly, that Poverty soon overtakes him,* as we read in *Poor Richard,* who adds, *Drive thy Business, let not that drive thee;* and *Early to Bed, and early to rise, makes a Man healthy, wealthy, and wise.*

So what signifies *wishing* and *hoping* for better Times. We may make these Times better, if we bestir ourselves. *Industry need not wish*, as *Poor Richard* says, *and he that lives upon Hope will die fasting*. *There are no Gains without Pains; then Help Hands, for I have no Lands*, or if I have, they are smartly taxed. And, as *Poor Richard* likewise observes, *He that hath a Trade hath an Estate; and he that hath a Calling, hath an Office of Profit and Honour;* but then the *Trade* must be worked at, and the *Calling* well followed, or neither the *Estate* nor the *Office* will enable us to pay our Taxes. If we are industrious we shall never starve; for, as *Poor Richard* says, *At the working Man's House Hunger looks in, but dares not enter*. Nor will the Bailiff or the Constable enter, for *Industry pays Debts, while Despair encreaseth them*, says *Poor Richard*. What though you have found no Treasure, nor has any rich Relation left you a Legacy, *Diligence is the Mother of Goodluck* as *Poor Richard* says *and God gives all Things to Industry*. *Then plough deep, while Sluggards sleep, and you shall have Corn to sell and to keep*, says *Poor Dick*. Work while it is called To-day, for you know not how much you may be hindered To-morrow, which makes *Poor Richard* say, *One to-day is worth two To-morrows*, and farther, *Have you somewhat to do To-morrow, do it To-day*. If you were a Servant, would you not be ashamed that a good Master should catch you idle? Are you then your own Master, *be ashamed to catch yourself idle*, as *Poor Dick* says. When there is so much to be done for yourself, your Family, your Country, and your gracious King, be up by Peep of Day; *Let not the Sun look down and say, Inglorious here he lies*. Handle your tools without Mittens; remember that *The Cat in Gloves catches no Mice*, as *Poor Richard* says. 'Tis true there is much to be done, and perhaps you are weak-handed, but stick to it steadily; and you will see great Effects, for *Constant Dropping wears away Stones*, and by *Diligence and Patience the Mouse ate in two the Cable;* and *Little Strokes fell great Oaks*, as *Poor Richard* says in his Almanack, the Year I cannot just now remember.

Methinks I hear some of you say, *Must a Man afford himself no Leisure?* I will tell thee, my friend, what *Poor Richard* says, *Employ thy Time well, if thou meanest to gain Leisure; and, since thou art not sure of a Minute, throw not away an Hour*. Leisure, is Time for doing something useful; this Leisure the diligent Man will obtain, but the lazy Man never; so that, as *Poor*

Richard says, *A Life of Leisure and a Life of Laziness are two Things.* Do you imagine that Sloth will afford you more Comfort than Labour? No, for as *Poor Richard* says, *Trouble springs from Idleness, and grievous Toil from needless Ease.* Many without Labour, would live by their Wits only, but they break for want of Stock. Whereas Industry gives Comfort, and Plenty, and Respect: *Fly Pleasures, and they'll follow you.* The diligent Spinner has a large Shift; and now I have a Sheep and a Cow, everybody bids me good Morrow; all which is well said by *Poor Richard.*

But with our Industry, we must likewise be *steady, settled,* and *careful,* and oversee our own Affairs *with our own Eyes,* and not trust too much to others; for, as *Poor Richard* says

> *I never saw an oft-removed Tree,*
> *Nor yet an oft-removed Family,*
> *That throve so well as those that settled be.*

And again, *Three Removes is as bad as a Fire;* and again, *Keep thy Shop, and thy Shop will keep thee;* and again, *If you would have your Business done, go; if not, send.* And again

> *He that by the Plough would thrive,*
> *Himself must either hold or drive.*

And again, *The Eye of a Master will do more Work than both his Hands;* and again, *Want of Care does us more Damage than Want of Knowledge;* and again, *Not to oversee Workmen, is to leave them your Purse open.* Trusting too much to others' Care is the Ruin of many; for, as the Almanack says, *In the Affairs of this World, Men are saved, not by Faith, but by the Want of it;* but a Man's own Care is profitable; for, saith *Poor Dick, Learning is to the Studious,* and *Riches to the Careful,* as well as *Power to the Bold,* and *Heaven to the Virtuous,* and farther, *If you would have a faithful Servant, and one that you like, serve yourself.* And again, he adviseth to Circumspection and Care, even in the smallest Matters, because sometimes *A little Neglect may breed great Mischief;* adding, *for want of a Nail the Shoe was lost; for want of a Shoe the Horse was lost; and for want of a Horse the Rider was lost, being overtaken and slain by the Enemy; all for want of Care about a Horse-shoe Nail.*

So much for Industry, my Friends, and Attention to one's

own Business; but to these we must add *Frugality*, if we would make our *Industry* more certainly successful. A Man may, if he knows not how to save as he gets, *keep his Nose all his Life to the Grindstone*, and die not worth a *Groat at last. A fat Kitchen makes a lean Will*, as *Poor Richard* says; and

> *Many Estates are spent in the Getting,*
> *Since Women for Tea forsook Spinning and Knitting,*
> *And Men for Punch forsook Hewing and Splitting.*

If you would be wealthy, says he, in another Almanack, *think of Saving as well as of Getting: The Indies have not made Spain rich, because her Outgoes are greater than her Incomes.*

Away then with your expensive Follies, and you will not then have so much Cause to complain of hard Times, heavy Taxes, and chargeable Families; for, as *Poor Dick* says,

> *Women and Wine, Game and Deceit,*
> *Make the Wealth small and the Wants great.*

And farther, *What maintains one Vice, would bring up two Children.* You may think perhaps, that a *little* Tea, or a *little* Punch now and then, Diet a *little* more costly, Clothes a *little* finer, and a *little* Entertainment now and then, can be no *great* Matter; but remember what *Poor Richard* says, *Many a Little makes a Mickle;* and farther, *Beware of little Expences; A small Leak will sink a great Ship;* and again, *Who Dainties love, shall Beggars prove;* and moreover, *Fools make Feasts, and wise Men eat them.*

Here you are all got together at this Vendue of *Fineries* and *Knicknacks.* You call them *Goods;* but if you do not take Care, they will prove *Evils* to some of you. You expect they will be sold *cheap,* and perhaps they may for less than they cost, but if you have no Occasion for them, they must be *dear* to you. Remember what *Poor Richard* says, *Buy what thou hast no Need of, and ere long thou shalt sell thy Necessaries.* And again, *At a great Pennyworth pause a while:* He means, that perhaps the Cheapness is *apparent only,* and not *Real;* or the bargain, by straitening thee in thy Business, may do thee more Harm than Good. For in another Place he says, *Many have been ruined by buying good Pennyworths.* Again, *Poor Richard* says, *'tis foolish to lay out Money in a Purchase of Repentance;* and yet this

Folly is practised every Day at Vendues, for want of minding the Almanacks. *Wise Men*, as *Poor Dick* says, *learn by other's Harms, Fools scarcely by their own;* but *felix quem faciunt aliena pericula cautum*.[1] Many a one, for the Sake of Finery on the Back, have gone with a hungry Belly, and half-starved their Families. *Silks and Sattins, Scarlet and Velvets,* as *Poor Richard* says, *put out the Kitchen Fire.*

These are not the *Necessaries* of Life, they can scarcely be called the *Conveniences;* and yet only because they look pretty, how many *want* to *have* them! The *artificial* Wants of Mankind thus become more numerous than the *Natural;* and, as *Poor Dick* says, *for one poor Person, there are an hundred indigent.* By these, and other Extravagancies, the Genteel are reduced to poverty, and forced to borrow of those whom they formerly despised, but who through Industry and Frugality have maintained their Standing; in which Case it appears plainly, that *A Ploughman on his Legs is higher than a Gentleman on his Knees,* as *Poor Richard* says. Perhaps they have had a small Estate left them, which they knew not the Getting of, they think, *'tis Day, and will never be Night;* that a little to be spent out of *so much,* is not worth minding; *a Child and a Fool,* as *Poor Richard* says, *imagine Twenty shillings and Twenty Years can never be spent* but, *always taking out of the Meal-tub, and never putting in, soon comes to the Bottom;* as *Poor Dick* says, *When the Well's dry, they know the Worth of Water.* But this they might have known before, if they had taken his Advice; *If you would know the Value of Money, go and try to borrow some; or, he that goes a borrowing goes a sorrowing;* and indeed so does he that lends to such People, when he goes *to get it in again. Poor Dick* farther advises, and says,

> *Fond Pride of Dress is sure a very Curse;*
> *E'er Fancy you consult, consult your Purse.*

And again, *Pride is as loud a Beggar as Want and a great deal more saucy.* When you have bought one fine Thing, you must buy ten more, that your Appearance may be all of a Piece; but *Poor Dick* says, *'Tis easier to suppress the first Desire, than to satisfy all that follows it.* And 'tis as truly Folly for the Poor to ape the Rich, as for the Frog to swell, in order to equal the ox.

[1] Fortunate is he whom the misfortunes of another makes cautious.

> *Great Estates may venture more,*
> *But little Boats should keep near Shore.*

'Tis, however, a Folly soon punished; for *Pride that dines on Vanity, sups on Contempt,* as *Poor Richard* says. And in another Place, *Pride breakfasted with Plenty, dined with Poverty, and supped with Infamy.* And after all, of what Use is this *Pride of Appearance,* for which so much is risked, so much is suffered? It cannot promote Health, or ease Pain; it makes no Increase of Merit in the Person, it creates Envy, it hastens Misfortune.

> *What is a Butterfly? At best*
> *He's but a Caterpillar drest*
> *The gaudy Fop's his Picture just,*

as *Poor Richard* says.

But what Madness must it be to *run in Debt* for these Super-fluities! We are offered, by the Terms of this Vendue, *Six Months' Credit;* and that perhaps has induced some of us to attend it, because we cannot spare the ready Money, and hope now to be fine without it. But, ah, think what you do when you run in Debt; *you give to another Power over your Liberty.* If you cannot pay at the Time, you will be ashamed to see your Creditor; you will be in Fear when you speak to him; you will make poor pitiful sneaking Excuses, and by Degrees come to lose your Veracity, and sink into base downright lying; for, as *Poor Richard* says, *The second Vice is Lying, the first is running in Debt.* And again, to the same Purpose, *Lying rides upon Debt's Back.* Whereas a free-born *Englishman* ought not to be ashamed or afraid to see or speak to any Man living. But Poverty often deprives a Man of all Spirit and Virtue: *'Tis hard for an empty Bag to stand upright,* as *Poor Richard* truly says.

What would you think of that Prince, or that Government, who should issue an Edict forbidding you to dress like a Gentle-man or a Gentlewoman, on Pain of Imprisonment or Servitude? Would you not say, that you were free, have a Right to dress as you please, and that such an Edict would be a Breach of your Privileges, and such a Government tyrannical? And yet you are about to put yourself under that tyranny, when you run in Debt for such Dress! Your Creditor has Authority, at his Pleasure to deprive you of your Liberty, by confining you in Gaol for Life, or to sell you for a Servant, if you should not be able to pay him! When you have got your Bargain, you may, perhaps, think little of Payment; but *Creditors, Poor Richard* tells us, *have better Memories than Debtors;* and in another Place says, *Creditors are a superstitious Sect, great Observers of set Days and Times.* The Day comes round before you are aware, and the Demand is made before you are prepared to satisfy it; or if you bear your Debt in Mind, the Term which at first seemed so long, will, as it lessens, appear extreamly short. *Time* will seem to have added Wings to his Heels as well as Shoulders. *Those have a short Lent,* saith *Poor Richard, who owe Money to be paid at Easter.* Then since, as he says, *The Borrower is a Slave to the Lender, and the Debtor to the Creditor,* disdain the Chain, preserve your Freedom; and maintain your Independency: Be *Industrious* and *free;* be *frugal* and *free.* At present, perhaps, you may think yourself in thriving Circumstances, and that you can bear a little Extravagance without Injury; but,

> *For Age and Want, save while you may;*
> *No Morning Sun lasts a whole Day,*

as *Poor Richard* says. Gain may be temporary and uncertain, but ever while you live, Expence is constant and certain; and *'tis easier to build two Chimnies, than to keep one in Fuel,* as *Poor Richard* says. So, *Rather go to Bed supperless than rise in Debt.*

> *Get what you can, and what you get hold;*
> *'Tis the Stone that will turn all your lead into Gold,*

as *Poor Richard* says. And when you have got the Philosopher's Stone, sure you will no longer complain of bad Times, or the Difficulty of paying Taxes.

This Doctrine, my Friends, is *Reason* and *Wisdom;* but after all, do not depend too much upon your own *Industry,* and *Frugality,* and Prudence, though excellent Things, for they may all be blasted without the Blessing of Heaven; and therefore, ask that Blessing humbly, and be not uncharitable to those that at present seem to want it, but comfort and help them. Remember, *Job* suffered, and was afterwards prosperous.

And now to conclude, *Experience keeps a dear School, but Fools will learn in no other, and scarce in that;* for it is true, *we may give Advice, but we cannot give Conduct,* as *Poor Richard* says: However, remember this, *They that won't be*

counselled, can't be helped, as *Poor Richard* says: and farther,
That, *if you will not hear Reason, she'll surely rap your
Knuckles."*

Thus the old Gentleman ended his Harangue. The People
heard it, and approved the Doctrine, and immediately practised
the contrary, just as if it had been a common Sermon; for the
Vendue opened, and they began to buy extravagantly, notwithstanding his Cautions and their own Fear of Taxes. I found
the good Man had thoroughly studied my Almanacks, and
digested all I had dropt on these Topicks during the Course of
Five and twenty Years. The frequent Mention he made of me
must have tired any one else, but my Vanity was wonderfully
delighted with it, though I was conscious that not a tenth Part
of the Wisdom was my own, which he ascribed to me, but
rather the *Gleanings* I had made of the Sense of all Ages and
Nations. However, I resolved to be the better for the Echo of
it; and though I had at first determined to buy Stuff for a new
Coat, I went away resolved to wear my old One a little longer.
Reader, if thou wilt do the same, thy Profit will be as great as
mine. I *am, as ever, thine to serve thee.*

RICHARD SAUNDERS.

July 7, 1757

The Sale of the Hessians

FROM THE COUNT DE SCHAUMBERGH TO THE
BARON HOHENDORF, COMMANDING THE HESSIAN
TROOPS IN AMERICA

*⊰ Since England's use of Hessian mercenaries caused
great anger in America, Franklin's powerfully ironic essay
was an effective piece of wartime propaganda, widely reprinted. Whether or not Hessian officials actually profited
from death indemnities has not been proved, but generally
suspected.*

Rome, February 18, 1777.

MONSIEUR LE BARON:

On my return from Naples, I received at Rome your letter of
the 27th December of last year. I have learned with unspeak-
able pleasure the courage our troops exhibited at Trenton,[1] and
you cannot imagine my joy on being told that of the 1,950
Hessians engaged in the fight, but 345 escaped. There were just
1,605 men killed, and I cannot sufficiently commend your prudence in sending an exact list of the dead to my minister in
London. This precaution was the more necessary, as the report
sent to the English ministry does not give but 1,455 dead. This
would make 483,450 florins instead of 643,500 which I am entitled to demand under our convention. You will comprehend
the prejudice which such an error would work in my finances,
and I do not doubt you will take the necessary pains to prove
that Lord North's list is false and yours correct.

The court of London objects that there were a hundred
wounded who ought not to be included in the list, nor paid for
as dead; but I trust you will not overlook my instructions to you
on quitting Cassel, and that you will not have tried by human
succor to recall the life of the unfortunates whose days could
not be lengthened but by the loss of a leg or an arm. That would
be making them a pernicious present, and I am sure they would
rather die than live in a condition no longer fit for my service.

[1] On Christmas night, 1776, Washington's army soundly whipped the
Hessians at the Battle of Trenton, taking nearly a thousand prisoners.

I do not mean by this that you should assassinate them; we should be humane, my dear Baron, but you may insinuate to the surgeons with entire propriety that a crippled man is a reproach to their profession, and that there is no wiser course than to let every one of them die when he ceases to be fit to fight.

I am about to send to you some new recruits. Don't economize them. Remember glory before all things. Glory is true wealth. There is nothing degrades the soldier like the love of money. He must care only for honour and reputation, but this reputation must be acquired in the midst of dangers. A battle gained without costing the conqueror any blood is an inglorious success, while the conquered cover themselves with glory by perishing with their arms in their hands. Do you remember that of the 300 Lacedæmonians who defended the defile of Thermopylæ, not one returned? How happy should I be could I say the same of my brave Hessians!

It is true that their king, Leonidas, perished with them; but things have changed, and it is no longer the custom for princes of the empire to go and fight in America for a cause with which they have no concern. And besides, to whom should they pay the thirty guineas per man if I did not stay in Europe to receive them? Then, it is necessary also that I be ready to send recruits to replace the men you lose. For this purpose I must return to Hesse. It is true, grown men are becoming scarce there, but I will send you boys. Besides, the scarcer the commodity the higher the price. I am assured that the women and little girls have begun to till our lands, and they get on not badly. You did right to send back to Europe that Dr. Crumerus who was so successful in curing dysentery. Don't bother with a man who is subject to looseness of the bowels. That disease makes bad soldiers. One coward will do more mischief in an engagement than ten brave men will do good. Better that they burst in their barracks than fly in a battle, and tarnish the glory of our arms. Besides, you know that they pay me as killed for all who die from disease, and I don't get a farthing for runaways. My trip to Italy, which has cost me enormously, makes it desirable that there should be a great mortality among them. You will therefore promise promotion to all who expose themselves; you will exhort them to seek glory in the midst of dangers; you will say to Major Maundorff that I am not at all content with his saving the 345 men who escaped the massacre of Trenton. Through the whole campaign he has not had ten men killed in consequence of his orders. Finally, let it be your principal object to prolong the war and avoid a decisive engagement on either side, for I have made arrangements for a grand Italian opera, and I do not wish to be obliged to give it up. Meantime I pray God, my dear Baron de Hohendorf, to have you in his holy and gracious keeping.

Three Bagatelles

Franklin, during his residence at Passy, near Paris, had a small press on which he amused himself by printing occasional "bagatelles," or light personal essays for circulation among his friends. The urbanity, wit, and graceful humor displayed in them indicate why Franklin was generally accounted as one of the world's most charming companions.

THE EPHEMERA

An Emblem of Human Life

(1778)

You may remember, my dear friend, that when we lately spent that happy day in the delightful garden and sweet society of the Moulin Joly,[1] I stopt a little in one of our walks, and staid some time behind the company. We had been shown numberless skeletons of a kind of little fly, called an ephemera, whose successive generations, we were told, were bred and expired within the day. I happened to see a living company of them on a leaf, who appeared to be engaged in conversation. You know I understand all the inferior animal tongues; my too great application of the study of them is the best excuse I can give for the little progress I have made in your charming language. I listened through curiosity to the discourse of these little creatures; but as they, in their national vivacity, spoke three or four together, I could make but little of their conversation. I found, however, by some broken expressions that I heard now and then, they were disputing warmly on the merits of two foreign musicians, one a *cousin*, the other a *moscheto;* [2] in which dispute they spent their time, seemingly as regardless of the shortness of life as if they had been sure of living a month. Happy people! thought I, you live certainly under a wise, just, and mild government, since you have no public grievances to complain of, nor any subject of

[1] An island in the Seine. The person addressed is Madame Brillon de Jouy, one of his Passy neighbors and a favorite chess partner.
[2] One a gnat, the other a mosquito.

contention but the perfections and imperfections of foreign music. I turned my head from them to an old grey-headed one, who was single on another leaf, and talking to himself. Being amused with his soliloquy, I put it down in writing, in hopes it will likewise amuse her to whom I am so much indebted for the most pleasing of all amusements, her delicious company and heavenly harmony.

"It was," said he, "the opinion of learned philosophers of our race, who lived and flourished long before my time, that this vast world, the Moulin Joly, could not itself subsist more than eighteen hours; and I think there was some foundation for that opinion, since, by the apparent motion of the great luminary that gives life to all nature, and which in my time has evidently declined considerably towards the ocean at the end of our earth, it must then finish its course, be extinguished in the waters that surround us, and leave the world in cold and darkness, necessarily producing universal death and destruction. I have lived seven of those hours, a great age, being no less than four hundred and twenty minutes of time. How very few of us continue so long! I have seen generations born, flourish, and expire. My present friends are the children and grandchildren of the friends of my youth, who are now, alas, no more! And I must soon follow them; for, by the course of nature, though still in health, I cannot expect to live above seven or eight minutes longer. What now avails all my toil and labor, in amassing honey-dew on this leaf, which I cannot live to enjoy! What the political struggles I have been engaged in, for the good of my compatriot inhabitants of this bush, or my philosophical studies for the benefit of our race in general! for, in politics, what can laws do without morals? Our present race of ephemeræ will in a course of minutes become corrupt, like those of other and older bushes, and consequently as wretched. And in philosophy how small our progress! Alas! art is long, and life is short! My friends would comfort me with the idea of a name, they say, I shall leave behind me, and they tell me I have lived long enough to nature and to glory. But what will fame be to an ephemera who no longer exists? And what will become of all history in the eighteenth hour, when the world itself, even the whole Moulin Joly, shall come to its end, and be buried in universal ruin?"

To me, after all my eager pursuits, no solid pleasures now remain, but the reflection of a long life spent in meaning well, the sensible conversation of a few good lady ephemeræ, and now and then a kind smile and a tune from the ever amiable *Brillante*.

B. FRANKLIN.

THE WHISTLE
To Madam Brillon

PASSY, November 10, 1779.

I received my dear friend's two letters, one for Wednesday and one for Saturday. This is again Wednesday. I do not deserve one for to-day, because I have not answered the former. But, indolent as I am, and averse to writing, the fear of having no more of your pleasing epistles, if I do not contribute to the correspondence, obliges me to take up my pen; and as Mr. B. has kindly sent me word, that he sets out to-morrow to see you, instead of spending this Wednesday evening as I have done its namesakes, in your delightful company, I sit down to spend it in thinking of you, in writing to you, and in reading over and over again your letters.

I am charmed with your description of Paradise, and with your plan of living there; and I approve much of your conclusion, that, in the mean time, we should draw all the good we can from this world. In my opinion, we might all draw more good from it than we do, and suffer less evil, if we would take care not to give too much for *whistles*. For to me it seems, that most of the unhappy people we meet with, are become so by neglect of that caution.

You ask what I mean? You love stories, and will excuse my telling one on myself.

When I was a child of seven years old, my friends, on a holiday, filled my pocket with coppers. I went directly to a shop where they sold toys for children; and, being charmed with the sound of a *whistle*, that I met by the way in the hands of another boy, I voluntarily offered and gave all my money for one. I then came home, and went whistling all over the house, much pleased with my *whistle*, but disturbing all the family. My brothers, and sisters, and cousins, understanding the bargain I had made, told me I had given four times as much for it as it was worth; put me in mind what good things I might have bought with the rest of the money; and laughed at me so much for my folly, that I cried with vexation; and the reflection gave me more chagrin than the *whistle* gave me pleasure.

This however was afterwards of use to me, the impression continuing in my mind; so that often, when I was tempted to buy some unnecessary thing, I said to myself, *Don't give too much for the whistle;* and I saved my money.

As I grew up, came into the world, and observed the actions of men, I thought I met with many, very many, who *gave too much for the whistle.*

When I saw one too ambitious of court favour, sacrificing his time in attendance on levees, his repose, his liberty, his virtue, and perhaps his friends, to attain it, I have said to myself, *This man gives too much for his whistle.*

When I saw another fond of popularity, constantly employing himself in political bustles, neglecting his own affairs, and ruining them by that neglect, *He pays, indeed,* said I, *too much for his whistle.*

If I knew a miser, who gave up every kind of comfortable living, all the pleasure of doing good to others, all the esteem of his fellow-citizens, and the joys of benevolent friendship for the sake of accumulating wealth, *Poor man,* said I, *you pay too much for your whistle.*

When I met with a man of pleasure, sacrificing every laudable improvement of the mind, or of his fortune, to mere corporeal sensations, and ruining his health in their pursuit, *Mistaken man,* said I, *you are providing pain for yourself, instead of pleasure; you give too much for your whistle.*

If I see one fond of appearance, or fine clothes, fine houses, fine furniture, fine equipages, all above his fortune, for which he contracts debts, and ends his career in a prison, *Alas!* say I, *he has paid dear, very dear, for his whistle.*

When I see a beautiful, sweet-tempered girl married to an ill-natured brute of a husband, *What a pity,* say I, *that she should pay so much for a whistle!*

In short, I conceive that great part of the miseries of mankind are brought upon them by the false estimates they have made of the value of things, and by their *giving too much for their whistles.*

Yet I ought to have charity for these unhappy people, when I consider, that, with all this wisdom of which I am boasting, there are certain things in the world so tempting, for example, the apples of King John, which happily are not to be bought; for if they were put to sale by auction, I might very easily be led to ruin myself in the purchase, and find that I had once more given too much for the *whistle.*

Adieu, my dear friend, and believe me ever yours very sincerely and with unalterable affection,

B. FRANKLIN.

MORALS OF CHESS [1]
(*1779*)

[Playing at chess is the most ancient and most universal game known among men; for its original is beyond the memory of history, and it has, for numberless ages, been the amusement of all the civilised nations of Asia, the Persians, the Indians, and the Chinese. Europe has had it above a thousand years; the Spaniards have spread it over their part of America; and it has lately begun to make its appearance in the United States. It is so interesting in itself, as not to need the view of gain to induce engaging in it; and thence it is seldom played for money. Those therefore who have leisure for such diversions, cannot find one that is more innocent: and the following piece, written with a view to correct (among a few young friends) some little improprieties in the practice of it, shows at the same time that it may, in its effects on the mind, be not merely innocent, but advantageous, to the vanquished as well as the victor.]

The Game of Chess is not merely an idle Amusement. Several very valuable qualities of the Mind, useful in the course of human Life, are to be acquir'd or strengthened by it, so as to become habits, ready on all occasions. For Life is a kind of Chess, in which we often have Points to gain, & Competitors or Adversaries to contend with; and in which there is a vast variety of

---

[1] An avid chess player, Franklin once played at Passy from sunset to sunrise. His remarks on the game of chess, of course, reflect something of his attitude toward life. This bagatelle was printed first in *The Columbian Magazine* for 1786.

good and ill Events, that are in some degree the Effects of Prudence or the want of it. By playing at Chess, then, we may learn,

I. *Foresight,* which looks a little into futurity, and considers the Consequences that may attend an action; for it is continually occurring to the Player, "If I move this piece, what will be the advantages or disadvantages of my new situation? What Use can my Adversary make of it to annoy me? What other moves can I make to support it, and to defend myself from his attacks?"

II. *Circumspection,* which surveys the whole Chessboard, or scene of action; the relations of the several pieces and situations, the Dangers they are respectively exposed to, the several possibilities of their aiding each other, the probabilities that the Adversary may make this or that move, and attack this or the other Piece, and what different Means can be used to avoid his stroke, or turn its consequences against him.

III. *Caution,* not to make our moves too hastily. This habit is best acquired, by observing strictly the laws of the Game; such as, *If you touch a Piece, you must move it somewhere; if you set it down, you must let it stand.* And it is therefore best that these rules should be observed, as the Game becomes thereby more the image of human Life, and particularly of War; in which, if you have incautiously put yourself into a bad and dangerous position, you cannot obtain your Enemy's Leave to withdraw your Troops, and place them more securely, but you must abide all the consequences of your rashness.

And *lastly,* we learn by Chess the habit of not being discouraged by present appearances in the state of our affairs, the habit of hoping for a favourable Change, and that of persevering in the search of resources. The Game is so full of Events, there is such a variety of turns in it, the Fortune of it is so subject to sudden Vicissitudes, and one so frequently, after long contemplation, discovers the means of extricating one's self from a supposed insurmountable Difficulty, that one is encouraged to continue the Contest to the last, in hopes of Victory from our own skill, or at least [of getting a stale mate] from the Negligence of our Adversary. And whoever considers, what in Chess he often sees instances of, that [particular pieces of] success is [are] apt to produce Presumption, & its consequent Inattention, by which more is afterwards lost than was gain'd by the preceding Advantage, while misfortunes produce more care and attention, by which the loss may be recovered, will learn not to be too much discouraged by any present success of his Adversary, nor to despair of final good fortune upon every little Check he receives in the pursuit of it.

That we may therefore be induced more frequently to chuse this beneficial amusement, in preference to others which are not attended with the same advantages, every Circumstance that may increase the pleasure of it should be regarded; and every action or word that is unfair, disrespectful, or that in any way may give uneasiness, should be avoided, as contrary to the immediate intention of both the Players, which is to pass the Time agreeably.

Therefore, first, if it is agreed to play according to the strict rules, then those rules are to be exactly observed by both parties, and should not be insisted on for one side, while deviated from by the other — for this is not equitable.

Secondly, if it is agreed not to observe the rules exactly, but one party demands indulgencies, he should then be as willing to allow them to the other.

Thirdly, no false move should ever be made to extricate yourself out of difficulty, or to gain an advantage. There can be no pleasure in playing with a person once detected in such unfair practice.

Fourthly, if your adversary is long in playing, you ought not to hurry him, or express any uneasiness at his delay. You should not sing, nor whistle, nor look at your watch, nor take up a book to read, nor make a tapping with your feet on the floor, or with your fingers on the table, nor do any thing that may disturb his attention. For all these things displease; and they do not show your skill in playing, but your craftiness or your rudeness.

Fifthly, you ought not to endeavour to amuse and deceive your adversary, by pretending to have made bad moves, and saying that you have now lost the game, in order to make him secure and careless, and inattentive to your schemes: for this is fraud and deceit, not skill in the game.

Sixthly, you must not, when you have gained a victory, use any triumphing or insulting expression, nor show too much pleasure; but endeavour to console your adversary, and make him less dissatisfied with himself, by every kind of civil expression that may be used with truth, such as, "you understand the game better than I, but you are a little inattentive;" or, "you play too fast;" or, "you had the best of the game, but something happened to divert your thoughts, and that turned it in my favour."

Seventhly, if you are a spectator while others play, observe the most perfect silence. For, if you give advice, you offend both parties, him against whom you give it, because it may cause the loss of his game, him in whose favour you give it, because, though it be good, and he follows it, he loses the pleasure he might have had, if you had permitted him to think until it had occurred to himself. Even after a move or moves, you must not, by replacing the pieces, show how they might have been placed better; for that displeases, and may occasion disputes and doubts about their true situation. All talking to the players lessens or diverts their attention, and is therefore unpleasing. Nor should you give the least hint to either party, by any kind of noise or motion. If you do, you are unworthy to be a spectator. If you have a mind to exercise or show your judgment, do it in playing your own game, when you have an opportunity, not in criticizing, or meddling with, or counselling the play of others.

Lastly, if the game is not to be played rigorously, according to the rules above mentioned, then moderate your desire of victory over your adversary, and be pleased with one over yourself. Snatch not eagerly at every advantage offered by his unskillfulness or inattention; but point out to him kindly, that by such a move he places or leaves a piece in danger and unsupported; that by another he will put his king in a perilous situation, &c. By this generous civility (so opposite to the unfairness above forbidden) you may, indeed, happen to lose the game to your opponent; but you will win what is better, his esteem, his respect, and his affection, together with the silent approbation and good-will of impartial spectators.

Information for Those
Who Would Remove to America

◌§ Written probably in 1782, this tract for prospective Americans was widely translated and reprinted in Europe.

Many Persons in Europe, having directly or by Letters, express'd to the Writer of this, who is well acquainted with North America, their Desire of transporting and establishing themselves in that Country; but who appear to have formed, thro' Ignorance, mistaken Ideas and Expectations of what is to be obtained there; he thinks it may be useful, and prevent inconvenient, expensive, and fruitless Removals and Voyages of improper Persons, if he gives some clearer and truer Notions of that part of the World, than appear to have hitherto prevailed.

He finds it is imagined by Numbers, that the Inhabitants of North America are rich, capable of rewarding, and dispos'd to reward, all sorts of Ingenuity; that they are at the same time ignorant of all the Sciences, and, consequently, that Strangers, possessing Talents in the Belles-Lettres, fine Arts, &c., must be highly esteemed, and so well paid, as to become easily rich themselves; that there are also abundance of profitable Offices to be disposed of, which the Natives are not qualified to fill; and that, having few Persons of Family among them, Strangers of Birth must be greatly respected, and of course easily obtain the best of those Offices, which will make all their Fortunes; that the Governments too, to encourage Emigrations from Europe, not only pay the Expence of personal Transportation, but give Lands gratis to Strangers, with Negroes to work for them, Utensils of Husbandry and Stocks of Cattle. These are all wild Imaginations; and those who go to America with Expectations founded upon them will surely find themselves disappointed.

The Truth is, that though there are in that Country few People so miserable as the Poor of Europe, there are also very few that in Europe would be called rich; it is rather a general happy Mediocrity that prevails. There are few great Proprietors of the Soil, and few Tenants; most People cultivate their own

Lands, or follow some Handicraft or Merchandise; very few rich enough to live idly upon their Rents or Incomes, or to pay the high Prices given in Europe for Paintings, Statues, Architecture, and the other Works of Art, that are more curious than useful. Hence the natural Geniuses, that have arisen in America with such Talents, have uniformly quitted that Country for Europe, where they can be more suitably rewarded. It is true, that Letters and Mathematical Knowledge are in Esteem there, but they are at the same time more common than is apprehended; there being already existing nine Colleges or Universities, viz. four in New England, and one in each of the Provinces of New York, New Jersey, Pensilvania, Maryland, and Virginia, all furnish'd with learned Professors; besides a number of smaller Academies; these educate many of their Youth in the Languages, and those Sciences that qualify men for the Professions of Divinity, Law, or Physick. Strangers indeed are by no means excluded from exercising those Professions; and the quick Increase of Inhabitants everywhere gives them a Chance of Employ, which they have in common with the Natives. Of civil Offices, or Employments, there are few; no superfluous Ones, as in Europe; and it is a Rule establish'd in some of the States, that no Office should be so profitable as to make it desirable. The 36th Article of the Constitution of Pensilvania, runs expressly in these Words; "As every Freeman, to preserve his Independence, (if he has not a sufficient Estate) ought to have some Profession, Calling, Trade, or Farm, whereby he may honestly subsist, there can be no Necessity for, nor Use in, establishing Offices of Profit; the usual Effects of which are Dependance and Servility, unbecoming Freemen, in the Possessors and Expectants; Faction, Contention, Corruption, and Disorder among the People. Wherefore, whenever an Office, thro' Increase of Fees or otherwise, becomes so profitable, as to occasion many to apply for it, the Profits ought to be lessened by the Legislature."

These Ideas prevailing more or less in all the United States, it cannot be worth any Man's while, who has a means of Living at home, to expatriate himself, in hopes of obtaining a profitable civil Office in America; and, as to military Offices, they are at an End with the War, the Armies being disbanded. Much less is it adviseable for a Person to go thither, who has no other Quality to recommend him but his Birth. In Europe it has indeed its Value;

but it is a Commodity that cannot be carried to a worse Market than that of America, where people do not inquire concerning a Stranger, *What is he?* but, *What can he do?* If he has any useful Art, he is welcome; and if he exercises it, and behaves well, he will be respected by all that know him; but a mere Man of Quality, who, on that Account, wants to live upon the Public, by some Office or Salary, will be despis'd and disregarded. The Husbandman is in honor there, and even the Mechanic, because their Employments are useful. The People have a saying, that God Almighty is himself a Mechanic, the greatest in the Univers; and he is respected and admired more for the Variety, Ingenuity, and Utility of his Handyworks, than for the Antiquity of his Family. They are pleas'd with the Observation of a Negro, and frequently mention it, that *Boccarorra* (meaning the White men) *make de black man workee, make de Horse workee, make de Ox workee, make ebery ting workee; only de Hog. He, de hog, no workee; he eat, he drink, he walk about, he go to sleep when he please, he libb like a Gentleman.* According to these Opinions of the Americans, one of them would think himself more oblig'd to a Genealogist, who could prove for him that his Ancestors and Relations for ten Generations had been Plough-men, Smiths, Carpenters, Turners, Weavers, Tanners, or even Shoemakers, and consequently that they were useful Members of Society; than if he could only prove that they were Gentlemen, doing nothing of Value, but living idly on the Labour of others, mere *fruges consumere nati*,[1] and otherwise *good for nothing*, till by their Death their Estates, like the Carcass of the Negro's Gentleman-Hog, come to be *cut up*.

With regard to Encouragements for Strangers from Govern-ment, they are really only what are derived from good Laws and Liberty. Strangers are welcome, because there is room enough for them all, and therefore the old Inhabitants are not jealous of them; the Laws protect them sufficiently, so that they have no need of the Patronage of Great Men; and every one will enjoy securely the Profits of his Industry. But, if he does not bring a Fortune with him, he must work and be industrious to live. One or two Years' residence gives him all the Rights of a Citizen; but the government does not at present, whatever it may have done in former times, hire People to become Settlers, by Paying their

[1] ". . . born merely to eat up the corn." — WATTS [*Franklin's note.*]

Passages, giving Land, Negroes, Utensils, Stock, or any other kind of Emolument whatsoever. In short, America is the Land of Labour, and by no means what the English call *Lubberland*, and the French *Pays de Cocagne*, where the streets are said to be pav'd with half-peck Loaves, the Houses til'd with Pancakes, and where the Fowls fly about ready roasted, crying, *Come eat me!*

Who then are the kind of Persons to whom an Emigration to America may be advantageous? And what are the Advantages they may reasonably expect?

Land being cheap in that Country, from the vast Forests still void of Inhabitants, and not likely to be occupied in an Age to come, insomuch that the Propriety of an hundred Acres of fertile Soil full of Wood may be obtained near the Frontiers, in many Places, for Eight or Ten Guineas, hearty young Labouring Men, who understand the Husbandry of Corn and Cattle, which is nearly the same in that Country as in Europe, may easily establish themselves there. A little Money sav'd of the good Wages they receive there, while they work for others, enables them to buy the Land and begin their Plantation, in which they are assisted by the Good-Will of their Neighbours, and some Credit. Multitudes of poor People from England, Ireland, Scotland, and Germany, have by this means in a few years become wealthy Farmers, who, in their own Countries, where all the Lands are fully occupied, and the Wages of Labour low, could never have emerged from the poor Condition wherein they were born.

From the salubrity of the Air, the healthiness of the Climate, the plenty of good Provisions, and the Encouragement to early Marriages by the certainty of Subsistence in cultivating the Earth, the Increase of Inhabitants by natural Generation is very rapid in America, and becomes still more so by the Accession of Strangers; hence there is a continual Demand for more Artisans of all the necessary and useful kinds, to supply those Cultivators of the Earth with Houses, and with Furniture and Utensils of the grosser sorts, which cannot so well be brought from Europe. Tolerably good Workmen in any of those mechanic Arts are sure to find Employ, and to be well paid for their Work, there being no Restraints preventing Strangers from exercising any Art they understand, nor any Permission necessary. If they are poor, they begin first as Servants or Journeymen; and if they are sober, industrious, and frugal, they soon become Masters, establish themselves in Business, marry, raise Families, and become respectable Citizens.

Also, Persons of moderate Fortunes and Capitals, who, having a Number of Children to provide for, are desirous of bringing them up to Industry, and to secure Estates for their Posterity, have Opportunities of doing it in America, which Europe does not afford. There they may be taught and practise profitable mechanic Arts, without incurring Disgrace on that Account, but on the contrary acquiring Respect by such Abilities. There small Capitals laid out in Lands, which daily become more valuable by the Increase of People, afford a solid Prospect of ample Fortunes thereafter for those Children. The writer of this has known several Instances of large Tracts of Land, bought, on what was then the Frontier of Pensilvania, for Ten Pounds per hundred Acres, which after 20 years, when the Settlements had been extended far beyond them, sold readily, without any Improvement made upon them, for three Pounds per Acre. The Acre in America is the same with the English Acre, or the Acre of Normandy.

Those, who desire to understand the State of Government in America, would do well to read the Constitutions of the several States, and the Articles of Confederation that bind the whole together for general Purposes, under the Direction of one Assembly, called the Congress. These Constitutions have been printed, by order of Congress, in America; two Editions of them have also been printed in London; and a good Translation of them into French has lately been published at Paris.

Several of the Princes of Europe having of late years, from an Opinion of Advantage to arise by producing all Commodities and Manufactures within their own Dominions, so as to diminish or render useless their Importations, have endeavoured to entice Workmen from other Countries by high Salaries, Privileges, &c. Many Persons, pretending to be skilled in various great Manufactures, imagining that America must be in Want of them, and that the Congress would probably be dispos'd to imitate the Princes above mentioned, have proposed to go over, on Condition of having their Passages paid, Lands given, Salaries appointed, exclusive Privileges for Terms of years, &c. Such Persons, on reading the Articles of Confederation, will find, that the Congress have no Power committed to them, or Money put into their Hands, for such purposes; and that if any such Encouragement is given, it must be by the Government of some separate State. This, however, has rarely been done in America; and, when it has been done, it has rarely succeeded, so as to establish a Manufacture, which the Country was not yet so ripe for as to encourage private Persons to set it up; Labour being generally too dear there, and Hands difficult to be kept together, every one desiring to be a Master, and the Cheapness of Lands inclining many to leave Trades for Agriculture. Some indeed have met with Success, and are carried on to Advantage; but they are generally such as require only a few Hands, or wherein great Part of the Work is performed by Machines. Things that are bulky, and of so small Value as not well to bear the Expence of Freight, may often be made cheaper in the Country than they can be imported; and the Manufacture of such Things will be profitable wherever there is a sufficient Demand. The Farmers in America produce indeed a good deal of Wool and Flax; and none is exported, it is all work'd up; but it is in the Way of domestic Manufacture, for the Use of the Family. The buying up Quantities of Wool and Flax, with the Design to employ Spinners, Weavers, &c., and form great Establishments, producing Quantities of Linen and Woollen Goods for Sale, has been several times attempted in different Provinces; but those Projects have generally failed, goods of equal Value being imported cheaper. And when the Governments have been solicited to support such Schemes by Encouragements, in Money, or by imposing Duties on Importation of such Goods, it has been generally refused, on this Principle, that, if the Country is ripe for the Manufacture, it may be carried on by private Persons to Advantage; and if not, it is a Folly to think of forcing Nature. Great Establishments of Manufacture require great Numbers of Poor to do the Work for small Wages; these Poor are to be found in Europe, but will not be found in America, till the Lands are all taken up and cultivated, and the Excess of People, who cannot get Land, want Employment. The Manufacture of Silk, they say, is natural in France, as that of Cloth in England, because each Country produces in Plenty the first Material; but if England will have a Manufacture of Silk as well as that of Cloth, and France one of Cloth as well as that of Silk, these unnatural Operations must be supported by mutual Prohibitions, or high

Duties on the Importation of each other's Goods; by which means the Workmen are enabled to tax the home Consumer by greater Prices, while the higher Wages they receive makes them neither happier nor richer, since they only drink more and work less. Therefore the Governments in America do nothing to encourage such Projects. The People, by this Means, are not impos'd on, either by the Merchant or Mechanic. If the Merchant demands too much Profit on imported Shoes, they buy of the Shoemaker; and if he asks too high a Price, they take them of the Merchant; thus the two Professions are checks on each other. The Shoemaker, however, has, on the whole, a considerable Profit upon his Labour in America, beyond what he had in Europe, as he can add to his Price a Sum nearly equal to all the Expenses of Freight and Commission, Risque or Insurance, &c., necessarily charged by the Merchant. And the Case is the same with the Workmen in every other Mechanic Art. Hence it is, that Artisans generally live better and more easily in America than in Europe; and such as are good Œconomists make a comfortable Provision for Age, and for their Children. Such may, therefore, remove with Advantage to America.

In the long-settled Countries of Europe, all Arts, Trades, Professions, Farms, &c., are so full, that it is difficult for a poor Man, who has Children, to place them where they may gain, or learn to gain, a decent Livelihood. The Artisans, who fear creating future Rivals in Business, refuse to take Apprentices, but upon Conditions of Money, Maintenance, or the like, which the Parents are unable to comply with. Hence the Youth are dragg'd up in Ignorance of every gainful Art, and oblig'd to become Soldiers, or Servants, or Thieves, for a Subsistence. In America, the rapid Increase of Inhabitants takes away that Fear of Rivalship, and Artisans willingly receive Apprentices from the hope of Profit by their Labour, during the Remainder of the Time stipulated, after they shall be instructed. Hence it is easy for poor Families to get their Children instructed; for the Artisans are so desirous of Apprentices, that many of them will even give Money to the Parents, to have Boys from Ten to Fifteen Years of Age bound Apprentices to them till the Age of Twenty-one; and many poor Parents have, by that means, on their Arrival in the Country, raised Money enough to buy Land sufficient to establish themselves, and to subsist the rest of their

Family by Agriculture. These Contracts for Apprentices are made before a Magistrate, who regulates the Agreement according to Reason and Justice, and, having in view the Formation of a future useful Citizen, obliges the Master to engage by a written Indenture, not only that, during the time of Service stipulated, the Apprentice shall be duly provided with Meat, Drink, Apparel, washing, and Lodging, and, at its Expiration, with a compleat new Suit of Cloaths, but also that he shall be taught to read, write, and cast Accompts; and that he shall be well instructed in the Art or Profession of his Master, or some other, by which he may afterwards gain a Livelihood, and be able in his turn to raise a Family. A Copy of this Indenture is given to the Apprentice or his Friends, and the Magistrate keeps a Record of it, to which recourse may be had, in case of Failure by the Master in any Point of Performance. This desire among the Masters, to have more Hands employ'd in working for them, induces them to pay the Passages of young Persons, of both Sexes, who, on their Arrival, agree to serve them one, two, three, or four Years; those, who have already learnt a Trade, agreeing for a shorter Term, in proportion to their Skill, and the consequent immediate Value of their Service; and those, who have none, agreeing for a longer Term, in consideration of being taught an Art their Poverty would not permit them to acquire in their own Country.

The almost general Mediocrity of Fortune that prevails in America obliging its People to follow some Business for subsistence, those Vices, that arise usually from Idleness, are in a great measure prevented. Industry and constant Employment are great preservatives of the Morals and Virtue of a Nation. Hence bad Examples to Youth are more rare in America, which must be a comfortable Consideration to Parents. To this may be truly added, that serious Religion, under its various Denominations, is not only tolerated, but respected and practised. Atheism is unknown there; Infidelity rare and secret; so that persons may live to a great Age in that Country, without having their Piety shocked by meeting with either an Atheist or an Infidel. And the Divine Being seems to have manifested his Approbation of the mutual Forbearance and Kindness with which the different Sects treat each other, by the remarkable Prosperity with which He has been pleased to favour the whole Country.

Speech in the Convention

AT THE CONCLUSION OF ITS DELIBERATIONS

⮳ Written September 17, 1787. Since Franklin's speaking voice was weak, he asked James Wilson, another delegate from Pennsylvania, to read his remarks, which summarize a lifetime of experience in politics and of human nature.

MR. PRESIDENT: I confess that I do not entirely approve of this Constitution at present; but, Sir, I am not sure I shall never approve it; for, having lived long, I have experienced many instances of being obliged, by better information or fuller consideration, to change my opinions even on important subjects, which I once thought right, but found to be otherwise. It is therefore that, the older I grow, the more apt I am to doubt my own judgment of others. Most men, indeed, as well as most sects in religion, think themselves in possession of all truth, and that wherever others differ from them, it is so far error. Steele, a Protestant, in a dedication, tells the Pope that the only difference between our two churches in their opinions of the certainty of their doctrine is the Romish Church is *infallible* and the Church of England is *never in the wrong.* But, though many private persons think almost as highly of their own infallibility as of that of their Sect, few express it so naturally as a certain French Lady who, in a little dispute with her sister, said, "But I meet with nobody but myself that is *always* in the right." *"Je ne trouve que moi qui aie toujours raison."*

In these sentiments, Sir, I agree to this Constitution, with all its faults — if they are such; because I think a general Government necessary for us, and there is no *form* of government but what may be a blessing to the people, if well administered; and I believe, farther, that this is likely to be well administered for a course of years, and can only end in despotism, as other forms have done before it, when the people shall become so corrupted as to need despotic government, being incapable of any other. I doubt, too, whether any other Convention we can obtain may be able to make a better constitution; for, when you assemble a number of men, to have the advantage of their joint wisdom, you inevitably assemble with those men all their prejudices, their passions, their errors of opinion, their local interests, and their selfish views. From such an assembly can a *perfect* production be expected? It therefore astonishes me, Sir, to find this system approaching so near to perfection as it does; and I think it will astonish our enemies, who are waiting with confidence to hear that our councils are confounded like those of the builders of Babel, and that our States are on the point of separation, only to meet hereafter for the purpose of cutting one another's throats. Thus I consent, Sir, to this Constitution, because I expect no better, and because I am not sure that it is not the best. The opinions I have had of its *errors* I sacrifice to the public good. I have never whispered a syllable of them abroad. Within these walls they were born, and here they shall die. If every one of us, in returning to our Constituents, were to report the objections he has had to it, and endeavor to gain partisans in support of them, we might prevent its being generally received, and thereby lose all the salutary effects and great advantages resulting naturally in our favor among foreign nations, as well as among ourselves, from our real or apparent unanimity. Much of the strength and efficiency of any government, in procuring and securing happiness to the people, depends on *opinion*, on the general opinion of the goodness of that government, as well as of the wisdom and integrity of its governors. I hope, therefore, for our own sakes, as a part of the people, and for the sake of our posterity, that we shall act heartily and unanimously in recommending this Constitution, wherever our influence may extend, and turn our future thoughts and endeavors to the means of having it *well administered*.

On the whole, Sir, I cannot help expressing a wish, that every member of the Convention who may still have objections to it, would with me on this occasion doubt a little of his own infallibility, and, to make *manifest* our *unanimity*, put his name to this instrument.

RIVERSIDE EDITIONS

* In preparation